DATE DUE

DEMCO 38-296

THE EUROPEAN UNION AND ITS CITIZENS

THE EUROPEAN UNION AND ITS CITIZENS

THE SOCIAL AGENDA

Beverly Springer

CONTRIBUTIONS IN POLITICAL SCIENCE, NUMBER 349

Greenwood Press
Westport, Connecticut • London

Library of Congress Cataloging-in-Publication Data

Springer, Beverly.
     The European union and its citizens : the social agenda / Beverly
Springer.
        p.   cm.—(Contributions in political science, ISSN 0147–1066
; no. 349)
     Includes bibliographical references and index.
     ISBN 0–313–28815–1 (alk. paper)
     1. European Economic Community countries—Social policy.
2. Environmental policy—European Economic Community countries.
3. Labor policy—European Economic Community countries.   4. Regional
planning—European Economic Community countries.   5. Citizenship—
European Economic Community countries.   6. Europe 1992.   I. Title.
II. Series.
HN380.5.A8S697   1994
361.6′1′094—dc20   94–11223

British Library Cataloguing in Publication Data is available.

Library of Congress Catalog Card Number: 94–11223
ISBN: 0–313–28815–1
ISSN: 0147–1066

First published in 1994

Greenwood Press, 88 Post Road West, Westport, CT 06881
An imprint of Greenwood Publishing Group, Inc.

Printed in the United States of America

The paper used in this book complies with the
Permanent Paper Standard issued by the National
Information Standards Organization (Z39.48–1984).

10 9 8 7 6 5 4 3 2 1

Contents

Acknowledgments

I want to thank the people in the European Union who helped me in my research. They shared their insights and provided me with important documents. I cannot name all the persons, but I want to mention, in particular, Ivor Roberts and Jasmin Sozen in the Commission and Wolfgang Gaede in the Council.

The librarians at the American Graduate School of International Management introduced me to the miracle of modern technology so that I was able to obtain current reports via Agence Europe to supplement the information that I obtained on my research trips to Brussels. I want to acknowledge their skill and their patience.

I owe a special thanks to Zed Lanham for once again using his red pen to edit my manuscript and to my husband, Lee, who did not find it beneath his male dignity to help on all the details that are involved in completing a manuscript.

Introduction

In December 1991, the leaders of the European Community met in Maastricht, Netherlands, to sign a treaty for post-1992 Europe. They called the new document the Treaty on European Union. The document gives citizenship in the new European Union to the citizens of the member states. It gives authority to the institutions of the European Community to make policies of immediate concern to the new Eurocitizens. Regionalism, the environment, the rights of individuals in a borderless Europe, and the status of employees in an integrated economy are all covered in the new treaty. They are issues which take on new importance in an integrating Europe and which were previously handled primarily by national governments. How the European Community handles those issues, and the processes and politics which will develop around them, will determine the Europolity of the future.

The subject of this book is the European Union mandated by the Maastricht Treaty. (See Chapter 3 for an explanation of European Union and European Community.) The subject encompasses both practical and theoretical topics. Issues, such as the environment and the new regionalism, are covered through research which includes interviews with relevant actors and an analysis of primary sources. The politics of policy making in the European Community are examined and attention is given to the importance of traditional European values in forming current policies. Relevant concepts are utilized in order to provide a framework for analyzing the European Union now under construction.

The study of the European Community (EC) is difficult because it is a unique entity. Efforts to compare it to federalist structures or international organizations fail because it is neither a federal system nor an international organization. As many scholars have noted, it has some features of both, but it lacks certain essential attributes of a federal system yet has more claims to sovereignty than do international organizations (Tushnet, 1990). Scholars have struggled for decades to devise concepts for the study of the EC which do not distort its unique aspects, but which contribute to the general knowledge of politics. The work of Ernst Haas was seminal in devising those concepts (Haas, 1964).

The EC is a work "in progress." European leaders have not yet agreed on a final form for it, and they periodically remodel the EC still without defining a long-term objective. The EC is now undergoing another stage of construction. It has just completed the ratification of the Treaty on European Union (the Maastricht Treaty), which provides for economic and monetary union, as well as for a greater degree of political integration. Once again, however, the final goal of the effort is left undefined. Europe is to have a union but the essence of the union will only take form through implementing the provisions of the treaty.

Scholars must study the treaty, but they also must study the implementation of its provisions in order to discern the Union which is under construction. The provisions which the treaty makes for policies directly affecting citizens are the most important ones to study because they are the ones which have the potential for forging stronger ties between the Union and those citizens.

The task of implementing the new treaty is complicated because the atmosphere in Europe has changed so quickly and dramatically. The treaty was drafted in an era of optimism. It is being implemented in an era of political uncertainty and economic gloom. It was drafted in an era when the ideal of integration was in ascendancy. It is being implemented when nationalism, in a variety of guises, is reasserting itself throughout Europe.

As previously mentioned, the focus of this book is on the ties between the EC and the citizens in the member countries and specifically on the policies provided by the Maastricht Treaty which directly relate to citizens. National governments have generally been the intermediaries between the institutions of the EC and the citizens, but the EC has some direct ties with those citizens. Individuals have standing in the European Court of Justice. They have rights and obligations under EC law, and they participate, to a limited extent, in EC politics through European interest groups and political parties. The task of this book is to examine the range of EC actions available under the Maastricht Treaty which directly affect the people residing in the member states. The book focuses primarily on EC policies which may be called "people policies." The term may seem awkward, but it distinguishes the policies relevant to this book. Social policy is not used except to refer to employment policies, as it customarily does in the EC.

The era under scrutiny is the early 1990s as the EC prepares to implement the Treaty on European Union. The era is a crucial one for the future of European union. In order to implement the treaty, the EC must reform its institutions and assume new roles. The success of the effort is in doubt because of the changes noted above. Those changes are explored more fully in Chapter 1. Chapter 2 presents a discussion of some concepts and approaches useful in studying people policies. Chapter 3 provides an assessment of the Maastricht Treaty. Chapter 4 delves into social history to ascertain the cultural underpinnings of integration. The idea of Europe needs to be revisited in order to provide a sociological underpinning to the discussion of the relationship between the EC and its citizens.

Chapters 5 through 8 deal with different types of people policies. As noted above, those policies directly affect people in their daily lives. They include long-established EC policies, such as those affecting employment, and the new policies, such as European citizenship. The chapters include discussions of such problems as poverty, immigration, and seemingly intractable unemployment because those problems, with their threat to social stability, concern Europeans today. The EC cannot have relevance for ordinary people if it ignores those problems or, even worse, if its policies appear to exacerbate them.

The focus in each of the policy chapters is on the development of policy under the Treaty on European Union. The focus also encompasses the actors involved in forming the policy. All of the policy chapters have a common conceptual framework in order to provide the readers with a basis for comparison and for generalizations about policy formulation in the EC. The concepts and the framework are explained in Chapter 2.

The book concludes with an assessment, in Chapter 9, of the contribution of the people policies to European integration. The scope of the study is limited to policy making, so the assessment cannot be complete. A more complete assessment will have to wait for studies which can consider also the implementation of the relevant policies. I hope that the current study, although incomplete, contributes to a deeper understanding of the EC and the dynamics of European integration.

ADDENDUM

The following information is provided for readers who are new to the study of the EC.

The EC was created by treaty among the member states. The member states agree to give some limited attributes of sovereignty to the EC. They also agree to share or pool sovereignty in order to achieve mutual objectives. The division of authority between the EC and the member governments is guided by the principle of subsidiarity. Laws shall be made by the lowest possible authority or by the appropriate authority.

The EC has the authority to make and adjudicate laws as determined by the basic treaties. The two primary forms of EC law are directives and regulations. A directive is a framework law which requires every member state to enact a law to meet the objective of the directive. A regulation is an EC law which is directly enforceable in the member states. Members are bound by treaty to respect and enforce EC law. The scope of EC law is determined by its basic treaties.

The basic treaties of the EC are the Treaty of Rome (1958), which established the institutions of the EC and provided the mandate for creating an economic community; the Single European Act (1987), which reformed the policy-making process, expanded the legal competencies, and provided for the creation of the internal market; and the Treaty on European Union (1993).

The policy making of the EC starts with the Commission, which provides the EC bureaucracy. The seventeen commissioners who head it are not under the direction of member governments and generally present the Community view. The Council is the voice of the member governments and has the primary authority for enacting EC policies. (The European Council, comprised of the heads of the member governments and the president of the Commission, meets several times a year to decide major policies. Such meetings are often called European Summits or referred to in the press by the name of the city in which the Council meets.) Questions in the Council are usually decided by unanimous votes or by a qualified majority. According to the latter, a measure must have fifty-four votes out of a possible seventy-six. The votes are apportioned so that Germany, France, Italy, and the United Kingdom each have ten; Spain has eight; Belgium, the Netherlands, Greece, and Portugal have five each; Ireland and Denmark each have three; and Luxembourg has two. The European Parliament, which is directly elected, has the right to be consulted on most proposals for EC law. For some types of proposals, Parliament has more authority, according to the cooperation procedure established by the Single European Act or the co-decision procedure established by the Treaty on European Union. (The European Court of Justice, the other major institution of the EC, hears cases arising from Community law.) Two other EC bodies play minor roles in policy making. The Economic and Social Committee prepares opinions on many proposals. Its members represent different types of economic interests. A new Committee of the Regions will also prepare opinions on relevant proposals.

REFERENCES

Haas, E. 1964. *Beyond the Nation State*. Stanford, CA: Stanford University Press.
Tushnet, Mark, ed. 1990. *Comparative Constitutional Federalism*. Westport, CT: Greenwood Press.

Chapter 1

Europe in the 1990s:
The Crisis of Uncertainties

The political and economic climate in Europe has evolved through a number of major changes since the 1980s. The history of the era forms the backdrop against which the current status of European integration must be measured. In the early 1980s, leaders sought national solutions to economic recession, and European integration was in low regard. Later in the decade, the climate changed dramatically when economic recovery and new initiatives from Brussels led to "Europhoria," as the press called the remarkable state of confidence in Europe. Another reversal took place in the 1990s and Europe is now in a crisis of uncertainties. The norms, patterns, and institutions, which had organized European life from the personal to the international levels, are in disarray as a result of the dislocations following the end of the Cold War and a return of economic troubles. Leaders are once again seeking solutions to serious problems. They may seek European solutions or national ones. The choices that they make will determine the course of European integration in the decades ahead.

The decade of the 1990s opened in the European Community (EC) on a wave of optimism. Few were even aware of impending crises. The 1992 program to create the internal market was on schedule, and economic indicators were promising. The EC served as a magnet attracting the newly freed countries of Eastern Europe toward democracy and liberal capitalism. The formerly aloof members of the European Free Trade Association signaled an interest in closer relations with the EC. The EC took its place as an equal participant along with the United States and Japan in the triad which was to shape the new global economy. On that wave of optimism, two Intergovernmental Conferences (IGCs) set to work to draft the Treaty on European Union, which was to provide the EC with the means to move to a new stage of integration. The treaty was signed by the heads of government of the member states at the European Council meeting at Maastricht in February 1992. The heads of government gathered in Maastricht had good reasons for congratulating one another on their achievements.

The year 1992 began on an optimistic note, but closed on a pessimistic one as an *annus horribilis*. Europhoria collapsed in a crisis of uncertainties. In retrospect, officials should have paid more attention to the warnings of an economic slowdown and to public confusion over the proposed treaty, but most did not. They were shocked when the Danes rejected the treaty in a popular referendum in June. They were disturbed by worsening economic indicators throughout the summer and lost their last illusions about an easy road to integration when a currency crisis spread throughout Europe in September. The feeble "yes" vote in a French referendum, a short time later, did little to restore confidence. The wave of confidence which had carried the EC forward since 1985 seemed to end as abruptly as it had begun. The heads of government, meeting at an EC summit in Edinburgh at the end of 1992, tried to alleviate public uncertainties, but they were not able to stop the growing pessimism in Europe.

January 1993 opened with celebrations, long scheduled, to mark the completion of the internal market, but they did not lighten the gloom cast by grim economic indicators and by public disillusion with the promise of European integration. Although the Treaty on European Union was ratified later in the year, the bitter fight over ratification harmed its public image. The work of implementing the treaty began as the year ended, and the economic and political indicators continued to be negative.

The situation in Europe in the 1990s needs to be assessed against the ebbs and flows of European integration during the previous decade. (For a more complete consideration, see Pryce, 1987.) The optimism of the years 1985 to 1991 was linked to two related developments: the recovery of the economy during those years and the adoption of the 1992 program on the completion of the internal market. Both of those developments were linked to a preceding cycle of economic and political stagnation in the EC. Integration in the EC appeared to have reached a plateau. Policy making in the EC was slow and the outcomes were frequently disappointing. The economies in the member states were experiencing difficulties, but few national leaders looked to Brussels for solutions. When national policies did not reverse the economic decline, however, some politicians and business people began to reconsider integration as a means of restoring competitiveness in Europe. Their interest was matched by that of the new team in the Commission in Brussels headed by Jacques Delors (Colchester and Buchan, 1990). The result was an agreement to revitalize the EC by adopting the 1992 program and the Single European Act. The objective of the former was to remove national barriers to trade. One of the purposes of the latter was to facilitate policy making in the EC on issues related to creating the single market. The 1992 program gave the EC a mission and made the EC relevant to leaders in the member states. Economic revitalization accompanied (or resulted from) the revitalization of the EC, and a cycle of optimism and confidence commenced.

The 1992 program was based on the famous "White Paper on Completing the Internal Market," which was drafted in the Commission and accepted by the Council (CEC, 1985).The White Paper is a remarkable document: part rallying cry and part work schedule. The text of the document exhorted the member states to join together in eliminating barriers to an internal market and extolled the benefits which will result from the elimination. The annex to the document contained a list of EC actions which would be needed in order to sweep away the barriers. Each action was given a due date, with the entire list of almost three hundred measures to be completed by the end of 1992.

The White Paper was greeted with a great deal of skepticism, but it had the support of crucial actors in the EC, in the member governments, and perhaps most important, in international business (Green, 1993). Public skepticism changed to enthusiasm as the implementation started and proceeded at an unprecedented rate. Excitement grew, and the EC flag with the twelve gold stars appeared on car bumpers, umbrellas, and lapel pins throughout the member states. Some businesses even began to restructure in response to the opportunities which would be created by the single market. Business confidence increased as did investments. Business groups supported the efforts of the Commission to implement the measures in the White Paper (Coutu, Hladik, Meen, and Turcq, 1993). Even European labor unions gave support to the 1992 program in hope that it would increase employment opportunities in the EC.

Economic recovery coincided with a new era in Brussels. The number of unemployed dropped significantly between 1986 and 1990 (CEC, 1990, p. 21). The growth in investments for the period was about 6 percent annually (CEC, 1992, p. 42). Annual growth in gross domestic product (GDP) averaged 3 percent during those years compared to rates between 0 and 2 percent in the preceding five years (CEC, 1991, p. 27).

Economists will argue for years about the relationship between the 1992 program and the economic revitalization, but the public and many leaders in the EC credited the good economic performance to the 1992 program. The linkage helped to promote the program as long as the economic indicators were good, but it helped to discredit the program when the indicators started to turn down in 1991. More significantly, the idea of Europe itself was tarnished. Many turned away from the EC and sought solutions to their problems closer to home. The brief era of optimism had ended, and Europe had entered a watershed period when new structures and new ideas had to be found to replace those which served the Cold War era.

A crisis of uncertainties gripped the EC in 1992, and it persists in putting at risk the optimistic forecasts about integration, which were so widely accepted in the preceding years. Uncertainties are a norm in life, but the number and depth of the uncertainties now confronting the EC are overwhelming. The uncertainties are economic, political, financial, and social. Each will be discussed in the following pages.

The economic malaise in the EC is deep and destructive. Almost every economic indicator, such as growth, investment, budget deficits, and current accounts, is negative. Slow growth is harming the fragile fabric which binds the member states together. Many blame Germany, the economic powerhouse of the EC, for pursuing domestic policies in disregard to the consequences for the EC and the exchange rate mechanism; meanwhile governments from the poorer countries in the EC blame the rich ones for failing to provide more regional aid. As the malaise continues, many leaders have doubts about the 1992 program and turn to national solutions for economic problems.

Unemployment, which is widespread and apparently chronic, probably causes the most uncertainty in the EC. Even the years of recovery did not solve the problem. The unemployment rate never fell below 7.7 percent during the recovery and rose above 10 percent by 1993. Experts now recognize that the problem is complex and structural and that economic growth alone will not solve it. Many fear that the formation of the internal market will actually exacerbate unemployment. Even those who have jobs fear that they will lose them. The fear is fed by a growing awareness of poverty. Throughout much of the EC, little evidence of poverty has existed in recent decades and most people believed that the welfare state had ended the worst forms of poverty. The belief has now eroded. The EC has more than fifty million in the poverty class. Every country has socially marginalized groups and many people worry about the emergence of a permanent underclass.

Political uncertainty is added onto economic uncertainty in Europe today. Many commentators have noted that the norms of postwar politics have lost their hold. A schism exists between citizens and their traditional political parties. Citizens no longer trust their leaders, and their lack of trust creates many ramifications for domestic politics as well as for the EC. Traditional political parties and their leaders, almost without exception, support the EC, but they can no longer ensure that citizens will follow them in that support. The Danish rejection of the Treaty on European Union is a good example of citizens' lack of trust. The major political parties and their leaders endorsed the treaty and urged their supporters to ratify it. The rejection, even though it was by a small margin, came as a surprise to Danish leaders. If the EC can no longer rely on political parties and national leaders to mobilize support for the EC among Europeans, the EC will have to develop other means if it is to progress in the current climate.

Another cause of political uncertainty arises from the failure of leadership in the EC. In the late 1980s, the EC had a plentiful supply of vigorous leaders, with vision and confidence, at both the national and the EC levels. Jacques Delors, as president of the Commission, demonstrated leadership when he guided the development of the 1992 program. He was matched at the national level by such leaders as Felipe Gónzales Marquez of Spain, François Mitterrand of France, and Helmut Kohl of Germany. The British also had the strong leadership of Margaret Thatcher, who, although she opposed the idea of integration, was firm in her support of the internal market for the EC. Now, just a few years later, those leaders are either gone or tired and uninspired. The Commission has not regained the initiative which it showed in the late 1980s, and national leaders have not filled the void. Europe appears ready for a generational change in leadership, but no new, younger leaders have yet appeared.

Another area of uncertainty centers on the currency question. The exchange rate mechanism (ERM) closely linked most of the currencies of the states of the EC. Member governments intervened in the market to limit the fluctuation of their currencies. They also tried to reform their economic policies in order to bring about stability and convergence. The system worked well in the early years of the 1992 program. The success encouraged members to discuss currency unification and to provide for it in the new Treaty on European Union. The ERM came under pressure in 1992, but the warning signs were ignored. The exchange rate crisis, which occurred in September 1992, devastated confidence in monetary union and public belief in integration. The ERM, the 1992 program, and the EC are inextricably linked for many people. Leaders had failed to foresee and to act jointly to prevent the crisis. Even after the crisis, they were not able to restore confidence in the ERM. Their failure to act also left in place exchange rates which harmed many member states. The system came under attack again at the end of July 1993. Leaders agreed to allow much wider fluctuations in exchange rates rather than dismantle the system. The two options were the only ones politically possible. Leaders chose the one which provided at least a facade of a system, but they could not prevent further loss of confidence in the currency unification and the treaty associated with it.

Eastern Europe causes great uncertainty in the EC. A successful transition to capitalism in Eastern Europe could revitalize Western Europe, but a failed transition would threaten Western Europe politically, economically, and so-cially. The EC was to mentor the countries of Eastern Europe and to pull them into the Western system. The EC failed its first test as a world political leader when it failed to meet the crisis in Yugoslavia. It did not find the necessary unity or policies to perform well. It has performed better as a provider of aid, but its generosity in aid has been countered by its protectionism in trade. The social uncertainty centers on the immigrant question. People in the EC fear that large numbers of unemployed Eastern Europeans will enter their countries if steps are not taken to prevent them from doing so. Their fear nurtures xenophobia and extremist politics, and every member country has experienced them. The only acceptable solution is to create prosperity in the East, but the cost may be unacceptably high. Poor members of the EC oppose using limited funds outside the EC when they themselves need those funds. The uncertainties associated with the changes in Eastern Europe will continue to challenge the EC, and failure to find solutions will erode respect for it among its citizens.

Another major uncertainty to trouble the EC in the *annus horribilis* was the question of whether the Treaty on European Union would be ratified. Ratification, however, did not end the uncertainty. The process was too bitter and the conditions too difficult to ensure that the treaty would be implemented even though it had been ratified. The currency crisis has caused many to doubt that the provisions of the treaty providing for currency unification will be implemented as intended. If doubt exists, then the credibility of the entire treaty is at risk.

CONCLUSION

Europe in the 1990s faces numerous uncertainties and must dramatically change its economy, politics, and society for the era which is commencing. The EC should guide the changes. It has a new treaty to provide it with more authority, but that treaty was drafted in a different era. In the 1980s, Jacques Delors and others were confident that the EC was the proper agent to restore Western Europe to global competitiveness. The means was the internal market. Economic success, progress on the internal market, and confidence in the EC were all related. All rose in the prosperity of the 1980s, and all plunged in the fateful year of 1992.

The pessimism and uncertainties in Europe in the 1990s create a harsh environment in which to implement the Treaty on European Union. The treaty is designed to create a union, but current conditions evoke nationalism and xenophobia. The treaty is designed to build bridges between the EC and its citizens, but if the EC fails to remedy the problems troubling Europe, the foundations for the bridges may be destroyed. Observers agree that the conditions in Europe in the 1990s are not propitious for implementing a new treaty. The questions which remain to be answered concern the quality of the treaty itself and the plans to implement it.

REFERENCES

CEC (Commission of the European Communities). 1985. "White Paper on Completing the Internal Market." COM(85)310 final.
———. 1990. *Basic Statistics of the Community*. 27th ed. Brussels: Statistical Office of the European Communities.

————. 1991. *Employment in Europe, 1991*. Brussels: CEC.

————. 1992. *Employment in Europe, 1992*. Brussels: CEC.

Colchester, N., and David Buchan. 1990. *Europower*. New York: The Economist Book—Random House.

Coutu, D., K. Hladik, D. Meen, and D. Turcq. 1993. "Views of the Business Community on Post–1992 Integration in Europe." *The European Challenges Post 1992*, ed. by Alexis J. Jacquemin and David Wright. Aldershot, England: Edward Elgar.

Green, Maria. 1993. "The Politics of Big Business in the Single Market Program." Paper presented at the annual conference of the European Community Studies Association, Washington, D.C., May 27, 1993.

Pryce, Roy, ed. 1987. *Dynamics of European Union*. London: Croom Helm.

Chapter 2

Conceptualizing European Integration

P olitical scientists have grappled for decades with the problem of studying
European integration. They have searched for answers to two basic and
related questions: What drives integration and where is it going? Scholars try
to discern why national governments relinquish portions of their sovereignty.
They want to understand the factors which encourage integration as well as to
foresee the future of European integration. They pose questions about the
viability of the European Community (EC) and its institutions as the primary
agent of integration. They have defined a field of study which is immensely
challenging and one which takes on new importance in the 1990s as Europe
undergoes major changes and moves into an uncertain future.

Political scientists find their work complicated because they must develop
new concepts and approaches to studying an entity which is neither a sovereign
state nor an international organization. The search for valid methods of study
has extended over more than three decades. The first political scientists to study
the EC gave us useful insights and concepts, but their approaches failed to
provide explanations when the course of integration was disrupted in the 1970s.
(See Mally, 1973, or Pentland, 1973, for more details.) Neo-functionalism was
the most widely accepted approach or "pre-theory" for the study of European
integration in the early period of study. Neo-functionalists took as their starting
point the motives of the founders of the EC, who believed that integration
needed to start with small, practical steps. Ernst Haas wrote several influential
works on neo-functionalism. He and other neo-functionalists believed that once
functional integration had begun, the process would take on its own dynamic
and integration would spread into related areas. Incrementalism, linkage, and

spillover characterize integration for neo-functionalists. They provided a relatively positive vision of the evolution of European integration (Haas, 1968).
Ernst Haas revised neo-functionalism in the 1970s to account for unforeseen
developments in that decade (Haas, 1975). He noted that integration could result
from a deliberate linkage of policies as well as from functional linkage. In
functional linkage, political actors, holding constant their objectives, decide to
extend their activity. In deliberate linkage, political actors alter "the objectives
which gave rise to their efforts at regional integration" (Haas, 1975, p. 15). For
example, participants agreed on the objective of a common market, so they
accepted proposals to extend integration through the harmonization of product
standards (functional linkage). The decision was an incremental extension of
integration and not controversial. In contrast, when participants, who agreed to
provide for the free movement of labor, began to consider the effect of national
redistributive policies on the movement of labor, they found that a common
policy was not easy to formulate. The consideration of redistributive policies
took the actors beyond their original objective of creating a common market
into a consideration of social justice where they had no common objective
(Haas, 1975, p. 23). Haas introduced the concept *turbulent fields* for "the
confused and clashing perceptions of organizational actors who find themselves
in a setting of great social complexity: the number of actors is large; each actor
pursues a variety of objectives which are mutually incompatible, but each is
unsure of the trade-offs between the objectives; each actor is tied into a network
of interdependencies with other actors who are as confused as he, yet some of
the objectives sought by each cannot be obtained without cooperation from
others" (p. 18). The concepts which Haas introduced in his 1975 book helped
to correct the impression that integration would evolve almost automatically
and provided a view of the EC which appears more valid today.

Few contributions were made to the study of the EC following the early,
creative period. The first theorists posed the questions which still trouble
scholars today. They broadened the field of inquiry beyond the usual confines
of political science into such subjects as communications theory and sociology.
Later students of the EC, however, retreated from the broad approach and
frequently studied specific institutions or policies. Theorists generally ne-
glected developments in the EC.

Scholars have recently renewed their interest in the theory of European
integration. Most of them agree that the EC entered a new era as a result of
the adoption of the Single European Act (SEA) and the 1992 program. The
subsequent revitalization of the EC surprised most observers and intrigued
scholars. Theorists have returned once again to the study of European
integration seeking to explain the sea change in the 1980s and to forecast the
course of integration. The new work on integration theory closely relates
either to the earlier neo-functionalism or to the realist theory of international
relations. The work of Andrew Moravcsik is often cited as an example of the

latter (see for example, Moravcsik, 1991). Martin Holland bases his latest study of the EC on the concepts and assumptions of neo-functionalism (Holland, 1993). Robert Keohane and Stanley Hoffmann have written an important study in which they argue that both neo-functionalist and realist concepts are valid for analyzing aspects of recent developments in the EC (Keohane and Hoffmann, 1991). They believe that the neo-functionalists were correct in discerning elements of supranationalism in the EC; however, they do not find that neo-functionalist concepts account for the recent changes in the EC. They propose a hypothesis which they call the "preference-convergence hypothesis" to account for the change. According to their hypothesis, the change resulted from "intergovernmental bargains made possible by convergence of preferences of major European states" (p. 25). Keohane and Hoffman believe that European integration can progress either by major steps or incrementally and that the two forms result from different policy processes. The EC takes major steps when member states agree that the steps are in their national self-interest. It takes incremental steps according to the processes outlined by the neo-functionalists and includes the participation of nongovernmental as well as governmental actors.

Philippe Schmitter is another scholar who has reconsidered the theory of EC integration (Schmitter, 1992). Although he was one of the contributors to neo-functionalism, he agrees with Keohane and Hoffmann that its concepts do not account for the transformation during the 1980s. He believes that political life in the EC is unique and involves a complex mixture of actors, interests, and conditions. He is less certain than Keohane and Hoffmann about defining the role of national governments. He writes about a "post-sovereign, poly-centric, incongruent, neo-medieval arrangement of authority" and adds, "Its core lies in the growing dissociation between authoritative allocations, territorial constituencies, and functional competences" (p. 48). Integration is not a single process but a composite of processes depending on the subject, and each process entails its own blend of actors and interests. He has developed an interesting scheme of possible outcomes for European integration. Integration does not have, and may not be susceptible to, determined objectives. His work does not constitute a theory of integration, but it represents a significant advance in the preparation for such a theory. It is innovative and conceptualizes the unique quality of European integration.

The scholars discussed above are theorists, but they offer important insights and concepts to guide the study of European union as proposed in this book. They agree that integration is a reality and needs to be understood on its own terms. They warn against simple assumptions about the objectives of integration or about why integration evolves as it does. They agree that policy making in the EC is a complex process involving formal and informal actors, but they do not agree about which actors or factors ultimately determine the results. They provide grounds for considering that the old questions about intergovernmentalism versus supranationalism are still open and that no one approach is preeminent in the field of European integration studies.

Roy Pryce and Wolfgang Wessels offer another approach to the study of European integration (Pryce and Wessels, 1987). Their approach does not provide a theory about integration, but it provides a practical framework for the study of the process. They developed their framework in order to study the history of European union since 1973. (The European Council agreed in 1973 to proceed toward a union.) According to Pryce and Wessels, studying the integration process should include three major categories: (1) the goals, content, and method involved in an EC initiative for integration, (2) the actors involved in the initiative, (3) the environment in which the initiative takes place.

The authors draw a number of relevant conclusions from their study. They note that integration may serve one of two strikingly different objectives—to replace member states or to assist them—but they find that the latter objective was more common in the period covered by their study. They also observe that integration is more successful when member governments perceive that integration offers solutions to mutual problems. Pryce and Wessels also find that the concept of national interest must be used carefully. It is neither stable nor cohesive. Government leaders, members of parliament, and other relevant national actors frequently have different interpretations of national interest, and definitions can change with changes of government. The authors also note that the politics of European union do not operate in separate spheres for national actors and EC actors but rather that national bureaucrats and EC bureaucrats have a long-term working relationship which has become the focus for related political activity and creates a new kind of politics. In considering the politics of European union, they find it useful to distinguish between propulsive elites and supportive elites. The former "conceive, launch, and take the lead in promoting initiatives designed to achieve closer union" (p. 16). The latter are individuals and organizations which mobilize and orchestrate support for an initiative.

The preceding discussion has focused on approaches to the study of the EC as the agent for European integration. Other approaches, either more limited in scope or focused on a single aspect of the EC, also offer useful tools for studying the EC. During the late 1970s and the 1980s most studies of the EC focused on specific policies of the EC and were largely descriptive. EC policies may, however, be analyzed with the aid of concepts borrowed from policy studies. Policy studies focuses on process, so concepts developed for policy studies may be adapted for studies of the policy process in the EC (with due regard for the unique character of EC policy as neither international nor national).

Regime theory was developed in the 1970s for the study of international relations but has been adapted for studying policy making in the EC. A regime is a set of principles, norms, rules, and decision-making procedures around which the expectations of actors converge on a specific issue (Krasner, 1983, p. 2). Behavior in international relations is shaped, in part, by regimes. The principles and values, as well as the decision-making process, help to shape outcomes. Outcomes do not result solely from the relative power of the actors, according to some regime theorists (Puchala and Hopkins, 1983, pp. 62 and 86).

Regime theory has been used to study environmental policy (List and Rittberger, 1992). Regimes involve sociological phenomena, such as norms and shared interests among international groups, and also political phenomena, such as rules and the decision-making procedure necessary to make the rules. Regime theory has three characteristics which make it a promising tool for studying EC environmental policy:

1. It provides the researcher with a manageable focus for research. The study of a single policy process, like the examination of a single cell, can provide insights into the whole.

2. It assumes a relationship between sociological phenomena and political phenomena. (Studies of regional integration dating back to the work of Karl Deutsch have included sociological phenomena.)

3. A comparison of the findings of a number of policy studies employing regime theory may provide evidence to support Philippe Schmitter's theory that the EC integration process is really a composite of processes and that integration should not be considered a unit.

Another approach, which was borrowed from the field of policy studies and which may be useful, is the advocacy coalition approach of Paul Sabatier (Sabatier, 1988, 1991). Two characteristics of his approach hold promise for the study of the development of European union. The first requires the study of the development of a policy over a number of years, and it requires the researcher to look for evidence of policy-related learning as a causal factor in the development of the policy. The second, public policy, is conceptualized as a belief system with value priorities and causal assumptions about how to realize them (Sabatier, 1988, p. 131). The researcher needs to focus on three different sets of variables:

1. The stable system parameters which also affect or restrain the policy subsystem. The parameters are set by the legal structure, the basic attributes of the problem, and fundamental cultural values.

2. The external environment, that is, changes outside the subsystem, such as changing socioeconomic conditions, which may affect or restrain the policy subsystem.

3. The policy subsystem which includes competing advocacy coalitions, policy brokers, and decision makers.

The Sabatier approach provides a useful framework on which to organize a study of an EC policy (see Figure 2.1). The framework accommodates the variables which need to be considered. The requirement to consider a policy over a number of years and to look for policy-related learning also accords with the idea that integration grows incrementally; on the other hand, the approach makes no assumption about goals, so it avoids the controversy over intergovernmentalism versus supranationality.

In this eclectic discussion of general theories in political science and policy studies, one more scholar will be considered. The work of that scholar is derived from the study of law, but it encompasses the basic questions of integration and its goals which concern the scholars discussed earlier in this chapter. Joseph Weiler is a noted authority on law and on the EC who has contributed important insights into the integration process. He posits three possible outcomes for integration:

1. Integration may lead to the creation of a superstate through the merger of the member states into the new entity. In that outcome, the new entity takes on the characteristics of a national state with all the associated strengths and flaws.

2. Integration may create an EC which functions solely to service the member states. It would exist in order to enhance the powers of the member states. Margaret Thatcher envisioned such an EC.

3. Integration may create a community composed of member states which still have significant functions but exercise self-restraint to form a unique relationship with one another. The member states and the peoples of the EC are joined through shared values and aspirations. (Weiler, 1992, pp. 36–39)

Weiler believes that supranationalism is in ascendancy and that the Thatcher approach to the EC has been defeated. He thinks that the community form of integration promises a more constructive and peaceful future.

One of the most important contributions of Joseph Weiler is his elaboration of the concept of legitimacy in regard to integration. He foresaw that the legitimacy of the EC would be challenged when the EC moved to implement the Maastricht Treaty. He distinguishes formal (legal) legitimacy from social (empirical) legitimacy. Legal legitimacy occurs when a constitution or a treaty provides a political entity with the legitimate right to act, and it may exist without social legitimacy. The latter occurs when citizens perceive that their government respects and guarantees values which are part of a political culture (p. 20). Social legitimacy enhances the stability and strength of a system. In order for the EC to acquire social legitimacy, it must demonstrate to the people that integration enhances their welfare, ensures democracy, and does not submerge important differences among the peoples who make up the Community. A governing body may have legal legitimacy long before it has social

Figure 2.1
A Diagram of Policy Development in the EC Based on the Sabatier Approach

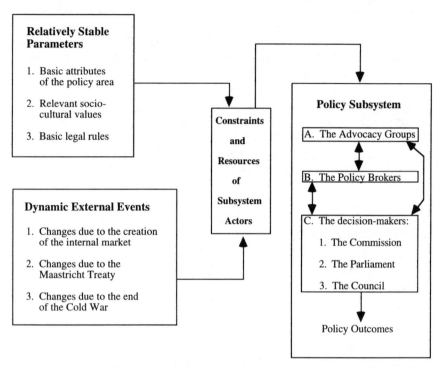

legitimacy. Legal legitimacy results from a political act, but social legitimacy requires changes in the perceptions of a people.

The Treaty on European Union will lead to a legitimacy crisis in the EC, according to Weiler, because the treaty gives the EC increased responsibility in matters of direct concern to the peoples of the EC. It also expands the use of majority voting in the Council. In the past, the EC adopted policies without concern for the public because the policies did not affect most people. Controversial proposals were quietly shelved in the Council under the threat of veto. Removing the right to veto changes the political dynamics just as the treaty increases the right of the EC to act in areas of public concern. A concerned majority in a member state used to be able to stop an EC proposal through pressure on its national government, but this is no longer true. National majorities have lost power and may have to accept EC policies which directly concern them and which they oppose. The possibility threatens traditional ideas of democracy and could lead to crises. The threat would be lessened if the EC had social legitimacy in addition to the legal legitimacy which the treaty provides. In order to obtain social legitimacy, however, the EC must succeed in adopting the new policies, and success is doubtful.

The extension of majority voting in the Council will change the political culture of the EC, according to Joseph Weiler. In the past, the ideologies of left and right were kept out of the Council. Members of the Council belonged to different political parties, but they left their ideologies outside the Council room. The need for unanimity led to a politics of consensus building. When the Council adopted the 1992 program, it accepted the values of the market, efficiency and competition, as EC values, but those values will conflict with the social values associated with new areas for EC policy making. The choices of the future will directly affect the left and the right in their views about markets versus social welfare. The members of the Council will not be constrained by the need for consensus but rather by the need for allies among the members in order to obtain a majority who will support the policies which the Council hopes to adopt. The political culture of consensus will be replaced by a more contentious one. Joseph Weiler has pinpointed a dangerous dilemma for the EC. It needs to move into social policy more strongly than it has if it is to establish social legitimacy, but the move threatens the consensus politics of the EC and may undermine public support for integration.

CONCLUSION

One thread runs through all of the approaches which have been discussed in this chapter. A study of the EC or of an EC policy needs to include a wide range of factors, external and nonpolitical as well as internal and political, informal as well as formal. The studies discussed here do not represent all the approaches for studying the EC. They were selected because they appear to hold the most promise for a study of European union. *Union*, as will be discussed more fully in the next chapter, is a vague word without a precise meaning. The member governments of the EC have ratified a document which commits them to a European Union but does not clarify the nature of that union. Indeed, one authority calls the treaty "an untidy compromise between two strands of thinking about how the Community should develop, the federalists and the inter-governmentalists" (Morris, 1993). (He believes that the federalists gained more in the treaty than the intergovernmentalists.) A study of the European Union of the Maastricht Treaty needs to encompass both strands of thinking. In order to do so, it needs to include approaches and concepts which do not prematurely exclude relevant factors.

A useful concept for initiating the study of European union is social legitimacy. If the European Union is to have a supranational quality, the peoples of the Union must accord it social legitimacy. One of the ways an entity gains social legitimacy is by providing people with policies which directly relate to them; therefore, the policies provided by the treaty which directly relate to people become the focus of study. A study of each of the relevant policies should provide a general overview of the potential effect of the new treaty on the people and should provide a basis for considering whether the development of the European Union is likely to deepen the legitimacy of European integration.

The relevant policies need to be studied separately and without expectations. As Keohane, Hoffmann, and Schmitter have noted, integration is a composite of processes, and different processes may have different politics. The different policies will be separately studied using concepts borrowed from policy studies. Each study of a policy will be structured according to the three categories defined by Sabatier: the stable system parameters, the effects of the environment, and the policy subsystem. The effect of policies on member states will also be noted. As Richard Rose noted, "In order to establish Community regulations, there must be a common fund of knowledge about programs already in effect in each country" (Rose, 1993, p. 70). The time will be long enough to show the evolution of a policy through the major eras of transformation in the EC. The concept of regime, particularly as discussed by List and Rittberger, will also be employed because it focuses on sociological factors and thereby relates to the discussion of social legitimacy.

REFERENCES

Haas, E. 1968. *The Uniting of Europe.* Stanford: Stanford University Press.
——— . 1975. *The Obsolescence of Regional Integration Theory,* 2d ed. Berkeley, CA: University of California Press.
Holland, M. 1993. *European Community Integration.* New York: St. Martin's Press.
Keohane, R., and S. Hoffmann. 1991. "Institutional Change in Europe in the 1980s." In *The New European Community,* ed. by R. Keohane and S. Hoffmann. Boulder, CO: Westview Press.
Krasner, S. 1983. "Structural Causes and Regime Consequences." In *International Regimes,* ed. by S. Krasner. Ithaca, NY: Cornell University Press.
List, M., and Rittberger, V. 1992. "Regime Theory and International Environmental Management." In *The International Politics of the Environment,* ed. by A. Hurrell and B. Kingsbury. Oxford: Clarendon Press.
Mally, G. 1973. *The European Community in Perspective.* Lexington, MA: Lexington Books.
Moravcsik, A. 1991. "Negotiating the Single European Act." In *The New European Community,* ed. by R. Keohane and S. Hoffmann. Boulder, CO: Westview Press.
Morris, A. 1993. "Europe 2000: Union or Fragmentation?" Occasional Papers, no. 14. The Jean Monnet Council—George Washington Forum in European Studies. Washington, DC.
Pentland, C. 1973. *International Theory and European Integration.* New York: Free Press.
Pryce, R., and W. Wessels. 1987. "The Search for an Ever Closer Union: A Framework for Analysis." In *The Dynamics of European Union,* ed. by R. Pryce. London: Croom Helm.
Puchala, D., and R. Hopkins. 1983. "International Regimes: Lessons from Inductive Analysis." In *International Regimes,* ed. by S. Krasner. Ithaca, NY: Cornell University Press.
Rose, Richard. 1993. *Drawing Lessons in Public Policy.* Chatham, NJ: Chatham House Publishers.
Sabatier, P. 1988. "An Advocacy Coalition Framework of Policy Change and the Role of Policy-Oriented Learning Therein." *Policy Sciences* 21: 129–169.
——— . 1991. "Towards Better Theories of the Policy Process." *PS: Political Science and Politics* (June): 147–156.

Schmitter, Philippe. 1992. "Interests, Powers and Functions: Emergent Properties and Unintended Consequences in the European Polity." Unpublished paper.
Weiler, J. 1992. "After Maastricht: Community Legitimacy in Post-1992 Europe." In *Singular Europe*, ed. by William James Adams. Ann Arbor: University of Michigan Press.

Chapter 3

Understanding the Treaty on European Union

The Treaty on European Union (or the Maastricht Treaty as it is more commonly known) is the third major treaty in the history of the European Community (EC). The Treaty of Rome established the European Economic Community. The Single European Act (SEA) provided the basis for the creation of the internal market. The purpose of the Maastricht Treaty is to give the EC the means to continue integration after 1992. The first two treaties were drafted and ratified in relative obscurity, but this was not the case for the Maastricht Treaty. It became the center of a storm which threatened to bring the EC into disrepute and to undermine the integration process. The problem arose only partly from weaknesses and ambiguities in the document itself. As noted in Chapter 1, the treaty was ratified at a time of great political and economic turmoil, which affected consideration of the treaty. Provisions of the treaty, such as monetary union, which might have been acceptable in a prosperous EC appeared highly risky to Europeans threatened by recession and the costs of ending the Cold War.

The treaty has now been ratified and the implementation is under way. The treaty provides for a Union with a vast range of responsibilities, the most famous of which are monetary union and a common foreign and security policy. It has major implications for the future of European integration, but the implications are not obvious. They must be found through an examination of the compromises which shaped the treaty and an understanding of the principles on which it is based. Any final assessment of the treaty must also consider its implementation under the difficult conditions existing in Europe. The purpose of this chapter is to examine the background of the treaty, its major provisions, and its basic principles. The discussion is not, however, equally balanced among the provisions of the treaty. Monetary union and a common foreign policy, although major provisions, are not relevant to the topic of this study.

DRAFTING THE TREATY ON EUROPEAN UNION

The Treaty on European Union was forged in a long and semipublic process which left scars on the final document. The stages of the process were determined by the Council. The foundation was laid by working groups and the treaty was completed in a marathon European summit in Maastricht in December 1991. The media provided extensive coverage of developments but full publicity was not possible because most of the work was not conducted publicly.

The major actors involved in drafting the Treaty on European Union were:

1. The national governments of the member states. Each government had its own agenda which it pursued in Council meetings and through its representatives in the working groups for the Intergovernmental Conferences.

2. The European Council. It is composed of the heads of governments of the member states with the participation of the president of the Commission. The Council meets to determine major policies for the EC, and it took the formal steps necessary to initiate the drafting of the treaty and to sign the final document. The presidency of the Council rotates every six months among the member governments. Each government which held the presidency during the relevant stages of the process played a role in shaping the process.

3. The Commission and its president, Jacques Delors. They played a significant role in promoting monetary union but were less successful in regard to political union. The Commission did not initiate the discussion on political union, and the Commission failed to obtain a commitment to federalism for the Union.

4. The European Parliament. It was able to place political union on the agenda for the treaty but it did not gain all that it sought in regard to an increase of its own powers.

5. Interest groups. They were not overt actors in the process; however, later studies may find, as they have in the case of the Single European Act, that interest groups were effective behind the scenes in shaping the provisions of concern to them. As one might expect, business groups were interested in monetary union.

6. A large number of experts. They participated in the working groups and were especially important in providing the studies for monetary union.

A glance at the history of the drafting process illustrates why the treaty is an unwieldy instrument. The initiative for the Treaty on European Union came from a number of sources. Jacques Delors and many business leaders wanted a new treaty in order to provide for monetary integration. They believed that a common currency was the logical capstone to the internal market. The twelve member states of the EC had liberalized financial services and removed controls on the movement of capital in the late 1980s. In 1988, they agreed to establish a committee to study monetary union and made Jacques Delors chairman of the committee. At a meeting of the European Council the next year, a majority of the heads of government voted to call an Intergovernmental Conference (IGC) to consider a new treaty on economic and monetary union. The Commission supported the move.

Once the European Council set the process in motion, other actors sought to broaden the process. The European Parliament (EP) requested that the Council add the topic of political union to the agenda of the IGC (EP, 1990a). The governments of Belgium and Italy supported the initiative of Parliament. President Mitterrand of France and Chancellor Kohl of Germany sent a letter to the European Council requesting that the Council consider creating a separate IGC on political union at its next meeting. When the Council met in Dublin in June 1990, the members agreed to establish an IGC to consider political union. The two IGCs would work simultaneously but separately. The two IGCs did not begin work, however, on equal terms. The IGC on monetary union benefited from the preliminary work of the Delors committee and it had a more specific task before it. The IGC on political union started work without a preliminary document and without specific objectives. Foreign policy, security policy, institutional reform, and the democratic deficit were all on its agenda.

According to David Williamson, secretary general of the Commission and a participant on the IGC on political union, the working group dealt with these five major elements: (1) the redefinition and extension of Community competences, (2) democratic legitimacy, (3) the efficiency of the Union, (4) a common foreign and security policy, and (5) European citizenship (Williamson, 1991, p. 18). Each of the five elements constituted a large and highly controversial topic. All of the actors had a significant stake in the outcome because what was decided would directly affect the division of authority between national governments and the EC, and among the institutions of the EC. Because the public was aware of the issues, public expectations were raised as well. The situation compelled compromise and made coherence unlikely.

The preparations for the IGCs continued throughout 1991. The leaders of the two countries which held the presidency of the Council during that crucial year tried to guide the work. Luxembourg held the presidency during the first half of the year. Its government produced a draft treaty which was "based on the prevailing drift emerging from the work of the two conferences" (*Draft*

Treaty on the Union, 1991). The Council accepted the draft as the basis for discussion.

The Luxembourg draft resembled in many respects a national constitution. It included articles on citizenship, human rights, and police powers. It also stated that the treaty marked a stage in the process leading to a federal goal (Article A). (The British government fought and won a battle to delete any mention of a federal goal in the final treaty.) The draft gave more power to Parliament, provided for a new Committee of the Regions, and made subsidiarity a general principle to guide EC policy making. The sum of the provisions would have been a new, more democratic, multilayered policy process.

When the Dutch took over the presidency of the Council, they produced a document which changed some provisions in the Luxembourg draft, particularly those dealing with the powers of the institutions. It increased the powers of the Commission and gave Parliament a veto over much of EC legislation. The draft was not accepted, however, by the Council as a basis for discussion. Indeed, it seemed to obstruct rather than to facilitate the discussion. Some sources stated that the draft did not even have the agreement of all relevant members of the Dutch government. Others stated that different versions of it were supplied to different member governments. The Dutch government failed to provide effective, coherent leadership in the crucial period leading to the Maastricht conference in December 1991.

The main actors in the IGCs were representatives of the national governments, an important fact to remember. The final treaty bears the imprints of different national concerns. By the end of the summer of 1991, most of the governments had made clear their objectives for the treaty. The British, Danish, and Portuguese governments fought to lessen federalist tendencies. German participants wanted to increase the powers of Parliament in exchange for their support of monetary union. The French were not enthusiastic about a strong Parliament, but they wanted monetary union. The poor members, under the leadership of Spain, worked together to ensure cohesion by which they meant the transfer of money from the rich members to the poor ones. The small states obstructed proposals to reform EC institutions if the reforms lessened their influence. No single ideal united the twelve with enough force to overcome individual national self-interest, and no leader had the charisma or authority to force the debate onto a higher plateau. The drafting process differed greatly from the processes which had shaped the Treaty of Rome and the SEA. In the former, participants fervently desired unity both for reasons of security and for the ideal of European integration (Mowat, 1973, pp. 114–115). In the latter, actors were united by their belief that integration had to be revitalized in order to bring about economic recovery (Taylor, 1989).

The member governments gathered in Maastricht in December 1991 with their differences still unresolved. They spent two days (and nights) in intense negotiations in order to produce a treaty which surprised most people who had followed the preparations. Observers were surprised by the division of the treaty into a main text and a number of protocols. In particular, they were surprised to learn that the important topics of monetary policy and social policy were covered in protocols, which meant that not all members would have to participate in EC policies on those topics. The effect was to establish a two-speed EC, a structure long rejected by leaders of the EC. According to the *Economist*, the Germans proposed opt-out clauses (the term used for the protocol structure) to the British so that the British would not prevent the inclusion of federalist elements in the treaty ("The Federalists Fight Back," November 30, 1991, p. 48). Social policy proved to be the most difficult problem. The British would not agree to give the EC more power to enact social policies. Late in the final night of negotiations, the other members agreed to a protocol by which they could make common social policies without British participation. The formal signing of the treaty took place in Maastricht on February 7, 1992. The treaty then had to be ratified by each member country according to its own constitutional provisions for treaty ratification.

Probably no international treaty since the one for the League of Nations encountered as much public debate and acrimony as did the Maastricht Treaty. Citizens who had supported the idea of integration suddenly became fearful of its reality. They had liked the 1992 logo and the EC flag, but they were not necessarily ready to abandon their borders or their currencies. Public attention peaked in June 1992 when the Danes voted against ratification. Bad publicity continued to gather during the summer of that year along with worsening economic news. The currency crisis in September raised serious doubts about monetary unification, the hallmark provision of the treaty. The feeble support which the treaty gained in the French referendum did not enhance its image. Inside the EC institutions, no effective leader emerged to capture public confidence as Jacques Delors had in the formative stage of the 1992 project. Perhaps only inertia saved the treaty. Ratification in most European countries is routine. Once government leaders set it in motion, mobilizing opposition to it is difficult. Even in Britain, where opposition was the strongest, government leaders were able to overcome it. John Major, facing a split in his own party and a united opposition party, still had the weapon of a no-confidence vote. He forced recalcitrant members of the Conservative Party to support the treaty or to defeat their own government on a no-confidence vote. They reluctantly fell in line rather than face a general election, which they knew would bring defeat to their party and return a Labour government. The last obstacle to ratification was removed on October 12, 1993, when the German high court ruled that the treaty is not incompatible with the German constitution.

PROVISIONS OF THE TREATY

The Treaty on European Union, including its protocols, is a document of some 250 pages (CEC, 1992b). The text of the treaty is divided into seven titles. Its signatories bind themselves to continue integration as indicated in the separate titles of the treaty as well as in the protocols. The institutions of the EC are given new tasks and new authority. The treaty establishes more than twenty procedures by which policies may be made. The treaty strengthens European integration but also evokes the principle of subsidiarity to protect the prerogatives of the member states. It adds two new layers to European politics through provisions for regions and European citizens. It is a much more complex and ambiguous document than either of its predecessors (see Figure 3.1).

The Union plays a major role in the treaty. It encompasses all the actors and policies provided by the treaty; however, the precise meaning of the Union is not clear. Participants in the negotiations differed in their definition of the Union according to their beliefs about the authority of the member states and of EC institutions. The Union meant intergovernmental cooperation to some and integration to others. Some argued that the Union should be compared to a tree with EC institutions providing the trunk from which would branch all policies of the Union. Others argued that the Union should be perceived as an entity resting on separate pillars. In a Union based on intergovernmental cooperation, the roles of the member states and of EC institutions would differ according to the policy (pillar) under consideration, but sovereignty would remain primarily with the nation states. (The political cooperation procedure established by the SEA for foreign policy is an example of this conception of the Union.) The Commission argued against the concept of separate pillars, but its argument did not prevail (CEC, 1990).

The previous treaties of the EC refer to union as well. The Treaty of Rome opens with a statement of purpose: "Determined to lay the foundation of an ever closer union among the peoples of Europe . . . "; union is therefore an objective and the wording implies a dynamic quality to integration but without defining the goal. The Rome treaty does not develop the idea of union any further. The Community is the sole international entity created by it. The Single European Act opens with the following: "Moved by the will to continue the work undertaken on the basis of the Treaties establishing the European Communities and to transform relations as a whole among their States into a European Union, in accordance with the Solemn Declaration of Stuttgart of 19 June 1983 . . ." Article 1 of Title I of the SEA acknowledges two international entities—the European Communities and European Political Cooperation. European Political Cooperation is composed of the High Contracting Parties (the signers of the treaty). Title III of the SEA provides that the High Contracting Parties develop a common foreign policy by a procedure which is distinct from

Figure 3.1
Main Elements of the Maastricht Treaty on European Union

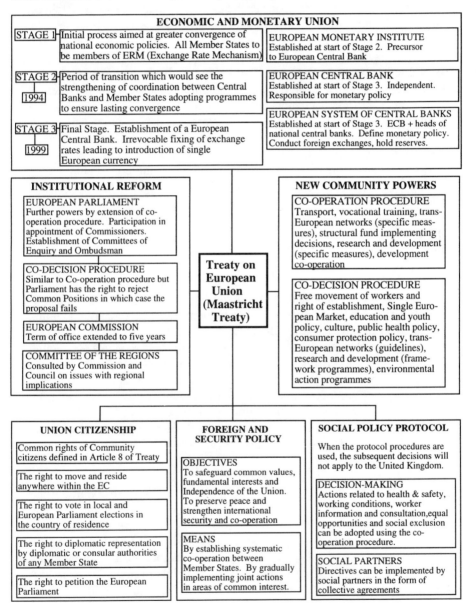

ECONOMIC AND MONETARY UNION	
STAGE 1 Initial process aimed at greater convergence of national economic policies. All Member States to be members of ERM (Exchange Rate Mechanism)	**EUROPEAN MONETARY INSTITUTE** Established at start of Stage 2. Precursor to European Central Bank
STAGE 2 1994 Period of transition which would see the strengthening of coordination between Central Banks and Member States adopting programmes to ensure lasting convergence	**EUROPEAN CENTRAL BANK** Established at start of Stage 3. Independent. Responsible for monetary policy
STAGE 3 1999 Final Stage. Establishment of a European Central Bank. Irrevocable fixing of exchange rates leading to introduction of single European currency	**EUROPEAN SYSTEM OF CENTRAL BANKS** Established at start of Stage 3. ECB + heads of national central banks. Define monetary policy. Conduct foreign exchanges, hold reserves.

INSTITUTIONAL REFORM

EUROPEAN PARLIAMENT
Further powers by extension of co-operation procedure. Participation in appointment of Commissioners. Establishment of Committees of Enquiry and Ombudsman

CO-DECISION PROCEDURE
Similar to Co-operation procedure but Parliament has the right to reject Common Positions in which case the proposal fails

EUROPEAN COMMISSION
Term of office extended to five years

COMMITTEE OF THE REGIONS
Consulted by Commission and Council on issues with regional implications

Treaty on European Union (Maastricht Treaty)

NEW COMMUNITY POWERS

CO-OPERATION PROCEDURE
Transport, vocational training, trans-European networks (specific measures), structural fund implementing decisions, research and development (specific measures), development co-operation

CO-DECISION PROCEDURE
Free movement of workers and right of establishment, Single European Market, education and youth policy, culture, public health policy, consumer protection policy, trans-European networks (guidelines), research and development (framework programmes), environmental action programmes

UNION CITIZENSHIP

Common rights of Community citizens defined in Article 8 of Treaty

The right to move and reside anywhere within the EC

The right to vote in local and European Parliament elections in the country of residence

The right to diplomatic representation by diplomatic or consular authorities of any Member State

The right to petition the European Parliament

FOREIGN AND SECURITY POLICY

OBJECTIVES
To safeguard common values, fundamental interests and Independence of the Union. To preserve peace and strengthen international security and co-operation

MEANS
By establishing systematic co-operation between Member States. By gradually implementing joint actions in areas of common interest.

SOCIAL POLICY PROTOCOL

When the protocol procedures are used, the subsequent decisions will not apply to the United Kingdom.

DECISION-MAKING
Actions related to health & safety, working conditions, worker information and consultation, equal opportunities and social exclusion can be adopted using the co-operation procedure.

SOCIAL PARTNERS
Directives can be implemented by social partners in the form of collective agreements

ALAN BURNETT: DONCASTER EBIU BRIEFING REPORT

the usual policy-making procedure in the EC, setting a precedent for the Union depicted in the Maastricht Treaty.

The Union created at Maastricht rests on three pillars. One pillar is composed of the EC itself and includes the competences and procedures covered by Title II of the treaty. The second and third pillars deal with foreign policy, and justice and home affairs, respectively, and each has a policy-making process based on cooperation among member governments and the EC.

The first paragraph of the treaty states:

> By this Treaty, the High Contracting Parties establish among themselves a European Union, hereinafter called "the Union." The treaty marks a new stage in the process of creating an ever closer union among the peoples of Europe, in which decisions are taken as closely as possible to the citizen. The Union shall be founded on the European Communities, supplemented by the policies and forms of co-operation established by this Treaty. Its task shall be to organize, in a manner demonstrating consistency and solidarity, relations between the Member States and between their peoples. (Article A, p. 7)

The Union as conceptualized in the treaty excludes a federalistic connotation. The first paragraph of the Luxembourg draft of the treaty had included the words "the Union with a federal goal," which add a more precise commitment to a greater degree of integration. In the final version, however, the commitment is deleted. Indeed, the inclusion of the phrase "in which decisions are taken as closely as possible to the citizen" gives a more restrained connotation to union than does the one in the Treaty of Rome.

The Union and the Community are not interchangeable concepts. According to Douglas Hurd, the British foreign secretary, the Union "embraces both the Community institutions and separate pillars of inter-governmental co-operation" (Hurd, 1992). Commission officials tried to delete the word "union" from the treaty. They warned that the Union and the Community would develop separately if the treaty did not provide a federalistic objective for the Union. Commission officials also warned that the word "union" has no legal personality in international law, so its use would complicate the development of a common foreign policy (CEC, 1991).

In Title I, Article B, the treaty assigns to the Union many important responsibilities, some of which will be exercised by the Union and some by the EC. Some will be shared with the member states. Title I provides two principles to guide the division of labor: subsidiarity and *acquis communautaire*. The principle of subsidiarity assigns responsibility for a policy to the most appropriate level of government. The principle of *acquis communautaire* operates to prevent any reversal of the existing authority of the Community.

In conclusion, the Union, as established by Title I, is an entity composed of the institutions of the EC and the member governments acting together in political cooperation. The powers assigned to the Union are not exclusive. The EC and the member governments continue to have separate and distinct responsibilities as well as those which they share when they act together as the Union. Union, so defined, is a unique and difficult concept but a vital one in European integration in the post-Maastricht era.

Title II of the treaty deals with the European Economic Community, which it renames the European Community. It is the longest part of the treaty and makes important changes in both the structure and the authority of the EC. The most famous power given to the Community by Title II is the power to establish a single currency, but Title II also gives the EC new powers to legislate on subjects such as European citizenship, education, culture, and public health. (Each of those subjects is discussed more fully in later chapters.) It makes complex and important changes in the policy process and adds subsidiarity as a guiding principle for policy making. Title II creates two new institutions: the Committee of the Regions and the European Central Bank. It makes a few gestures toward closer ties between the EC and citizens of the member states and toward removing the democratic deficit. (Democratic deficit refers to the failure of the EC to provide for democratic participation and, especially, to its failure to provide Parliament with full legislative powers.) Overall, with the exception of monetary union, provisions in Title II are extensions of provisions of previous treaties.

Title II does not make major changes in EC institutions even though many changes were proposed when the treaty was under discussion. Some people thought changes were necessary in order to remove the democratic deficit. Others thought changes were necessary in order to make the institutions more efficient and to prepare for the addition of new member states. Title II provides for few reforms for either the Council or for the Commission. The size of the Commission remains at seventeen, but the Council may change the number of Commissioners if all members agree. The reforms for Parliament, while more extensive than the reforms of the Council or of the Commission, fall far short of those sought by persons concerned about the democratic deficit. Parliament may initiate a procedure for uniform direct election of its members. It has a modest power of initiative and of oversight to investigate other institutions or bodies suspected of wrongdoing (Article 138b and c). It has the right to confirm the appointment of a new Commission. As a gesture to democracy, citizens may petition Parliament about matters which affect them directly and which are under the authority of the Community. Parliament will appoint an ombudsman who will have the power to investigate complaints received from citizens and to make other investigations when he believes that adequate grounds exist (Article 138e).

Title II does provide Parliament with more influence over EC policy making. Until 1985, Parliament had only the right to prepare an opinion on pending legislation. The SEA gave Parliament the right to participate in a cooperation procedure for enacting measures relating to creating the internal market (Article 100a of the SEA). The procedure gave Parliament the means to compel the Council to be more responsive to Parliament. Article 189, parts b and c, of the new treaty further expands the authority of Parliament vis-à-vis the Council (see Figure 3.2). The provisions do not make Parliament an equal partner, but they do give it the means by which Parliament can effectively participate.

Article 189b establishes a co-decision procedure according to which the Commission initiates a proposal, Parliament drafts an opinion, and the Council adopts a common position. Both the Council and the Commission next inform Parliament of their positions. Parliament then has three months to consider those positions. If Parliament approves the Council's common position or fails to act, the Council then adopts its common position as an EC directive. If Parliament rejects the common position by an absolute majority, the Council may convene a Conciliation Committee, composed of representatives of the Council and of Parliament and with the participation of the Commission. If Parliament continues to oppose the proposal after the Conciliation Committee, it has the power to kill it by a vote of an absolute majority of its members or it may propose amendments. In the latter case, the Council has three months in which it may approve the amended text by a qualified majority vote of its members or by a unanimous vote if the Commission disapproves the amended text. If the Council rejects the amendments, the Conciliation Committee is convened again. It has six weeks to draft a joint text which may be adopted by a majority vote in Parliament and a qualified majority vote in the Council. If either body fails to approve the measure, it is not adopted; on the other hand, if the Conciliation Committee fails to agree, the Council has six weeks to confirm its original position or a text which includes some of Parliament's amendments. The text becomes law unless Parliament votes within six weeks to reject it by an absolute majority.

The complicated procedure just described provides Parliament with some limited—but real—power. Parliament can kill proposals. The Council no longer is the final arbiter on EC directives in every case. The co-decision procedure also provides Parliament with the means to be more effective in shaping policies. The Council will be under a time constraint, so it will need to anticipate the demands of Parliament in order to ensure acceptance within the time frame set by the treaty. The co-decision procedure is also important to Parliament because it must be used for policies which particularly interest members of Parliament, such as education, culture, health, consumer protection, the free movement of workers, and some measures concerning the environment. Members of Parliament will undoubtedly use the opportunities provided by Article 189b to advance the legislative program of the EC in those important sectors.

Article 189c provides for a procedure similar to the cooperation procedure established by the SEA in which the initial steps are the same as those described

Figure 3.2
Procedures for Decision Making in the Maastricht Treaty

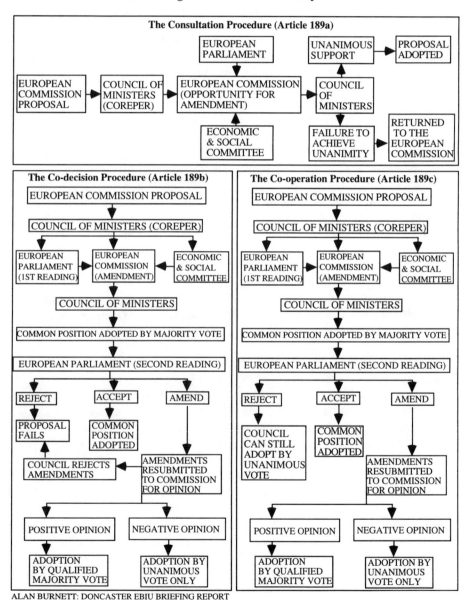

above; however, the procedure varies in situations where Parliament and the Council disagree. No Conciliation Committee is convened, and the Council can adopt the measure if all members agree. If Parliament adopts amendments to the proposal, the Commission has a month to consider them and to reexamine the Council's common position. It then sends the Council the reexamined proposal along with an explanation of the amendments which it has not accepted. The Council may accept the reexamined proposal by a qualified majority vote or amend it by a unanimous vote. The Council has three months to complete its task. The procedure established by Article 189c is to be used for proposals dealing with health, safety, and the environment at work (Article 118). (Measures concerning the internal market which used to be enacted under the cooperation procedure in the SEA are now subject to the new co-decision procedure of Article 189b.)

Further details on policy making are provided in sections of the treaty dealing with specific areas of competence such as the environment and consumer protection. The Economic and Social Committee must be consulted in many cases; in addition, the new Committee of the Regions must be consulted on policies of relevance to regional development. The treaty also states that some types of policy shall be made by the traditional policy process, which requires unanimous agreement by the Council and which limits the role of Parliament. Policies dealing with citizenship will be made by the traditional procedure, for example; some types of general policies are made by one procedure, and policies which implement the general policy are made by another. The multiannual framework programs for economic and social cohesion, for example, are adopted according to procedures established by Article 189b (except that decisions by the Council must be made unanimously), and measures to implement the program are adopted by a qualified majority of the Council after consultation with Parliament and the Economic and Social Committee. To add to the confusion, environmental policies are adopted by different procedures depending on their subjects.

In summary, Title II provides for more democratic policy making in the EC by increasing the power of Parliament and by limiting the number of cases in which a single member government can block action by the Council. The cost of the increased power, however, is high. The treaty provides for so many procedures that it fails to create the transparency or openness which is essential for democratic accountability. Interested citizens will have difficulty understanding the responsibilities of the various institutions. The provisions of the treaty also increase opportunities for disputes over the appropriate policy-making procedure. Such disputes have already occurred under the SEA over, for example, environmental policies. Given the greater complexity of the new treaty, one can foresee a vast increase in the number of disputes which will require a ruling by the European Court. What one cannot foresee is the consequences of the new procedures for the democratic legitimacy of the EC.

Many people policies will be easier to enact, thus increasing democratic legitimacy; on the other hand, the complexity and ambiguity of the process will confuse interested citizens, thus failing to lessen the distance between the EC and its citizens.

Titles III and IV extend the provisions of Title II to the European Coal and Steel Community and the European Atomic Energy Community. Title V provides for a common foreign and security policy. The details of the three titles are not relevant to this study and so will not be discussed.

Title VI of the treaty gives the Union responsibility for cooperation in home affairs including asylum policy, visa regulations, immigration policy and controls, drug trafficking, and judicial cooperation on criminal and civil matters. Such responsibilities are normal prerogatives of national governments and are of vital interest to citizens. Title VI assigns specific roles to EC institutions in implementing the provisions of the title. The Council has the power to initiate proposals dealing with subjects covered by Title VI except for visa policies, in which case the Commission has the power of initiative under Article 100c of Title II. Title VI contains an interesting provision whereby the Council may, if all members agree, make Article 100c of Title II the relevant article for other measures currently covered by Title VI. The provision makes possible the gradual transfer of responsibility for those measures from the Union to the EC.

Protocols play an important role in the Maastricht Treaty because they provide for flexibility in integration. As previously noted, protocols provide the means whereby EC monetary and social policy can proceed among members who are ready for the step. The protocol on social policy is especially important to the subject of this book. It allows eleven members of the EC to pursue the objectives of the 1989 Community Charter of the Fundamental Social Rights of Workers (see Chapter 5) despite the opposition of the United Kingdom. The policy-making procedure in the protocol is the same as the relevant one in the body of the treaty except that it is adjusted to exclude British participation. Under the protocol, policies which normally require a unanimous vote in the Council continue to do so, but the unanimity is among the eleven members rather than twelve. When a qualified majority vote is called for, the number necessary is reduced to forty-four; however, the protocol does not exclude British participation in Parliament.

The protocol on social policy was apparently a last-minute compromise drafted in the night by a small group and without the participation of persons from the Commission who are experts on EC social policies. Many believed that the protocol was a temporary expedient which would end when a new British government took office. The belief has not been fulfilled, and the EC faces confusion about social policy. Existing policies continue to apply to all twelve members. New policies may still be adopted by the twelve according to provisions in the text of the basic treaties and such policies will apply to all twelve members as well. Policies adopted under the protocol will apply only in the eleven member states but British subsidiaries operating in those states must implement the policies even though the parent firm in the United Kingdom does not. David Gardner called the social protocol "a Brussels benefit for the legal fraternity" (Gardner, 1991, p. 2). British multinational corporations are only beginning to realize the legal confusion created by the social protocol.

SUBSIDIARITY

The Maastricht Treaty contains references to a number of important principles such as cohesion and European citizenship. An understanding of the principles is essential to an understanding of the treaty. Most of the principles are discussed in later chapters dealing with the topic relevant to the principle. One principle is, however, fundamental to all provisions in the treaty and understanding it is essential to understanding European integration in the 1990s. The principle is subsidiarity which has already been mentioned but which requires a more careful examination.

Subsidiarity is first mentioned in the Treaty on European Union in Article B of the common provisions, which states: "The objectives of the Union shall be achieved as provided in this treaty and in accordance with the conditions and the timetable set out therein while respecting the principle of subsidiarity as defined in Article 3b of the treaty establishing the European Community." Article 3b of Title II of the Maastricht Treaty in turn states:

The Community shall act within the limits of the powers conferred upon it by this treaty and of the objectives assigned therein. In areas which do not fall with its exclusive competence, the Community shall take action, in accordance with the principle of subsidiarity, only if and in so far as the objective of the proposed action cannot be sufficiently achieved by the Member States and can therefore, by reason of the scale or effects of the proposed action, be better achieved by the Community. Any action by the Community shall not go beyond what is necessary to achieve the objectives of this Treaty.

Subsidiarity is therefore established by the treaty as a principle to guide action in the Union and to limit the action of the EC. The organizing principle of the treaty, subsidiarity applies to all actions of the EC except where it has exclusive competence. It implies a restraint on the EC and a protection for the role of the member states. Noting the implications of subsidiarity and the deletion of the word *federalism* from the treaty, one may reasonably conclude that the treaty sets limits to integration more clearly than the previous treaties, which had implied that integration was a process toward an undefined objective.

Subsidiarity is not mentioned in the Treaty of Rome. It is mentioned only once in the SEA and specifically in regard to environmental policy. Although authorities argue that subsidiarity was always implicit in the operation of the EC, the Maastricht Treaty is the first one to state it as a principle to guide all action in the Union. Subsidiarity is now discussed in numerous EC documents, but it was seldom mentioned in earlier decades (see, for example, CEC, 1992a; EP, 1990b; European Council in Lisbon, 1992). The attention to the concept perhaps indicates a reaction to the rapid expansion of EC activities resulting from the 1992 project. Subsidiarity is not an easy principle to implement. It does not define spheres of action for the participants in the Union; rather, it regulates the exercise of power. A special report prepared for the Commission lists these five criteria to guide the exercise of power under the principle of subsidiarity: need, effectiveness, proportionality, consistency, and communications (*The Internal Market after 1992*, 1992). The Commission should consider each of the criteria when it is considering proposing an EC policy.

The difficulty with the concept of subsidiarity arises in part from different definitions. According to one definition, that given by Jacques Delors, the concept relates to Roman Catholic social philosophy. He wrote: "Subsidiarity comes from a moral requirement which makes respect for the dignity and responsibility of the people which make up society the final goal of that society. . . . Subsidiarity, because it assumes that society is organized into groups and not broken down into individuals, rests, strictly speaking, on a dialectic relationship; the smaller unit's right to act is operative to the extent and only to the extent that it alone can act better than a large unit in achieving the aims being pursued" (Jacques Delors, 1991, p. 9). In contrast, Leon Brittan, another member of the Commission, stated: "Subsidiarity is a vital tool of self restraint" ("Subsidiarity in the Constitution of the EC," 1992). According to his concept, subsidiarity is a legally binding restriction on the scope of EC action. His definition derives from the individualistic, Anglo-Saxon tradition in contrast to the Catholic tradition implicit in the definition by Jacques Delors. The differences mark a fault line which underlies the different conceptions of integration and adds another element of ambiguity to the meaning of the Treaty on European Union.

THE PRYCE AND WESSELS CONCEPTUAL FRAMEWORK

If the Treaty on European Union is discussed within the framework that Roy Pryce and Wolfgang Wessels developed in 1987 in order to consider European union a number of insights are gained and some weaknesses are discerned (Pryce and Wessels, 1987; also see Chapter 2 of this book). They devised three categories for their study, the first of which comprises goals, content, and methods. If we consider the Maastricht Treaty in regard to the first category, certain problems become obvious. The authors wrote that goals should be clear. Member states should be able to see that the goals provide solutions to common problems (p. 26). The Maastricht Treaty fails in this regard. The Union is the goal of the treaty but, as we have seen, it is a goal without a precise meaning. The contents of the treaty includes measures intended to satisfy different national interests. Most interested parties can find in the treaty measures that are at least partially satisfactory to them. In this sense, the treaty is successful. The methods of the initiative contributed to the problems in the treaty. The separate consideration of monetary and political issues and the failure to provide coherent directions for the political discussions contributed to the adoption of a treaty which shows signs of hasty compromises and one whose provisions are poorly integrated.

The second category in the Pryce and Wessels framework concerns political actors. If the actors involved in the drafting of the Maastricht Treaty are compared with the actors associated with the SEA, several differences appear. Jacques Delors was a central figure both times, but he was older and less charismatic the second time around. In the 1980s he joined with Lord Cockfield to promote the 1992 program with a successful marketing campaign. The program and not the treaty caught the public attention. No popular proposal was on the horizon to excite interest in integration in the 1990s. Indeed, leaders of the EC did not make a concerted effort to win public support until after the failure of the Danish referendum. They did not seem to realize that the public was concerned and critical. The propulsive and supportive elites appear to have been less effective in the 1990s than in the 1980s. The Roundtable of European Industrialists, which played a major role in the 1980s, was less visible in the latest initiative. Other European interest groups were quiet as well. Indeed, it is difficult to discover an elite outside the Commission and, perhaps, banking circles that played a prominent role in promoting the treaty. The opponents were much more vocal than the proponents.

The third category in the Pryce and Wessels conceptual framework is the environment or the external conditions which affect integration. As noted earlier, economic conditions were not good during the ratification period; however, poor economic conditions do not necessarily threaten integration. Indeed, they were a factor in revitalizing interest in integration in the 1980s. The ratification of the Maastricht Treaty, however, took place within an environment combining poor economic conditions with public suspicion of Brussels. In the 1980s, the public did not blame Brussels for the bad economy, but many people did in the 1990s. Political conditions were also not conducive to integration. The turmoil in Eastern Europe raised serious questions about the future of Europe which the treaty did not address.

Roy Pryce described four conditions that encourage progress toward union (Pryce, 1987, pp. 273–294). The Treaty on European Union fails on three of them: (1) it fails to motivate actors to transcend narrow interests, (2) it lacks goals that will inspire supporters, and (3) it does not harness national interest to the goals of the union.

The only test that it meets is the one for flexibility. It provides a flexible strategy to meet the diverse needs of its members. The findings do not indicate a favorable prognosis for the next stage in the integration process.

CONCLUSION

The Treaty on European Union is a complex document characterized more by pragmatism and compromise than idealism and coherence. It gives to the Union important responsibilities but divides responsibilities for making policies between the institutions of the EC and the member states acting together in political cooperation. It implies that integration is a dynamic process but does not provide a direction for the process. It also introduces subsidiarity as a principle of restraint in integration. It addresses the democratic deficit by giving more power to Parliament but obscures democratic accountability by creating a policy-making morass. It provides for flexibility in the integration process through the addition of protocols, but the resulting two-speed Europe may not be feasible when it is superimposed on a single market. In short, it is a flawed instrument but one which can serve to provide the amount of integration possible in the current situation in Europe.

The Union is one of the most important features of the new system. The Union consists of the EC and its member states, but the demarcation of functions and responsibilities among the whole and the parts is not clear. Subsidiarity is the operational principle for determining the locus for policy making but is not an easy principle to apply. The treaty and its protocols provide an intricate map to the locations of the various responsible actors and the routes which they must take according to the circumstance or policy involved. The treaty provides for multilayered politics. Citizens, regions, political parties, national governments, and EC institutions have roles to play in the Union.

One may easily criticize the treaty as a bundle of compromises. One may even speculate that the EC might have been better if it had not been drafted. Once it was drafted, however, implementing it became essential to the future of the EC. The tenuous public support for integration would have plummeted in the face of a defeat in the ratification process. It could still plummet if implementation flounders on the complexities and ambiguities in the treaty; on the other hand, the treaty could encourage closer relations between the EC and citizens in the member states and lead to European union. The latter possibility is explored in the chapters which follow.

REFERENCES

CEC (Commission of the European Communities). 1990. "Commission Opinion of 21 October 1990 on the Proposal for Amendment of the Treaty Establishing the European Economic Community with a View to Political Union." COM(90)600 final.

———. 1991. "Declaration of the Commission on the Two Intergovernmental Conferences on Political Union and on Economic and Monetary Union." IP(91)1063.

———. 1992a. "The Principle of Subsidiarity." SEC(92)1990 final.

———. 1992b. "Treaty on European Union." Luxembourg Office for Official Publications of the European Communities.

Delors, J. 1991. "The Principle of Subsidiarity: Contribution to the Debate." *In Subsidiarity: The Challenge of Change*. Maastricht: European Institute of Public Administration.

Draft Treaty on the Union. 1991. 1722/1723 of Europe Documents Series: Agence Internationale D'Information Pour La Presse.

European Council in Lisbon. 1992. "Conclusions of the Presidency," June 26–27.

EP (European Parliament). 1990a. "Interim Report on the Intergovernmental Conference in the Context of Parliament's Strategy for European Union." Committee on Institutional Affairs. PE 137.068/final.

———. 1990b. "Interim Report on the Principle of Subsidiarity." Committee on Institutional Affairs. PE 139.293/final.

"The Federalists Fight Back." 1991. *Economist*, November 30, p. 48.

Gardner, David. 1991. "Astonishing Compromise Threatens to Create a Brussels Benefit for the Legal Fraternity." *Financial Times*, December 12, p. 2.

Hurd, Douglas. 1992. "Europe After Maastricht." Speech given at Cambridge University, February 7, 1992. Published by the British Information Services, February 10, 1992, New York.

The Internal Market after 1992. 1992. Report to the EEC Commission by the High Level Group on the Operation of the Internal Market (The Sutherland Report).

Mowat, R. 1973. *Creating the European Community*. New York: Harper & Row.

Pryce, R. 1987. "Past Experiences and Lessons for the Future." In *The Dynamics of European Union*, ed. by R. Pryce. London: Croom Helm.

Pryce, R., and Wolfgang Wessels. 1987. "The Search for an Ever Closer Union: A Framework for Analysis." In *The Dynamics of European Union*, ed. by R. Pryce. London: Croom Helm.

"Subsidiarity in the Constitution of the EC." 1992. Extract from a speech by Sir Leon Brittan to the European University, Florence, Italy, June 11, 1992.

Taylor, P. 1989. "The New Dynamics of EC Integration in the 1980s." In *The European Community and the Challenge of the Future*, ed. by Juliet Lodge. New York: St. Martin's Press.

Williamson, David. 1991. "General Strategy of EPU." In *The Agenda of the Intergovernmental Conferences: What Can Be Achieved?* Proceedings by Gabriele Jauernig. Brussels: Centre for European Policy Studies.

Chapter 4

The Cultural Basis of European Union

I s Europe a society? Is Europe becoming a society? These questions were posed in a recent book about European sociology (Bailey, 1992). Such questions are seldom asked in studies of the European Community (EC) but the answers are crucial. If the EC is composed of disparate societies, then EC institutions can formulate only general policies in order to win compliance from those societies. If the EC, however, is composed of peoples sharing certain social characteristics, then a closer link is possible between the EC and its citizens, and European union is a realistic objective. In the following discussion, Europe and the EC are used interchangeably. Many studies are based on Europe as a whole, others are based on Western Europe, and some are limited to the EC. In all cases, the meanings derived from the studies are discussed as they relate to the EC, so cumbersome references to Europe are omitted.

The question "Is Europe becoming a society?" is a particularly interesting one for the present study. The question raises the additional questions about what factors encourage the formation of a society and what the relationship between society and legitimacy is. Political culture is the relevant concept for the discussion because it concerns the aspect of society which deals with the set of subjective orientations to politics (Almond, 1993, p. 15). It comprises the expectations, behavior, and attitudes of a people toward their political system. Research demonstrates that political cultures change and that public policies can induce change in a political culture (Inglehart, 1990). Studies in Germany indicate that the success of German welfare policies, coupled with the effectiveness of political actors in the postwar era, led to positive changes in the political culture. The result is "the legitimation of the political system through its achievements" (Berg-Schlosser and Rytlewski, 1993, p. 326). A similar legitimation should be possible in the EC. Many who fought to insert "people policies" into the Treaty on European Union certainly believed in the possibility.

Headlines in Europe today cast doubt on assumptions about a common European society or even a common EC society. Nationalism, not social integration, appears ascendant. The rise of nationalistic political parties and of anti-immigrant demonstrations, as well as bitter campaigns against the Maastricht Treaty, demonstrates that nationalism remains a strong force in Europe. How does one determine, however, whether the surge in nationalism is fueled by short-term economic problems, the outrage of groups threatened by integration, or the expression of a deep and abiding social phenomenon? The history of nationalism in Europe has been so ugly and destructive that observers can easily forget that nationalism is modern, dating possibly only from the French Revolution. The current expression of nationalism, however, warns leaders that EC policies are testing the limits of public tolerance, so those leaders have tried to reassure the public that the EC will be guided by the principle of subsidiarity and not by centralized power in Brussels.

Competing nationalisms in Europe do not necessarily mean denying the existence of a European society or, at least, the embryo of one. The two can coexist. According to pluralistic theory, individuals can hold diverse values, or different groups of citizens can hold competing values and still exist within one society united by some common interests. Despite the signs of nationalism, people in the member states believe in European integration. (Both the EC and national governments are less popular than they were a decade ago.) Social scientists need to distinguish the shared values and attitudes of a common European society from deeply held national differences.

A society is a self-perpetuating group of people sharing interests, institutions, and culture. Everyone knows that societies exist, but no one has devised easy methods for proving their existence. In order to answer the questions posed in the first paragraph of this chapter, an interdisciplinary approach is necessary. Evidence must be provided by historians, anthropologists, and sociologists. A good starting point is with historians and anthropologists who have studied common characteristics of Europeans and with historians who have studied the idea of Europe. Sociologists provide findings from contemporary Europe. Finally, subsidiarity, a concept of vital importance to the topic, but one which does not fit into the categories of this chapter, is considered separately. When all of the findings are considered, one should be able to discern the outlines of a European society and also foresee limits which the society places on the EC.

UNIFYING FORCES IN EUROPEAN HISTORY

"Europe is a unity by virtue of having one Caesar and one God" (Martin, 1978, p. 228). The unifying influence of Rome on European administrative and legal traditions and of Christianity on European values is widely recognized. Roman roads and Roman laws lingered long after Rome fell, and traces of both can still be found from Britain to Greece. Christianity gave Europeans a common worldview and a system of ethics. It also bound them together. For centuries, Europeans referred to Europe as Christendom to distinguish it from other societies with which they came into contact.

Other factors unified Europeans as well. Recently, historians such as Janet Abu-Lughod have reexamined crucial eras, such as the thirteenth century, to uncover what bound Europeans together in a time when, according to conventional wisdom, people lived in isolated manors. She wrote that never had so many regions communicated with one another as in the thirteenth century. She argued that two qualities characterized that century: increased economic integration and cultural efflorescence (Abu-Lughod, 1989, pp. 2–3). Not only did merchants and traders move across Europe, but prospective guild members were also required to travel to learn their trade from masters in different places. (About 50 percent of the urban population belonged to a guild.) New skills or techniques developed in one location soon spread across much of the continent; for example, the diffusion of knowledge necessary to build the great cathedrals of the era came about through travel and communication among guild members. Common values and norms evolved to shape the classes which were to form the basis of the industrial revolution which followed centuries later (Cipolla, 1973, p. 9).

Throughout much of its history, Europe also had a common class system, groups of which were aristocrats, burghers, and peasants. Class, not locality, shaped people's values, behavior, and culture. An aristocrat had more in common with other European aristocrats than he had with the peasants on his land. Styles of socializing in that era created social networks for the aristocracy, which extended throughout Europe. The anthropologist Robert Anderson wrote, "These three pan-European cultures, aristocratic, burgher, and peasant, more than any and all others [factors] gave shape to that complex of cultures we call the traditional civilization of Europe" (Anderson, 1973, p. 5). He also argued that modern Europe is dominated by a single culture which derives through evolution from the traditional culture of the aristocracy (pp. 131–132).

None of the information above is new, but it needs to be reiterated to balance the emphasis today on nationalism. Europe was a society in the sense of having common values, attitudes, and institutions although it was divided politically before the age of nationalism. Norms which evolved over centuries persist and continue to provide a common social base despite strong national differences.

THE IDEA OF EUROPE

One aspect of European history that is particularly relevant to this study is the idea of Europe. Denis de Rougement wrote that a united Europe has been the ideal of great men for a thousand years (de Rougement, 1966, p. 3). Since the time of the Greeks, writers have referred to Europe as an entity distinguished from other geographical areas. After Rome fell, much of European history centered on attempts to provide unity for Europe. Intellectuals since Dante in the thirteenth century and Erasmus in the fifteenth century have argued that unity is a good that should be sought. Intellectuals and political actors have produced plans for a united Europe since the Duc de Sully wrote his Grand Design in the seventeenth century (Heater, 1992, p. 191).

Agnes Heller rejects the arguments that a European identity existed before the eighteenth century, but in that century a common European identity was forged. According to her, changes in social life and in political thought fused and reinforced one another to create a specific idea of Europe in which modernity and Europe were linked (Heller, 1992, p. 12). Her conception of Europe is dynamic, rational, and free; it flourished as a culture from the Napoleonic era until World War I (p. 15). She is uncertain about the fate of the European identity today but hopes that the drama of the previous era may now be followed by "the epic of settling in" (p. 25).

Intense nationalism characterizes the nineteenth century, but it was also the time when people tried to define and express the idea of Europe. Giuseppe Mazzini, the Italian patriot, organized the Young Europe movement in support of European unity. He saw no contradiction in simultaneously working for Italian independence and European unity because the two should coexist (Salvatorelli, 1970, p. 93). Victor Hugo, the famous French literary figure, tried to mobilize Europeans to create a united states of Europe in order to preserve peace. Pierre-Joseph Proudhon, known in the history of anarchist thought, wrote *The Federal Principle*, which was a plan for a federated Europe composed of nations, which in turn would be composed of confederations of local administrations. The higher levels would exist to coordinate the work of the lower units (Woodcock, 1956, pp. 248–249).

The impetus from the nineteenth century continued into the twentieth century and culminated in the writing of the Treaty of Paris, which established the European Coal and Steel Community. The story of the crucial era in postwar Europe, when the treaties for the three Communities were drafted and ratified, has been told by a number of authorities (see, for example, Haas, 1958, or Monnet, 1978). Two well-known points need to be reiterated, however, because of their relevance to the idea of Europe. As many authorities have noted, the men who fathered the Community shared many characteristics. They were Europeans for both philosophical and pragmatic reasons. They believed unity was necessary and morally right. They differed from earlier Europeanists, because they had practical political experience and knew the need for compromise. The participants also agreed that sovereignty is divisible and that national governments should cede a small portion of their sovereignty to the new entity.

One thread which runs through all the plans for a united Europe is the assumption that some degree of European social unity exists. Derek Heater wrote, "No project for voluntary political integration would be at all credible unless the putative member states shared some cultural and political traditions and values" (Heater, 1992, p. 180). The persons who, through the centuries, dreamed, planned, and worked for the idea of Europe ranged from aristocrats to anarchists, from literary figures to practical politicians, but all agreed that the peoples of Europe constituted a group distinct from others and that that group should have institutions to serve its needs.

THE EUROPE OF SOCIOLOGISTS

Sociologists, with their studies of social patterns, have some interesting findings to aid the consideration of European society. The literature on the subject is not extensive although the field is serviced by a journal, *The European Sociological Review*. One of the best sources is still the classic *Contemporary Europe,* edited by Salvador Giner and Margaret Archer in 1978. A more recent book (*Social Europe*, edited by Joe Bailey in 1992) considers unity and diversity in European society. The European Value Systems Study is the major source of survey data (Harding and Phillips, 1986). The data were compiled in 1981, but a new report is forthcoming.

According to sociologists, European society should not be regarded as a vast social monolith but rather as a mosaic of overlapping social patterns which do not necessarily conform to country boundaries. Indeed, the German sociologist Sven Papke asserts that purely national cultures do not exist in Europe (Papke, 1992, p. 64). The European Value Systems Study found that moral and personal values, religion, politics, the family, marriage and divorce, work, and well-being fall into diverging patterns: "Yet these diverging patterns across countries do not in our view indicate any fundamental disparity in value systems in Western Europe. The underlying organization of values is remarkably unified, demonstrating at a number of points an internal logic which clearly transcends national and linguistic boundaries" (Harding and Phillips, 1986, pp. 212–213).

Sociologists study a wide range of social phenomena to discover patterns but only three—religion, social stratification, and the welfare state—will be noted here. (Others will be considered in later chapters where the findings provide information necessary for the study of a particular EC policy.) Sociologists study not only patterns but also pressures which disturb those patterns. They examine how the society adapts to external factors and what mediators in the society facilitate the changes.

Sociologists agree with anthropologists and historians that a common religious heritage shaped the development of common values in Europe, but the question that particularly interests them is the extent to which religion has been replaced by secularism. If secularism is the norm, then a related question concerns the continued relevance of values which arose from religion. Many indicators support the change to secularism. Attendance at church services, participation in religious rituals, membership in a church, all show a decline; on the other hand, beliefs in the moral precepts of religion continue to hold firm (Harding and Phillips, 1986, p. 70). Grace Davie prefers to call Europeans unchurched rather than secular. She states that correlations between religious indicators and socioeconomic variables "confirm the existence of socio-religious patterning across national boundaries" (Davie, 1992, p. 223).

Sociologists note common trends in regard to social stratification in Europe. Inequality in the distribution of wealth continues to be a basis for social stratification, but ethnic and national characteristics constitute new and serious causes of social stratification. North Africans, gypsies, and Moslems are classed by their ethnic or religious identity as much as by their incomes (Davis, 1992, p. 18). Poverty is another factor exacerbating social stratification today. The number of people trapped in seemingly hopeless poverty has grown alarmingly, and poor people now constitute a new underclass throughout Europe (Gustafsson and Lindblom, 1993, pp. 33–34). One other trend regarding social stratification is important to note: Studies show that moral and religious values cut across class lines in the EC and, therefore, do not reinforce social stratification (Davis, 1992, p. 26).

Some of the common trends noted above pose serious threats to social stability. In the past, problems associated with social stratification were amenable to solutions provided by national governments. Reforms of national education systems, income tax policies, and social programs were effective national policies to lessen such social problems. The problems today are less amenable to national solutions. The two main problems, poverty and the social exclusion of persons from different religious or ethnic groups, cannot be solved at the national level when the causes are European.

The welfare state is a well-known feature of Western Europe. Countries in Western Europe are distinguished from other industrialized countries by the large amount of their national wealth which they commit to welfare programs. The development of the welfare state in postwar Europe and its present crisis have marked uniformity among the countries in Europe when perceived from the outside. The people throughout Western Europe value their welfare system. Although the welfare state is pervasive in Western Europe, one can discern three different categories. G. Esping-Andersen distinguishes between the liberal, social democratic, and conservative corporatist (Esping-Andersen, 1990). The liberal model, which is found in the United Kingdom, limits the role of the state and depends on voluntary programs and the operation of the free market to solve most problems. The social democratic model, or Scandinavian model, relies on state action to bring about social equality. The third model, which applies to both France and Germany, operates through social insurance programs. Employers, labor unions, and the government cooperate through corporatist structures to ensure welfare protection for most people. Today, all three systems are under attack because of budget limits, and authorities agree that major reforms will be necessary (Taylor-Gooby, 1993, p. 98). The EC is under pressure to solve the problems of the welfare state, but it will have difficulty devising common solutions given the differences among its member states.

SUBSIDIARITY

A buzzword in Brussels today, the word *subsidiarity* was seldom heard until a few years ago, and it still causes confusion. Subsidiarity concerns the sharing of responsibilities and powers among the EC, national governments, and other levels of government. The Single European Act is the first treaty to invoke subsidiarity as a principle, and it did so only in regard to environmental policy. In the Treaty on European Union, however, subsidiarity is the principle to guide all EC policy making. All policies being drafted in the EC today have a provision justifying action under the principle of subsidiarity.

A discussion of subsidiarity is appropriate in a chapter on European society because the word has roots in European values, and it is relevant to an understanding of European social organization. The search for its meaning leads back into European social history. An understanding of its meaning provides an insight into the mosaic which forms European society.

Subsidiarity is strongly linked to Catholic doctrine, but it also shows influences of Continental liberalism. During the nineteenth century, when the industrial revolution resulted in new social classes, labor unions, and philosophies, Catholic theologians sought to come to terms with the new social order. They had an organic view of society in contrast to the individualistic view which prevailed in Great Britain. They wrote about just relationships among the actors in the industrial revolution and urged cooperation and restraint (Misner, 1991). Catholic political parties and labor unions came into existence during the industrial revolution. The doctrine for the new age was given papal sanction in the famous encyclical *Rerum Novarum* in 1891. Forty years later, the pope issued another famous encyclical, *Quadragesimo Anno*, which again addressed the conditions for a just order. Subsidiarity is used in the document to instruct public authorities to leave to lower levels the right to act on subjects which can be handled at those lower levels. Public authorities should encourage, stimulate, supplement, and complement, but not destroy, the ability of the lower levels to function. Jacques Delors, the president of the Commission of the EC, echoes the religious precepts of the principle. He writes, "Subsidiarity comes from a moral requirement which makes respect for the dignity and responsibility of the people which make up society the final goal of that society" (Delors, 1991, p. 9).

Although subsidiarity belongs most clearly within Catholic social doctrine, other theorists of the time developed similar ideas. Paul Spicker argues that

Continental individualism, with its emphasis on local authority, decentralization, and diversity, influenced the doctrine (Spicker, 1991, p. 5). The British
claim that subsidiarity is an expression of Anglo-Saxon individualism. Lord
Mackenzie Stuart, former president of the European Court of Justice, claims
that the roots of subsidiarity are in the writings of John Stuart Mill (Mackenzie
Stuart, 1991, p. 38). Jacques Santer claims that Proudhon is one of the fathers
of subsidiarity through his ideas about federalism, which are discussed above
(Santer, 1991, p. 20). If we accept that each of the authorities is correct, then
the ideas on which the doctrine is based had to have been widely held in the
nineteenth century.

Subsidiarity is also widely held today. The Commission, the Council, and
Parliament have issued documents discussing their support for the principle.
Member governments have indicated their agreement as well. No one seems to
dispute the propriety of the principle as a guide to action by the EC. The
difficulty will come when the principle is invoked to set limits on EC actions.
Subsidiarity, perhaps even more so than federalism, is a difficult guide to follow.

CONCLUSION

Is Europe a society? Yes, Europe, or at least its core, the EC, is a society if
the term is used in a general sense. History provided Europeans with common
norms, a culture, and institutions which persist today; however, later history
also divided Europeans into competing nationalisms. The task of the EC has
always been to build on the foundation of the commonalities without challenging the differences.

Is Europe becoming a society? If we accept that Europe is already a society,
then the question is whether the society is becoming stronger? Sociologists do
not provide conclusive evidence, but they note common norms and institutions.
They also find that people in the EC are facing common social problems, many
of which are caused by developments outside national borders. Common
problems may compel Europeans to seek common solutions, thereby strengthening European society, but sociologists warn against optimism about such
common solutions. If European society is a mosaic of overlapping patterns,
then common solutions may not be acceptable even to common problems. Both
the Germans and the British want their welfare systems repaired, but neither
would accept a solution crafted on the system of the other.

For centuries, some Europeans have believed that Europe should unify, and
they have proposed plans for unification. They assumed that a unifying strand
of history runs through Europe and that the appropriate kinds of institutions
could nurture it. The findings of sociologists and of scholars of German political
culture give support to those assumptions. Societies are malleable, and careful
public actions can strengthen them. The European Community is heir to that
strand of European history. Its founders believed that a Europe of common

values and principles exists and that common institutions are necessary to protect and assist Europeans.

The question which remains to be answered is whether European society has enough commonalities to allow for common actions to meet common needs. The answer rests with subsidiarity, a vague and difficult concept. The Treaty on European Union mandates common action in sensitive social areas. The principle of subsidiarity stipulates that EC actions not intrude on effective local or national policies. If boundaries can be marked and the EC implements successful social policies, we may see the development of legitimacy based on achievement.

REFERENCES

Abu-Lughod, J. 1989. *Before European Hegemony*. New York: Oxford University Press.

Almond, G. 1993. "The Study of Political Culture." In *Political Culture in Germany,* ed. by D. Berg-Schlosser and R. Rytlewski. New York: St. Martin's Press.

Anderson, R. 1973. *Modern Europe: An Anthropological Perspective*. Palisades, CA: Goodyear Publishing.

Bailey, J., ed. 1992. *Social Europe*. London: Longman.

Berg-Schlosser, D., and R. Rytlewski. 1993. "Political Culture in Germany: A Paradigmatic Case." In *Political Culture in Germany*, ed. by D. Berg-Schlosser and R. Rytlewski. New York: St. Martin's Press.

Cipolla, C. 1973. *The Fontana Economic History of Europe*. Vol. 3. London: Collins/Fontana Books.

Davie, G. 1992. "God and Caesar: Religion in a Rapidly Changing Europe." In *Social Europe,* ed. by J. Bailey. London: Longman.

Davis, H. 1992. "Social Stratification in Europe." In *Social Europe*, ed. by J. Bailey. London: Longman.

Delors, J. 1991. "The Principle of Subsidiarity Contribution to the Debate." In *Subsidiarity: The Challenge of Change*. Maastricht: European Institute of Public Administration.

de Rougement, D. 1966. *The Idea of Europe*. New York: Macmillan.

Esping-Andersen, G. 1990. *The Three Worlds of Welfare Capitalism*. Cambridge, England: Polity Press.

Giner, S., and M. Archer, eds. 1978. *Contemporary Europe*. London: Routledge & Kegan Paul.

Gustafsson, B., and M. Lindblom. 1993. "Poverty Lines and Poverty in Seven European Countries, Australia, Canada and the USA." *Journal of Social Policy* 3, no. 1.

Haas, E. 1958. *The Uniting of Europe*. Stanford, CA: Stanford University Press.

Harding, S. P., and D. Phillips, with M. Fogarty. 1986. *Contrasting Values in Western Europe*. London: Macmillan.

Heater, D. 1992. *The Idea of European Unity*. Leicester, England: Leicester University Press.

Heller, Agnes. 1992. "Europe: An Epilogue?" In *The Idea of Europe*, ed. by B. Nelson, D. Roberts, and W. Veit. New York: Berg.

Inglehart, R. 1990. *Culture Shift in Advanced Industrial Society*, Princeton, NJ: Princeton University Press.

Mackenzie Stuart, Lord. 1991. "Assessment of the Views Expressed and Introduction to a Panel Discussion." In *Subsidiarity: The Challenge of Change*. Maastricht: European Institute of Public Administration.

Martin, D. 1978. *General Theory of Secularization*. Oxford: Blackwell.

Misner, P. 1991. *Social Catholicism in Europe*. London: Darton, Longman and Todd.

Monnet, J. 1978. *Memoirs*. Trans. by J. Mayne. New York: Doubleday.

Papke, S. 1992. "Who Needs European Unity and What Could It Be?" In *The Idea of Europe,* ed. by B. Nelson, D. Roberts, and W. Veit. New York: Berg.

Salvatorelli, L. 1970. *The Risorgimento: Thought and Action*. New York: Harper & Row.

Santer, J. 1991. "Some Reflections on the Principle of Subsidiarity." In *Subsidiarity: The Challenge of Change*. Maastricht: European Institute of Public Administration.

Spicker, P. 1991. "The Principle of Subsidiarity and the Social Policy of the European Community." *Journal of European Social Policy* 1, no. 1.

Taylor-Gooby, P. 1991. "Welfare State Regimes and Welfare Citizenship." *Journal of Social Policy* 1, no. 2.

Woodcock, G. 1972. *Pierre-Joseph Proudhon: His Life and Work*. New York: Schocken Books.

Chapter 5

Employees and European Union

In an era when most adults are also employees and when work is characterized by stress and insecurity, social policies serve as a major link between citizens and their government. In an earlier era, socialist and Christian democratic parties came to power on the strength of their programs for workers. The policies which they adopted strengthened the allegiance of the working class to the government. Today governments which fail to address the employment needs of voters generally do not get reelected, but governments frequently cannot fulfill the expectations of voters because of economic constraints. As a result, labor union leaders, representing the interests of employees, have turned to the European Community (EC) for social policies which national governments can no longer provide. A successful Community social policy could be an important factor in building European union.

The EC has had policies on employment for decades, but the policies do not constitute a coherent, developed social program. Rather they are a collection of directives adopted in response to a specific concern and requiring minimal amounts of harmonization in national practices. Voting practices in the Council impeded the adoption of more sweeping measures. Because each member state had a veto, with a few exceptions, supporters of an EC social policy fought for the elimination of the veto. They gained a partial victory with the ratification of the Maastricht Treaty. The way is now open for a more fully developed EC social policy.

The provisions for social policy are among the most complicated in the Maastricht Treaty. They bear the imprints of old struggles and persistent divisions. They both facilitate and complicate the making of EC social policy.

They offer the possibility of a comprehensive social policy, they offer the risk of exacerbating the struggles and divisions of the past, and they increase the probability that firms and governments will turn to the European Court for rulings on EC employment directives.

The purpose of this chapter is to provide a framework for understanding both the promise and the risk. The framework is based on the approach introduced in Chapter 2. Relevant information about EC social policy and the process by which it is formulated is separated into three categories in order to facilitate understanding. The three categories are as follows:

1. The stable system parameters of EC employment policy (basic attributes of the problem area, the relevant cultural values, and the legal structure within which the policy is made).

2. The dynamic external environment (changes in the socioeconomic system which affect social policy).

3. The policy subsystem (decision makers, policy brokers, and relevant advocacy groups involved in the making of EC social policy).

The concepts which were discussed in Chapter 2 (regime, social legitimacy, and subsidiarity) are also considered. The objective of this chapter is to determine how much EC social policy will contribute to the creation of the European Union.

Employment policy in the EC is generally known as social policy, and the term is used in the following discussion. The distinction which Giandomenico Majone makes between employment policy and social regulation is considered in the conclusion (Majone, 1993).

BACKGROUND

When the EC was formed in the 1950s, each member state had a comprehensive social policy, which continued to grow and adapt in response to new needs and demands. The framers of the Treaty of Rome did not believe that an EC social policy should replace the national ones. Their main concern about employment was to provide for the free movement of labor as a necessary part of the proposed common market. The free movement of labor is one of the basic freedoms of the EC. Articles 117 and 118 reaffirm the right of member states to regulate employment. Intervention was foreseen only to encourage cooperation among the member states (Article 118) and to ensure that different national policies did not obstruct the operation of a common market (Article 100).

The Treaty of Rome includes several other provisions which later provided the basis for a social policy. The preamble to the treaty gives the EC the task of providing for "the constant improvement of the living and working condition of the people." Article 119 provides for equal pay for men and women. Articles

123 to 128 establish a Social Fund which has the purposes of making "the employment of workers easier and of increasing their geographic and occupational mobility within the Community" (Article 123). The treaty also requires the Commission to prepare an annual report on social developments. These requirements, supplemented by Article 235 (which allows the EC to take appropriate measures to attain the objectives of the treaty even in the absence of a specific grant of power), provided an adequate base for the EC to propose an ambitious social policy in the 1970s, during an era of heightened social consciousness.

The Social Action Program for 1974–1976 marked the start of the EC effort to create a far-ranging social policy. (The EC had adopted a few measures before the program.) The programs are framework documents which provide an agenda for EC action. The first program called for action under three headings: full and better employment, improvement of living and working conditions, and employee participation. Some parts of the first program were adopted and provided the basis for later, successful EC policies; for example, a vocational training policy was mandated under the heading of full and better employment. The EC now is extensively involved in vocational training. Health and safety policy is another important topic for EC action that originated in the first action program. The principle of employee participation, the third heading, became the center of one of the longest running and most acrimonious struggles in EC history.

Although the Council accepted the first action program, its members were reluctant to adopt measures to implement it, partly because of the deep recession in Europe following the oil crisis in 1973. The recession, however, was not the only reason for their reluctance. The composition of the Council changed in the 1970s, and consensus was more difficult to achieve. The EC had expanded from its original six members to nine and, according to Michael Shanks, who was director general for social affairs in the Commission, "the divergence of objectives became more and more marked" (Shanks, 1977, p. 17). The Commission continued to make studies and to draft proposals, but many of them disappeared from view once they arrived in the Council.

Following the adoption of the famous 1992 program in the 1980s, Jacques Delors, the president of the Commission, proposed the addition of a "social dimension" to the program. He wanted the support of labor union leaders, as well as of employees, for the 1992 program. Most labor unions supported the 1992 program, but they were concerned about some of its consequences. In June 1988, the Council adopted the Commission proposal for a social dimension (CEC, 1988). The policy concerns social problems which may result from or be exacerbated by the internal market. Its purpose is to alleviate the consequences of the 1992 program, but not to undermine the effectiveness of it. The scope of the new social program is further limited by the inclusion of the principle of subsidiarity, which leaves the primary responsibility for social policy with the member states. The directives proposed in the document are generally noncontroversial and primarily concern training, health and safety, and the free movement of labor. Only four proposals are controversial. Two deal with employee participation, one is concerned with part-time work, and one proposes a charter of social rights.

The adoption of the social dimension marked a new era in the history of the EC, one in which the Commission launched a number of highly publicized proposals, many of which the Council refused to adopt. One of the most famous was the Community Charter of the Fundamental Social Rights of Workers, which the Council did adopt but only as a declaration, which means that it is a statement of principle without the force of law (CEC, 1989). The struggle between the Commission and the Parliament on one side and the Council on the other lasted into the 1990s. The Commission and the Parliament supported social initiatives, but the Council failed to adopt many of them. The division was partly the result of fear in the Council that social policies would undermine the 1992 initiative. The more basic explanation for the apparent division rests with the voting procedures in the Council. Throughout the era, a majority of the members of the Council supported proposals from the Commission, but many types of social policy required a unanimous vote in the Council. The British government steadfastly refused to support many of those proposals, especially the highly publicized ones involving employee participation. Many observers concluded that social policy in the EC was a failure (see, for example, Lange, 1993). Meanwhile, the work to create the internal market rapidly progressed. The imbalance between economic and social legislation became untenable for those who supported the social dimension. They believed that the EC had to reform its policy-making process in order to remove the threat of the British veto, so they began to draft a new treaty.

The EC adopted more social policies between 1987 and 1992 than many may realize. The Single European Act (SEA), ratified in 1987, provided for the adoption of some types of social policy by a qualified majority vote in the Council. Many of the proposals falling under the provision were adopted, but they did not receive much public attention. Health and safety directives provide the best example of a type of policy which benefited from the SEA. Member governments all accepted Article 118 of the SEA, which created a special status for health and safety directives. The directives adopted under Article 118 did not become a common denominator for national laws, but they did become a benchmark; for example, the EC protections for workers on computers are arguably the highest in the world. Despite the effect of those protections, they were adopted by the Council with little public attention and little public argument from member governments which opposed them.

The social policies which the EC considered between 1987 and 1992 can be divided into three categories:

1. Policies providing for the free movement of labor.
2. Policies to prevent social dumping. (Social dumping refers to a situation in which a firm relocates from one member state to another in order to escape a higher level of social regulation in the first country.)
3. Policies to encourage a dialogue between labor and management.

Proposals for the free movement of labor are seldom controversial. Member states adopted directives for the mutual recognition of education degrees and training certificates. They agreed not to discriminate against employment opportunities among citizens of their respective countries. Some policies related to social dumping were also not controversial. Members readily agreed to important measures on health and safety. Other policies designed to prevent social dumping, for example, a proposal dealing with part-time employees, have been highly controversial. Almost all measures about relationships between labor and management, the third category, aroused fierce opposition and usually faced a British veto in the Council. The most important examples are the Fifth Directive, the European Company Statute, and the Works Council Directive. All would have required management to provide for some form of employee participation in the workplace. All were opposed by business groups and by the British government; none was adopted.

By the end of the 1987–1992 era, social policy remained one of the most contentious areas in the EC. Some of the contention resulted from the obvious division between labor and management, but some appeared rooted in deep divisions among the member states. Supporters of social policy hoped that the new treaty would provide a solution to the struggle and enable the EC to develop a more comprehensive policy.

STABLE SYSTEM PARAMETERS

The parameters within which EC social policy is formulated consist of the basic attributes of the problem area, the relevant cultural values, and the legal structure.

Basic Attributes of the Problem Area

The basic attributes of the problem area refer to the "givens" the natural resources which are not under the direct control of policy makers but which are directly relevant to policy. In the case of social policy, the basic attributes are the nature of work or the job market in the EC and the composition of the workforce in the EC. Both these attributes are determined by demographic and economic forces which are largely outside the control of policy makers. Policy serves to alleviate the negative consequences of these forces on employees and also to lessen the effect of negative demographic trends on the economy. The resulting policies are frequently controversial and subject to failure because of the complexity of the subject.

The job market in the EC is a consequence of the postindustrial economy which prevails in much of the region. Almost 60 percent of jobs are in the service sector, 33 percent are in manufacturing, and only slightly more than 7 percent of jobs remain in the agricultural sector (CEC, 1992b, p. 112). The majority of jobs have been in the service sector for the last twenty years. The old image of work as a permanent job in industry requiring a skilled, male workforce has been replaced by the reality of flexible work in the service sector requiring a workforce consisting of men and women, and both educated employees and cheap, easily replaceable workers. Officials have been slow to change public policies adopted in an earlier era to make them accommodate the situation which has prevailed for the last twenty years.

A number of characteristics of the workforce in the EC are relevant for policy makers. One is the fact that the EC has a smaller proportion of adults of working age actually working than either of its main competitors, the United States and Japan. In 1990, only 60 percent of working-age people were working in the EC compared to 70 percent in the United States and almost 74 percent in Japan (CEC, 1992a, p. 21). The statistics indicate that a relatively large number of working-age people are dependent on some form of public support. Some people apparently do not work by choice, but many are unable to find work. Unemployment has been a chronic problem since the 1970s, and the EC has been concerned with the failure of employers to create jobs even during periods of economic growth. Job creation rates are much lower in the EC than in either the United States or Japan. Public programs to assist the unemployed are a heavy burden on national budgets in every member state.

Another characteristic has to do with the needs of the workplace. Employers need a trained and flexible workforce. The workforce in the EC is educated and trained, but employers have a chronic need for new skills and for employees able to cope with a dynamic work environment. The task of public policy is not only to train and educate but also to provide adequate security so that the workforce can respond to changing needs. Most Europeans expect job security, but fewer find it today than found it right after World War II. Part-time and temporary jobs in the service sector have replaced traditional, secure, manufacturing jobs. Part-time workers comprise about 13 percent of the workforce in the EC (CEC, 1992b, p. 116). Twelve percent of working women and 8 percent of working men are employed on temporary contracts (CEC, 1992a, p. 15).

A third characteristic of the workforce in the EC is that women and foreigners comprise important groups in it. Women, who comprise about 40 percent (CEC, 1992b, p. 113), are regarded as a permanent part of the workforce, and all member countries have accordingly made some adjustments in their employee policies. Foreigners are a more controversial group in the workforce. About five million of the foreigners are citizens of an EC country living in another EC country. They comprise about 2 percent of the workforce (CEC, 1992b, pp. 90 and 114). They are not legally foreigners and should be treated as nationals. Their presence causes little difficulty, because they are generally integrated into the local community, and they are frequently engaged in technical or white-collar work. The controversies center on the more than eight million foreigners from non-EC countries (CEC, 1992b, p. 90), who tend to be younger and less educated than EC citizens. They comprise about 3 percent of the workforce (CEC, 1992b, p. 114). Many of them find jobs in construction and low-skill service jobs. Foreigners have been a regular feature of the EC workforce for decades, but the EC largely ignored them.

A particularly worrisome aspect of the EC workforce is its costs, which exceed those of the workforce in the United States and Japan. The costs are explained by three facts:

1. Wage rates have remained high despite the loss of competitiveness in many sectors of the economy (Marsden and Silvestre, 1992, pp. 20–28).
2. Social costs are a high and fixed charge on employers. The welfare state, created when the workforce was young and firms were prosperous, has not adjusted to new conditions.
3. Benefits awarded in another era have not been adjusted to new conditions. EC employees work fewer hours per year than employees in competitor countries. They have long annual vacations and many public holidays for which they are paid and which add to the total labor cost.

Relevant Cultural Values

The history of social policy in Europe is long, with roots in the early years of the industrial revolution, if not before. Certain cultural values underpin the history and lead to public expectations that the legitimacy of a government rests, in part, on the effectiveness of social policy. In order to formulate an effective social policy, those responsible will need to find commonalities among the cultural values of the member countries, then use those commonalities as the basis for their policy. The existence of welfare states in all member countries indicates one commonality. Citizens do not believe that market forces provide the best assurance for their well-being. They expect government to set some limits to the operation of the market and to provide policies to protect individuals from market abuses. If national governments cannot provide effective social policies, then the EC would appear to be the legitimate actor; therefore, cultural values compel the EC to have a social policy when national policies cannot function effectively. What those values compel the EC to do is a question less easily answered. One approach to answering that question would be to cull through the social and cultural history of all the member states for commonalities, but the task would be enormous and the potential pitfalls numerous. A more manageable approach would be to seek clues in a study of the much more concise history of the EC to determine from EC actions what values beyond national self-interest shaped them.

Clues to the cultural values which set parameters for EC social policy can, perhaps, be discerned from examining the three different types of EC social policy. The examination should include both the successful policies and those which the EC has pursued over a period of years without success. The goal is to find patterns which extend over years. The three types of policy are equal rights for workers, health and safety, and worker participation. Each type distinctly differs from the others, but all aim at benefiting employees.

Equality has a special status among social policies in the EC, because it rests on a mandate provided by the Treaty of Rome. Article 119 provides for equal pay regardless of gender. Despite its status, however, the policy did not receive serious attention until the 1970s when the Commission began to issue regular action plans for women (Landua, 1985).

In addition to directives dealing with pay discrimination, the EC has adopted directives and programs to solve workplace problems of specific concern to women. When the policy is considered as a whole, three observations are relevant.

One observation is that the policy differs in several respects from equality policy in the United States. U.S. policy focuses on the need to ensure that women are fairly represented in different work categories. Affirmative action, enforced through adversarial court procedures, has been the primary mechanism for meeting that need. EC policy has been less legalistic and more indirect, addressing attitudes and providing support services such as maternity leave (Springer and Riddle, 1988). The EC has held seminars for bankers to consider how they could use their female employees more effectively. It has special funds to assist training programs for women. It even has a program to provide funds for women who want to open their own businesses.

Another observation concerns the actors and their motives in establishing policies for equality. The impetus for such policies generally does not come from member governments, but rather from a loosely knit group composed of persons working in the equality unit of the division of the Commission which deals with social policy (DG V), outside experts under contract from DG V, women's groups in the member countries, labor unions, and the Centre for Research on European Women (CREW). The European Parliament, certain commissioners, and even the European Court of Justice have played important supporting roles. No one member of the Council has emerged as a major proponent of equality in the workplace. At times, one government will play a significant role, as the Irish government did in regard to a report on sexual harassment, but the role is not constant and may be the result of special circumstances. The British have played perhaps the most consistent role by regularly rejecting proposals which stray beyond a narrow definition of discrimination in hiring and promotion practices.

The third observation concerns the objectives and the scope of equality policy. The policy, taken as a whole and including both proposals which have been accepted and those still in the "waiting room," constitutes an ambitious effort to go beyond a narrow concern about discrimination in the workplace to one about improving the quality of life of working women. In the terminology of Giandomenico Majone, it is a social regulation and not a social policy (Majone, 1992). It arose not from a market failure but from quality-of-life issues and "thus reflects the values and political culture of post-industrial societies" (p. 7). The continuity of activity on the subject, despite a lack of success in the Council, indicates that equality is a widely held value. Even the British government has carefully affirmed its support for the principle. The value of equality appears to provide one of the parameters for EC social policy.

Health and safety is another area in which EC activity appears to indicate that a widely held norm exists. As noted above, health and safety directives do not constitute a common denominator among national laws. They set a high standard despite the fact that implementing them will cost much in many member states; moreover, they include the development of a requirement that responsibility for implementing the measures shall be shared by workers and managers. That potentially significant development of worker participation was quietly accepted as other proposals for worker participation were blocked. Member states unanimously agreed to revise Article 118 when the SEA was drafted. The revised article allows health and safety measures the privilege of being adopted by a qualified majority vote in the Council. Health and safety is the only topic in the field of social policy to be accorded that privilege. Indeed, the entire political process surrounding health and safety policy is unique. The EC has acquired its impressive health and safety policy with little public fanfare. Health and safety does not have loyal promoters among interest groups as do women's issues. The topic does not have high-profile opponents either, in the way that worker participation issues do. Health and safety measures have been drafted in the relative obscurity of Luxembourg by specialists from DG V and quickly and quietly moved through the institutions to acceptance as policy. It seems justifiable to conclude that the policy rests on some consensus which may be called an EC norm.

The third policy area, worker participation, has some similarities with the previous two, but also important differences. In sharp contrast to the other two, worker participation has evoked heated debate. Some groups may hesitate to go on record as opposing equality or health and safety, but they do not hesitate to oppose an EC policy for worker participation. Many commentators have called the debate over worker participation the most heated one in the whole field of social policy debates in the EC, and in contrast to the directives on equality or health and safety the EC failed to enact any important directive on worker participation despite almost a quarter century of effort.

The EC has claimed for many years that worker participation policy is a "democratic imperative." As early as 1970, the EC had a formal proposal for worker participation in the draft regulation for a European Company Statute. In 1972 the Commission proposed the Fifth Directive, which would have required formal worker-participation schemes in all large enterprises. (For a more complete discussion, see Pipkorn, 1980, or Shanks, 1977.) In 1980 the Commission added the famous Vredeling Proposal to require multinational enterprises to inform and consult their workforces regularly. All three proposals met overt hostility from business groups and rejection from the British government.

In the 1980s worker participation received less public notice, but the issues never disappeared from the agenda of the EC; indeed, the Commission continued to revise and to seek a strategy to ensure the acceptance of its proposals. In the 1990s the Fifth Directive and the European Company Statute were revised yet again and a new proposal for European works councils was placed on the agenda of the Council. The Danish government promised action on the subject in 1993 when Denmark held the presidency of the Council. The Council discussed the European Company Statute for the sixteenth time in its history but failed to accept it or either of the other two. (The discussion of the fate of the proposed directive on works councils during the Belgian presidency in the fall of 1993 will be included in the discussion of the Maastricht Treaty.)

A goal which has been pursued as tenaciously as has worker participation in the EC has obvious importance for its advocates. The usual explanations for such a development include the following:

- The proposal represents the lowest common denominator among national laws, so its passage would not disturb existing national practices. Its acceptance would not harm any member states and would enhance the democratic credentials of the EC.
- The proposal is necessary for the creation of the internal market. In this case, the different forms of worker participation required by national law are said to constitute a barrier to the internal market.
- The proposal has the support of a powerful member government or a powerful constituency.

None of those explanations adequately explains the place of worker participation in the social policy agenda. Although the various proposals have been moderated through the years, they still would entail more than a ratification of the status quo if they were accepted. The proposals (except the one for works councils) predate the 1992 initiative, and business groups argue that the proposals would harm rather than aid the formation of the internal market. The proposals have benefited from the support of the German government. German governments of both the left and the right have supported EC efforts for worker participation, but none has exercised the full power of that country to try to force acceptance. Labor unions comprise the main constituency in support of the goal; however, they are neither a powerful influence in the EC nor an unqualified advocate of specific proposals. Divisions in the ranks of the European Trade Union Confederation (ETUC) prevented it from lobbying vigorously for either the European Company Statute or the Fifth Directive when they were discussed in the 1970s.

Because none of the usual explanations is adequate, perhaps some explanation can be found in a consideration of worker participation as a concept. Worker participation is a European phenomenon, practiced widely in Europe but almost unknown in the United States. Its roots reach back to the industrial revolution, and its evolution is closely intertwined with the evolution of European systems of industrial relations. The search to understand worker participation leads back into history and philosophy even though some classify participation as a postindustrial value. The clues which can be found to explain the importance of the issue in the EC can only be speculative with such a complex subject, because no method exists to provide definitive answers. The discussion which follows should be considered within the context of materials developed in Chapter 4.

The concept of worker participation derives from two very different philosophies of the nineteenth century. One is obviously socialism and the other, less noticed but perhaps more pervasive, is social Catholicism. As early as 1835, the Catholic social philosopher Franz von Baader proposed establishing committees of workers within firms in order to curtail the power of the manager. The encyclical *Rerum Novarum* of 1891 is the most famous hallmark in the development of social Catholicism. It states, "Working men have been given over, isolated and defenseless, to the callousness of employers and the greed of unrestrained competition." Pope Leo XIII stated that private property was a right, but that owners and workers had mutual obligations and should work together to provide just conditions at work. He wrote about boards or associations of workers or of workers and employers who would provide those just conditions. The roots of both worker participation and corporatism can be found in the document (Leo XIII, reprinted in Sigmund, editor, 1988, pp. 155–162). The ideals were incorporated in the Catholic labor unions which were organized throughout Western Europe at that time (Misner, 1991).

Socialist labor unions, which were larger and more powerful, built on the philosophies of Marx and French syndicalists to develop more militant concepts of worker participation (Lichtheim, 1970, p. 216). Worker self-management ideas evolved from those philosophies. In later decades, social-ist labor unions compromised on the right of private property but retained the belief that the right was to be tempered by some form of worker participation.

The different philosophical bases of the concept hampered the formation of worker participation policies until after World War II. In the postwar era, most countries in Western Europe enacted laws to require workers' councils in firms. The main exception was the United Kingdom, where both labor and manage-ment preferred to retain their traditional collective bargaining system. Follow-ing an era of worker militancy in the 1960s, interest in worker participation was revitalized on the Continent and evoked new literature and new laws on the subject. During that era, the Commission began to draft its proposals on the topic.

A number of scholars have noted that a certain unity shapes European economic history and distinguishes features of labor and management relations (see, for example, Bendix, 1974, or Chamberlain, 1980). Worker participation grew out of that unity. Its adoption by the Commission needs to be understood as not linked solely to the needs of the internal market. It was perceived as a "democratic imperative," to use the language of a Commission document (CEC, 1975, p. 9).

The role of the United Kingdom as the major opponent to an EC policy on worker participation needs to be considered. A worker participation policy began before the United Kingdom joined the EC, and many commentators expected the easy passage of the proposed European Company Statute. They were surprised by the vigorous opposition of the new member of the Council. The British opposition persisted even when a Labour government was in power. The British system of industrial relations and labor law drastically differs from Continental systems and not just because the British lack experience with worker participation. A whole bundle of factors make up the "British differ-ence." The British legal and welfare systems are fundamentally different from Continental systems (Marshall, 1975). The philosophical and sociological factors which shaped the British working class differed as distinctively from Continental factors as Karl Marx differed from Robert Owen (Thompson, 1963). According to an interesting recent article, even British capitalism differs from Continental or "Rhine" capitalism (Hodges and Woolcock, 1993). Some-where in the shadowy realm of culture is the explanation of the "British difference."

When the whole of EC social policy is considered, one finds that it is not an attempt to replicate the social welfare systems of the member states; rather, it is an attempt to express widely held values, many of which would be classified as postindustrial values. Equality, health, and safety are examples. Both the subjects of the EC's social policy and the way in which they developed have distinctive characteristics; for example, the equality policy developed through programs to bring about the conditions for equality rather than through the more individualistic approach followed in the United States. Continental cultural norms seem to prevail in both the topics selected for proposals and the way these proposals are to be implemented. Two important norms are based on the old belief, noted earlier in *Rerum Novarum*, that capitalism needs to be tempered by control by governments or other institutions and that corporatist traditions mandate institutionalized forms of participation.

Relevant Constitutional Rules

The Treaty of Rome provided a firmer basis for the development of policies for employees than it did for policies to protect the environment; however, the framers of the treaty did nothing to indicate that they foresaw the creation of a comprehensive social policy in the EC. The treaty deals with employee issues in two different sections. One is found in Part II, which concerns the foundations of the new Community. Title III of Part II concerns the free movement of persons, services, and capital. Articles 48 through 51 make both the member states and the EC responsible for removing barriers to the free movement of workers. Those articles have been implemented with little controversy. Part III, which concerns the policy of the Community, contains more important provisions for social policy. The role assigned to the EC is that of facilitator and coordinator among the member states, which retain the primary authority for social policy. The Commission is to promote cooperation among the member states on topics such as working conditions and vocational training, conduct studies in close contact with member states, and make an annual report to Parliament on social developments. Three of the five articles (Articles 117 through 122) on social policy deal primarily with responsibilities of the member states. One assigns some limited authority to Parliament and the Commission, and only one concerns the Council. Article 121 states that the Council, acting unanimously, may assign tasks to the Commission for implementing common measures. The European Social Fund is established in Articles 123 through 128 of the treaty. The fund, which is to be administered by the Commission, was created to assist social policies of member states by supplying 50 percent of the cost of programs for vocational training or relocation of displaced workers. One other measure in the treaty significantly relates to social policy. Article 235 gives the Council, acting unanimously, the right to adopt proposals from the Commission, after consulting Parliament, when such measures are necessary to meet an objective of the treaty and when the treaty does not provide a specific procedure to do so.

The provisions of the Treaty of Rome proved adequate for the EC to begin a significant social policy in the 1970s. The Single European Act (SEA) did not change the legal basis for social policy as significantly as it changed the legal basis for environmental policy. It made important additions to Article 118 to provide for the adoption of directives on health and safety at work by a qualified majority vote in the Council and to instruct the Commission to encourage negotiation between labor and management at the European level. The only other change which the SEA makes and which directly relates to social policy is to combine the Social Fund with the regional and agricultural modernization funds into the new Structural Funds.

Article 100a of the SEA provides that measures dealing with the formation of the internal market may be adopted by a qualified majority vote in the Council. Economic policies were thus placed in a privileged position in relation to social policy. As the number of directives adopted under Article 100a grew in the 1980s and early 1990s, supporters of social policy sought to revise the treaty in order to provide for similar entitlement for social policy. They also redrafted a number of social proposals so that they could be considered under the revised Article 118 (health and safety) or under Article 100a. Social measures which required a unanimous vote in the Council frequently failed because of the British veto. The dispute between the British government and supporters of social policy was carried into the negotiations for the Treaty on European Union. Both parties believed that the outcome of the negotiations was vital to them.

In conclusion, demographic, cultural, and legal factors together produce an environment which enables the EC to act to establish social policies, but its ability to act is constrained by strong national policies and its own rather modest legal authority. Citizens expect public policies to ameliorate the effect of difficult demographic and economic conditions on work life. A laissez-faire market system is not a cultural value for many Europeans. When the policies of national governments are not adequate to protect employees, then the EC appears to be the legitimate actor. The treaties provide the EC with the authority to act, but its ability to act has been limited by the necessity to obtain unanimity in the Council for most types of employment proposals.

THE DYNAMIC EXTERNAL ENVIRONMENT

Two recent major developments have led to a new era of EC social policy: the economic recession and the Treaty on European Union (the Maastricht Treaty).

The Effect of the Recession on the EC

From 1986 to 1990, economic growth created a supportive climate for the 1992 program; however, the economic climate has dramatically changed since then. Declining confidence in the economy has been matched by declining support for European integration. The allegiance of employees and labor unions to the 1992 initiative, always tenuous, has also weakened. European leaders had promoted the 1992 program as the means to economic prosperity. The recession has undermined their credibility as well as increased the problems which they must solve.

The recession has changed the environment in two ways which directly relate to EC social policy. One is increasing unemployment. Although not a new problem, as noted earlier, it is now an EC problem. In the past, unemployment mostly concerned national governments. The EC held public demonstrations in support of job creation and had separate and limited programs, primarily training programs, to assist the unemployed. It did not, however, have a full-scale social policy. For reasons noted in the previous paragraph, an ad hoc social policy no longer suffices. EC leaders promised that the 1992 initiative would bring job creation. The credibility both of EC leaders and of the 1992 initiative is linked to an effective social policy.

The other major change which the recession makes in EC social policy is shaped by current economic thinking. According to the prevailing economic doctrine, the appropriate response of governments to the recession should be a policy of austerity and liberalization. European governments have responded to the recession not with policies to encourage demand but rather with policies to curb public spending in order to control taxes. Social policies are perceived as an obstacle to recovery. The governments in the member states have all considered how to cut their social spending. Socialist as well as conservative and Christian democratic governments agree that economic recovery is essential and that austerity policies are necessary to achieve that recovery. European leaders carry their views into meetings in Brussels and have influenced EC social policy.

The Maastricht Treaty and Employment Policy

The provisions of the Maastricht Treaty dealing with social policy are confusing and novel. They provide for a "two-speed" Europe and open possibilities for endless legal wrangling. They do, however, have an important redeeming quality: They enable eleven member states to establish a more ambitious social policy than they could hitherto. For the first time, the EC may create a social dimension to match its economic dimension. Such a course is technically possible but politically unlikely.

Supporters of an EC social policy wanted the Maastricht Treaty to provide for more democratic participation in policy making, and they wanted the elimination of the veto in Council votes on all aspects of social policy. They obtained a partial success but only at the cost of allowing the British to opt out of agreements.

Social policy is dealt with in the treaty in a most unusual manner. The body of the treaty contains two brief provisions dealing directly with social policy, while the main provisions on social policy are found in a special protocol attached to the treaty. The distinction between the two parts is not clear. The text of the treaty applies to the "high contracting members" who "establish among themselves a European Union" (Article A). According to the protocol on social policy, the high contracting members (all twelve) authorize eleven member states to adopt an agreement to be attached to the protocol and to use the institutions, procedures, and mechanisms of the treaty in order to effect the agreement. The protocol stipulates that the United Kingdom shall not take part in the Council when it is dealing with matters raised under the protocol. Measures of the Council arising under the protocol shall be adopted by the vote of eleven members if requiring unanimity or forty-four votes if requiring a qualified majority vote.

The agreement the eleven members attached to the protocol contains seven articles which constitute revisions of Articles 117 through 122 of the Treaty of Rome as amended by the Single European Act (CEC, 1992c, pp. 10–11). The agreement makes the Community as well as the member states responsible for social objectives and provides an impressive list of objectives. They include the promotion of employment; improved living and working conditions; proper social protection; negotiations between management and labor; the development of human resources with a view to lasting, high employment; and the combating of social exclusion. Article 118 is modified to provide a number of topics, such as equal opportunity, under the cooperation procedure which allows the Council to adopt directives by a qualified majority vote. Other topics, such as worker participation measures and ones dealing with workers from non-EC countries employed in a member state, require a unanimous vote. The agreement provides, in revisions of Article 118a and 118b, possibly important new roles for representatives of labor and management. The Commission must consult them when preparing social proposals and assist the two in negotiating at the Community level. If labor and management agree, they may even preempt action by the EC and instead negotiate an agreement on the topic or they may be made responsible for implementing directives by collective agreements.

Although subsidiarity is not mentioned in the section of the treaty dealing with social policy, it is a general principle applicable to the formation of all policies dealt with in the treaty. If the EC shares its competence with member states, it may act only when action by member states cannot achieve the objective of the action or when, for reasons of scale or the effects of the proposed action, the EC can better achieve the objective (Article 3b). The agreement attached to the protocol states that social policy is a shared competence between the Community and the member states. The language indicates that the treaty does not provide a basis for a uniform set of practices relating to employees throughout the EC. The agreement states that measures shall respect the diverse forms of national practices. Member states may have more stringent national measures than those adopted by the EC. As an additional expression of subsidiarity, the protocol provides that the nongovernmental actors who are closest to labor and management (labor unions and employers' associations) shall have important powers to make policies instead of either the member states or the EC. In specifically providing for policy making outside the framework of government, the social protocol probably makes the most significant gesture to subsidiarity of any provision in the treaty.

The Maastricht Treaty does not abrogate the legal procedures of the Treaty of Rome or of legislation that has already been adopted or that will be adopted in the future under those procedures. The EC has social policy for twelve members and will have, in addition, social policy for eleven members. The EC may try to adopt measures under the Treaty of Rome, and, if it fails, it may then adopt them under the Maastricht Treaty, in which case the measure will apply only to eleven members. The measures adopted under the social protocol will not apply inside the United Kingdom, but they will apply to U.K. firms in their operations elsewhere in the EC. The result is a cumbersome, two-speed European system for social policy which surely will be a priority for modification in 1996, when the Maastricht Treaty is scheduled for revision.

The implications of the Maastricht Treaty for social policy are obviously enormous. The possible legal quagmire is readily apparent but so is the positive potential of the document. A major roadblock has been removed. In the past individual social-initiatives in the EC were almost invariably terminated in the Council under the threat of a British veto. Now eleven members have been empowered to proceed without the British. For many years, some observers have asserted that the eleven were happy to make Britain the scapegoat for policies which they did not really want. That assertion will soon be tested because the Commission is already preparing to reintroduce some of its earlier proposals.

Several possible developments could change the implications of the Maastricht Treaty for EC social policy. The British could decide to accept the new provisions in order to retain influence over the formation of social policy, but they probably will not soon do so given the present delicate balance inside the Conservative government. Another possibility is that the protocol will be challenged in the European Court. The relationship of the protocol to the treaty, the right of twelve member states to delegate to eleven member states the authority to add their own agreement to the treaty, the right of the eleven to use the institutions of the EC for policy making which does not extend to all members, the role of British members of Parliament and of the Economic and Social Committee to participate under the protocol when British participation in the Council is excluded, all raise unprecedented legal questions which the Court may have to decide and which may change or invalidate the protocol. Another possibility is that member governments will continue to act under the provisions in the text of the treaty and will ignore the option of the protocol. They might choose to ignore the option for two reasons: Either they may want to preserve unity in order to act on pressing issues, such as economic recovery, or they may not be eager, in the face of the recession, to adopt controversial social programs which might frighten potential investors.

The two changes, economic and legal, surrounding EC social policy dictate a new era in policy making. The new treaty opens the way to a more ambitious policy for eleven members, but the recession is not conducive to such a development. The treaty does, however, provide a range of actions. Advocates of social policy may seek in the treaty a means to action which is workable within the limits set by the recession. The provisions for negotiating social issues, coupled with the treaty principle of subsidiarity, will likely provide an alternative to new EC social legislation. Negotiating social issues brings to the EC level a practice which has long been known in many member states and which is within European corporatist norms.

THE POLICY SUBSYSTEM

The policy subsystem is composed of policy makers, advocacy groups, and policy brokers, all interacting within the framework provided by the EC treaties. Their interaction also appears to be influenced by the subject of the policy. In the case of environmental policy, for example, the interaction is moderated by the favorable aura which surrounds green issues in the EC. It is also affected by the scientific nature of many proposals, which forces policy makers to depend on specialists. The social policy subsystem has its unique characteristics. Unlike environmental policy, which is a relatively new policy area, social policy has a long history and is highly developed in member states. The subject does not engender the same supportive social consensus as environmental policy does, although the welfare state enjoyed broad support in the postwar era. One of the most striking characteristics of the EC social policy subsystem is the ideological fault line which divides British actors from Continental ones. The fault line was always there but was most apparent in the Thatcher era. It remains in the post-Thatcher era.

Decision Makers

The Commission has the most complex role of all the actors involved in making social policy. It is the initiator, drafter, political mastermind, advocate, and broker. If it is to be successful in its roles, the Commission must sense both what the EC needs and what the public will accept. It must also orchestrate and time the policy process in order to build support and approach other institutions, especially the Council, at the most auspicious moment. The Commission tries to time the arrival of a proposal before the Council during the presidency of a sympathetic member state; in addition, it has to perform its assigned duty of drafting sound, acceptable proposals. No one should feel surprised to learn that the Commission frequently fails to fulfill some of its duties.

One of the seventeen EC commissioners, the commissioner for employment, social affairs, and education, has the primary responsibility for social policy, which includes overseeing the directorate general for employment, social affairs, and education (DG V) and being the spokesperson for social policy in EC institutions and before relevant public groups. Few who have served as the commissioner have left a mark. In the vital years of the late 1980s, the commissioner for social affairs was Vasso Papandreou. The fact that she was both Greek and female indicates that not many potential commissioners contested the post. Despite a promising start, she was not able to distinguish herself in a period when Greece's reputation in the EC was at an ebb. In 1993, she was replaced by Padriag Flynn, an Irishman whose selection disappointed advocates of social policy and particularly women's groups. He later became a more effective proponent of social policy than many had expected and spearheaded the EC campaign for jobs.

From 1985 to 1992, Jacques Delors dominated the Commission. He epitomized the EC in the years of "Europhoria" when everyone scrambled to climb onto the 1992 bandwagon. He is most famous for the 1992 initiative, but he steered through the EC two major social policies as well: the Social Dimension and the Community Charter of the Fundamental Social Rights of Workers (Social Charter). He overshadowed Vasso Papandreou as an advocate of EC social policy with frequent appearances before European trade unions and other forums where social policy was under discussion. Tying social policy securely to the 1992 initiative, he advocated a type of social market-economy for the EC and had an obvious distaste for Thatcherite capitalism. His philosophical orientation was close to that of the French union, CFDT, and of social Catholicism. His ability to dominate the EC agenda weakened in 1992 in the face of the dual debacle of the first Danish referendum and the currency crisis, which undermined hopes for currency unification, his next major objective. Although he continued to head the new Commission which came to power in 1993, he did not seize the initiative again until the end of that year with the publication of what has been called his magnum opus, the White Paper on employment, competitiveness, and growth, which will be discussed below.

The Directorate General for social policy (DG V) is composed of civil servants who specialize in various aspects of social policy. Their efforts are supplemented by the services of other specialists on short-term contracts and by cooperation with national civil servants. Morale is seldom high. For much of its history, the DG V has had ineffective leadership and a low success-ratio for its initiatives. In frustration, one group broke away to form the autonomous Task Force for Human Resources, Education, Training, and Youth. Despite the problems, however, many parts of DG V continue to produce useful studies in addition to drafting new proposals for legislation. The output of the health and safety group, working in the relative isolation of Luxembourg, is impressive. The equality division is another part of DG V which issues respected reports. In the 1990s, DG V began to produce an annual volume called *Employment in Europe*, which is a valuable source of data and analyses of employment issues. Through the years, DG V has been the core of the effort to create an EC social policy. It has frequently suffered from inattention from the commissioners and from lack of visibility, but it has functioned as a low-key institutional interest group as *interest group* is defined by neo-functionalists.

The Commission and the Council appear to be less integrated on social policy than they are on environmental policy. The Commission has proposed many more social policies than the Council has accepted. The old description of the Council as the graveyard of Commission initiatives has certainly applied to social policy because of, for one reason, the opposition of the British government to the legitimacy of EC social policy. British governments, both Labour and Conservative, have not accepted the legitimacy of most social proposals which arrive before the Council. The chronic British opposition has obstructed efforts to establish a more cooperative relationship between the Council and the Commission comparable to the arrangement between the two institutions on their environmental policies. The British opposition is only part of the problem, however. Social policy does not enjoy general popularity as does environmental policy. Since the 1970s, Europeans have worried that social costs may be a major reason for economic ills. National governments have struggled to lighten the fiscal and regulatory burden on their industries. Their struggle was mandated by economic realities, as well as by public concerns, so they are cautious about reinstituting social expenses in the EC. In their view, a common environmental policy is more compelling for a common social policy because no group with expert knowledge argues for social policy as it does for environmental policy, in which scientific evidence demonstrates the futility of national efforts; Council members therefore have more constraints and fewer incentives to endorse EC social policy.

Two developments may bring a closer rapport between the Commission and the Council. First, the creation of the single market threatens the effectiveness of national social policies and may force national leaders to turn to Brussels for remedies. The first evidence appeared in the winter of 1993 when Hoover moved a facility from France to Scotland and cited high French social costs as the reason. The single market could compel member states to compete for investment by offering a lighter burden of social regulations, hardly a politically attractive course of action for national governments. The alternative is to set common levels of social protection in the EC, which is what the Commission is willing to design.

In addition, the Maastricht Treaty may encourage greater cooperation between the Council and the Commission. The treaty provides for a greater use of majority voting in the Council, which is likely to change the political dynamics between the two institutions. The Commission has an incentive to locate potential supporters in the Council and to draft legislation in such a way as to ensure their vote; moreover, the Commission no longer has to seek ways to avoid or sidestep the customary British veto. Now that the social protocol has removed the British problem, the Commission can shift its attention to focus more on potential collaborators in the Council. The new focus paves the way for a more ambitious social agenda.

The relationship between the Commission and relevant interest groups has a long and interesting history. In making policy, the Commission operates by what Michael Gorges calls a "corporatization process" (Gorges, 1992). Scholars have long argued about whether the relationship between the Commission and interest groups is pluralist or corporatist. Do multiple and changing groups of interests influence policy or are interest groups an integral part of the formation of policy? The Commission has always sought to bring interest groups into the policy process. It established a tripartite group to oversee the operation of the Social Fund. It advocated the creation of the Standing Committee on Employment in 1970. It influenced the establishment of the European Trade Union Confederation (ETUC) and continues to fund its operation. It maintains both formal and informal relations with the ETUC. The president of the Commission meets regularly with leaders of the ETUC. Informal contacts take place frequently between persons in DG V and persons in the ETUC (Barnouin, 1986, p. 70). The Commission was instrumental in establishing the social dialogue which is provided for by the SEA and which gives the ETUC new powers. It has programs to prepare labor leaders for their new roles, as prescribed by the Maastricht Treaty.

The relationship between the Commission and the Union of Industrial and Employers' Confederations of Europe (UNICE), the counterpart of the ETUC for employers, is less fully developed on social policy. The UNICE is more closely involved with other directorate generals of the Commission, who draft proposals of more immediate concern to them. The UNICE and the ETUC are, however, jointly consulted on major employment proposals. They have enough time to respond to proposals before these proposals take their final form. The proposal process is highly institutionalized and comprises the corporatization process discussed by Gorges. Proposals seldom leave the Commission without serious efforts to find an acceptable compromise between the interests of employers and employees.

The Commission seeks consensus and avoids confrontation. The Commission has sought the common ground between the interests of employees and employers. The output may not be impressive, but the persistence of the Commission in pursuit of acceptable policies has been; for example, the Commission has worked since the late 1960s to find a form of employee participation which is acceptable to labor unions and employers' associations. It has pursued that goal largely on its own initiative, with little or no support from the Council, employers' associations, or even the ETUC. (The ETUC was not united in support of early initiatives, but it has supported later ones.) The Commission proposed the European Company Statute, the Fifth Directive, the Vredeling Proposal, and the Works Council Directive, and, seeking agreement, it has revised each of them many times. The Commission has been patient and nonconfrontational. Despite the difficult nature of the subject, all parties have remained involved in the discussions. The history of the Commission's effort provides an excellent example of bureaucratic politics as discussed by Guy Peters. Through the years, Eurocrats from DG V have acted as "quasi-autonomous actors with their own goals, which they pursue through the policymaking process" (Peters, 1992, p. 115).

Laura Cram argues that the Commission's method of operation has created a constituency of support for social policy (Cram, 1993). She asserts that the Commission has gained support for an EC social policy by "purposeful opportunism." The Commission has engaged in activities which are useful to employers and labor unions through a broad interpretation of its role. It has gained recognition and legitimacy by being useful. The Commission has developed programs and research projects, which extend from sophisticated analyses of unemployment to studies of sexual harassment. Many of the research projects are useful to employers' associations, and many serve to focus public attention on social issues. The Commission has also involved employers and labor unions in other projects; for example, it held seminars for bankers on more efficient personnel policies in light of new patterns of female employment.

A recent study of the Council noted that it operates in a "European" and cooperative style in contrast to the popular perception of the Council as the EC institution which most fully represents national interests (Wessels, 1991). The author convincingly argues that we are in the era of the cooperative state, which is characterized by policy-led interdependence. Members of the Council seek to maintain a consensus even when they can act on the basis of a majority vote, but maintaining a consensus lessens the possibility that the Commission will be able to woo a majority of members in order to pursue social policies. The Council has seldom demonstrated much interest in social policy. It has held fewer meetings of the Social Affairs Council than of any other of the twenty-three specialized councils which it operates. A recent example is supplied by the British presidency of the Council in 1992. Only one meeting of the Social Affairs Council was held during the six-month period and it failed to adopt any of the pending directives of social policy. It only succeeded in adopting several resolutions which have no force of law. The British minister for employment even refused to schedule time for discussion of a proposed directive on working time when requested to do so by the Commission (CREW, 1992, p. 10). Once in a while, the Council made a public occasion of its endorsement of a social policy, as it did with the social charter, but usually social policy is not a priority for the Council; moreover, no member state or group of member states has emerged as an advocate of social policy as has happened in the case of regional policy. Given the current mood, the Council is likely to continue to give a low priority to social policy unless that policy also addresses more immediate concerns. A policy which deals with job creation holds the most promise for favorable attention in the Council.

Among the EC institutions, Parliament has been the strongest ally of the Commission for social policy. The socialist and Christian democratic groups which dominate Parliament have made common ground on the subject. Social proposals have benefited from the increased prestige and visibility of Parliament in recent years; for example, Parliament hosted a joint meeting with national parliamentarians in December 1992 to publicize the need for the EC social dimension. Members of Parliament routinely use question time in Parliament to call attention to weaknesses in social policy. Some members of Parliament maintain close ties with the ETUC as well as with national labor unions. The new powers which Parliament gains from the Maastricht Treaty should serve to strengthen the cause of social policies in the EC. The extension of the cooperation procedure to many types of social policies will give Parliament a greater power to insert its views into policies through its greater scope for amending proposals. Parliament has already shown how it can influence proposals through amendments in areas covered by the cooperation procedure in the SEA (Wessels, 1991, p. 144). It should exercise its influence even more vigorously on social policy given its demonstrated interest in the subject.

Advocacy Groups

The two main groups interested in EC social policy are the European Trade Union Confederation (ETUC) and the Union of Industrial and Employers' Confederations of Europe (UNICE), which are umbrella associations for national labor unions and employers' associations, respectively. (For more information on the two groups see Springer, 1992.) Both groups are important players in Brussels and have established entries into the EC. Through the years, they have contested with each other in a more openly aggressive style than was noted in the relationship among environmental interest groups. The UNICE has adamantly opposed proposals for worker participation, for example, and rejected attempts by the Commission to find an acceptable compromise. Both groups have been represented on EC standing committees on social policy, where they have often held bitter and public disputes. In many respects the two groups have behaved in ways normal for advocacy groups.

In the 1980s, the Commission began an effort to put the UNICE and the ETUC into a new, more constructive relationship. According to Article 118 of the Treaty of Rome as revised by the SEA, the Commission is responsible for establishing a dialogue between labor and management at the European level which could lead to European agreements if the partners wished.

Regular meetings were instituted between the two. The early efforts at negotiations were not promising, but after 1990, the social partners found some topics on which they could cooperate, such as training, employment, and the introduction of new technologies. On October 31, 1991, they entered into an important agreement to develop their role in formulating social policy. That agreement was then written into the Maastricht Treaty, in which it forms the basis for an important change in the way social policy is handled in the EC. The provisions in the Maastricht Treaty add a new form of EC policy making and involve the social partners in the policy process. Member governments may delegate to the social partners the responsibility for implementing directives on social policy, but the partners' potential role in policy formulation is the most novel and interesting of the new treaty provisions. The Commission must consult with the social partners when formulating relevant policies and must take measures to facilitate effective communications between the two sides. The consultation must take place twice during the process, first at the initial stage of consideration and again when a specific proposal is being drafted. The social partners are then to provide the Commission with an opinion or a recommendation. The new consultative procedure gives the social partners a role in the crucial formative stage of policy making. Potentially even more significant, however, the social partners may signal the Commission at the time of consultation that they want to enter into negotiations for the purposes of reaching an agreement. During the nine months they have to try to reach an agreement, the process in the EC is preempted. If the social partners accept the challenge provided by the treaty, their relationship can no longer be that of advocacy groups. They are being invited to enter into a corporatist arrangement which adds another dimension to the complex provisions for policy making in the Maastricht Treaty.

Policy Brokers

The Commission plays a role as a policy broker in addition to its formal role as a policy maker. The commissioners as a group are really the brokers. DG V acts as an internal interest group in the proposal of social policy, but the commissioners try to reconcile the interests of labor and management and, more important, they try to reconcile the need for social policy with other priorities. Jacques Delors played the role of broker publicly. He initiated the Social Dimension, in part because of his own beliefs but also because of his desire to ensure the support of employees for the internal market program. He then tried to ensure that both labor and management supported the internal market program and the Social Dimension. The commissioners largely succeeded in their efforts despite great difficulties. The brokering efforts of the Commission now take on a new facet as the social negotiation assumes its new role in the making of policy through direct agreements between labor and management.

The Council has not developed new attributes as a broker for social policy as it has for environmental policy. The presence of the British veto obstructed efforts to instill more flexibility in the Council's relations with the social partners. The Council does have a role in the new procedure of negotiating policy between labor and management. If the social partners so request, the Commission may propose to the Council measures to implement the negotiated agreement if it concerns a topic covered by Article 118 as amended by the Maastricht Treaty. The Council adopts the measure either by a qualified majority vote or unanimously, depending on the relevant provision in Article 118. The new role puts pressure on the Council to enter negotiations with the social partners in order to devise acceptable measures by which to implement the agreement.

EMPLOYMENT POLICY IN THE MAASTRICHT ERA

When the Commission presented its legislative agenda to Parliament in March 1993, the list contained thirty-seven proposals dealing with employment policy, which were contained under four subject areas—equal opportunities and equal treatment at work, employment and social protection, education and vocational training, and freedom of movement. Nearly half of the proposals (seventeen) were left over from previous years. Several dealt with proposed studies, and twelve were for new laws or amendments to existing laws. On closer examination, all were amendments or dealt with training programs. Everything on the list was familiar to persons concerned with the subject. Almost without exception, the proposed directives that did not concern training were ones that had been blocked in the Council by British opposition. Most of them now will be considered under the Maastricht Treaty and will be adopted via the Social Protocol. Some controversial legislation concerning working time was adopted, however, in the last days before the treaty went into force. The legislation provides for a maximum forty-eight-hour week and mandatory time off and limits working hours for children and adolescents. The British government threatened to challenge the working-time directive because, according to British spokesmen, it was adopted inappropriately as a health and safety measure in order to avoid the requirement for unanimity in the Council.

As noted previously, worker participation has long been a priority of the Commission. Eleven member states had affirmed their commitment to the principle when they signed the Community Charter of the Fundamental Social Rights of Workers. The most recent proposal relating to this subject is the proposed "Council Directive on the Establishment of a European Works Council in Community-scale Undertakings or Groups of Undertakings for the Purpose of Informing and Consulting Employees" (CEC, 1991). The proposal was first put forward in 1991 and was amended that same year to incorporate suggestions from Parliament and from the Economic and Social Committee. It would require companies or groups of companies with at least one thousand employees and with at least one hundred in two or more member states to establish elected works councils. Management would be required to hold an annual meeting with the works council and consult it on all issues likely to affect employees, including mergers, closures, relocations, organizational changes, and new work or production methods. Despite strong support from the Commission and Parliament, the proposal remained blocked in the Council because of British opposition. The Social Affairs Council considered the proposal again on October 13, 1993, and the British once again signaled their opposition. The measure appeared ripe to be the first one adopted under the social protocol once the Maastricht Treaty came into force on November 1, 1993. The social partners, however, were first asked if they wanted to try to negotiate an agreement. The UNICE agreed, but the ETUC wants the measure adopted as a directive. Its leaders hope that the measure will be adopted under the protocol when the Germans hold the presidency of the Council late in 1994.

The adoption of the directive under the provisions of the protocol will create a number of confusing and troubling consequences. The British government has already indicated that it will use its opt-out provision to entice investment from firms seeking to escape the law. Meanwhile, the EC has provided British labor unions with funds to create works councils in British firms. Those British firms that have operations in the other member states or in countries belonging to the European Economic Area and that meet the criteria set in the directive will have to provide works councils for their operations outside the United Kingdom. Similar problems will arise from other proposals if they are adopted by eleven members of an integrated market which has twelve participants. Commissioner Flynn has already indicated that the Commission will use the opt-out provision of the Maastricht Treaty only as a last result.

In November 1993 the Commission issued the "Green Paper: European Social Policy Options for the Union" (CEC, 1993b). Green Papers are discussion documents usually intended to prepare the ground for a framework policy. The November Green Paper was preparatory to the White Paper discussed below. The Commission invited 150 interested parties including member governments as well as private groups to make comments on a draft of the text or to suggest ideas. The subject of the paper is employment, the reasons for its decline in Europe, and possible solutions. The premise of the Green Paper is that "the next phase in the development of European social policy cannot be based on the idea that social progress must go into retreat in order for economic competitiveness to recover" (p. 7). The paper contains a survey of the accomplishments of EC social policy, but the main part of the text is devoted to an analysis of employment and related economic factors. Much of the analysis involves comparisons with the United States and Japan. The analysis, which is more objective than in some previous EC studies, honestly notes strengths in the United States and Japan. Previously taboo topics such as the costs of the welfare state are examined and defended, but the conclusions leave open the possibility that some cuts may be necessary. "Many of the questions which have emerged in the discussion imply that stark choices will have to be made if Europe is to cope with the fundamental structural changes taking place today" (p. 86). The paper indicates that the social partners and the member states must take responsibility to solve the employment problem and not rely on EC laws.

The "White Paper on Growth, Competitiveness, Employment" is the defining document in the current Maastricht era (CEC, 1993c). Before its publication, it was being called the magnum opus of Jacques Delors and compared to the "White Paper on Completing the Internal Market," the major document for European integration in the late 1980s. When the two documents are compared, however, it is obvious that the recent one lacks the coherence and conviction which made the earlier document so compelling. Both papers tackle one central problem, but the earlier paper provided a clear-cut remedy and the latter one does not.

In answer to the question of why the EC should have a new White Paper, the document contains a succinct answer: "The one and only reason is unemployment. We are aware of its scale, and of its consequences too. The difficult thing, as experience has taught us, is knowing how to tackle it" (p. 9). The paper examines various theories about job creation. For those who expected new insights or a new economics, the text makes disappointing reading. The critique of the existing system holds no surprises and the solutions offered are not radical, indeed they have been received favorably by business groups and even by a member of the British cabinet (Barber, 1993). The paper studies the relationships among growth, competitiveness and employment and probes the implications of the information for job creation. The paper concludes that growth must start with large investment programs to modernize European transportation, communication, and energy networks. The modern infrastructure will make EC firms more competitive and create jobs. At the same time, government must remove obstacles to competitiveness, such as laws that interfere with the operation of a flexible labor market. (In this regard the paper goes beyond the Green Paper.) Growth, competitiveness, and employment will then recover simultaneously. The most controversial part of the proposed solution is the investment fund which is to be provided by the EC, member states, and the private sector. If the fund is not created, then the crucial first impetus will be missing and the whole relationship is uncoupled. If the entire policy is implemented, however, the EC will have investments equal to 23 to 24 percent of GNP, an annual growth rate of 3 percent until the year 2000, and fifteen million new jobs (CEC, 1993a).

CONCLUSION

EC social policy enters a new era with the Maastricht Treaty and the "White Paper on Growth, Competitiveness, and Employment." The EC is set to be more assertive but along lines which differ from those of the past. The centerpiece of the new approach is job creation, an objective which appeals to both employees and employers. The EC is at the core of the effort, but responsibility is dispersed to many actors. Legislation plays a less prominent role than formerly. The Maastricht Treaty gives roles to the various participants and the White Paper defines the course of action. The new approach obviously draws inspiration from the earlier "White Paper on Completing the Internal Market." The EC will coordinate the removal of national barriers to job creation. Among its direct responsibilities, training and education for work assumes a prominent role. The most recent work program of the Commission lists thirteen EC initiatives for education and training, which have broad support.

Subsidiarity is an important aspect of the new approach. The meaning implied by the concept is closely linked with its original meaning in Catholic social doctrine. Subsidiarity implies that policy should be made at the lowest appropriate level, which in the EC consists of the national governments and the social partners. The assumption that the social partners share responsibilities and common interests is fundamental to the belief that they can fulfill those responsibilities and protect those interests. EC has reached this new approach after a long search, which was hampered by the existence in the member states of fully developed welfare systems, each with its unique national history and entrenched norms. Few desired the EC to replicate a national welfare state, and many feared even modest efforts to intervene in national practices. EC efforts to level the playing field and to set certain minimum standards for protecting at-risk groups have slowly gained legitimacy. The equality policy of the EC is a prime example. Public pressure made equality programs popular, but member states feared that their costs would make national firms less competitive in global competition. EC directives were a logical solution. Health and safety directives are another example. The controversy over worker participation tested the limits of legitimacy for the EC. A new approach was necessary in order to find a way around the controversy.

Although the Maastricht Treaty provides alternative paths to policy, it does not foreclose a future role for EC legislation. EC directives have made and continue to make a contribution to social protection in some areas. The contribution should not be measured by the standards used to assess national welfare programs. Giandomenico Majone, as mentioned previously, distinguishes between social policy—programs for the welfare state that involve redistribution of wealth—and social regulation—programs for the postindustrial society that balance concern for quality-of-life issues and the need for economic efficiency. Social regulations give priority to "the allocation function of public policy over distributional objectives" (Majone, 1993, p. 168). The EC has adopted and will continue to adopt social regulations to improve the quality of life for employees.

The question which is central to this book and which remains to be addressed is whether the new approach to social policy will serve to strengthen the European Union by increasing the ties between employees and the EC. The answer seems to be no, at least for the short term. The approach is one for the long term. Activities in Brussels today have little immediate relevance for employees. The effect of directives is always indirect. Individuals are more likely to be aware of the national legislation which implements a directive than of the directive itself; on the other hand, the opening of alternative channels to policy making does lessen the risk that Brussels will become the focus for bitter clashes over controversial issues as it has been previously. The possibility for labor unions to play a larger role may increase the legitimacy of the EC and may reduce the onus on it for failing to adopt policies which employees desire. To the extent that labor unions continue to represent employees and to develop as effective EC social partners, they will serve as a conduit for increasing the social legitimacy of the European Union. The success of their effort has greater promise for the EC than would a comparable effort in another part of the world without the norms and values which underpin those efforts, but the success, if it occurs, will arrive slowly and almost imperceptibly. The outcome may depend more on the new process for making social policy than it does on the policy.

REFERENCES

Barber, Lionel. 1993. "A New Lightness to His Touch." *Financial Times*. December 13.

Barnouin, Barbara. 1986. *The European Labour Movement and European Integration*. London: Frances Pinter.

Bendix, Reinhard. 1974. *Work and Authority in Industry*. Berkeley: University of California Press.

Chamberlain, Neil. 1980. *Forces of Change in Western Europe*. London: McGraw-Hill.

CEC (Commission of the European Community). 1975. "Employee Participation and Company Structure in the European Community." *Bulletin of the European Communities,* Supplement 8/75.

———. 1988. "Social Dimension of the Internal Market." SEC(88)1148 final.

———. 1989. *Community Charter of the Fundamental Social Rights of Workers*. COM(89)248 final.

———. 1991. "Amended Proposal for a Council Directive on the Establishment of a European Works Council in Community-scale Undertakings or Groups of Undertakings for the Purposes of Informing and Consulting Employees." COM(91)345 final. September 16.

———. 1992a. *Employment in Europe, 1992*. Brussels: CEC.

———. 1992b. *Europe in Figures*. 1992a. 3rd ed. Brussels: CEC.

———. 1992c. *Trade Union Information Bulletin* 4.

———. 1993a. "EU Launches Major Employment Creation Drive: 15 Million New Jobs Is the Target." Press release of the Office of Press and Public Affairs, Delegation of the Commission of the European Communities, Washington, DC, December 9.

———. 1993b. "Green Paper: European Social Policy Options for the Union." COM(93)551 final, November 17.

———. 1993c. "White Paper on Growth, Competitiveness, Employment." *Bulletin of the European Communities*, Supplement 6/93.

CREW (Centre for Research on European Women). 1992. *Crew Reports* 12, no. 12.

Cram, Laura. 1993. "Breaking Down the Monolith: The European Commission as a Multi-Organization." Paper presented to the European Community Studies Association, Washington, DC, May 27–29.

Gorges, Michael. 1992. "Euro-Corporatism after 1992." Paper presented to the American Political Science Association, Washington, DC, September 3–6.

Hodges, Michael, and Stephen Woolcock. 1993. "Atlantic Capitalism Versus Rhine Capitalism in the European Community." *West European Politics* 16, no. 3.

Landua, E. C. 1985. *The Rights of Working Women in the European Community*. Brussels: European Perspectives Series of the European Community.

Lange, Peter. 1993. "Maastricht and the Social Protocol: Why Did They Do It?" *Politics and Society* 21, no. 1.

Leo XIII (pope). 1891. *Rerum Novarum*. Reprinted in *St. Thomas Aquinas on Politics and Ethics*, ed. by Paul Sigmund. New York: W. W. Norton, 1988.

Lichtheim, George. 1970. *A Short History of Socialism*. New York: Praeger.

Majone, Giandomenico. 1993. "The European Community Between Social Policy and Social Regulation." *Journal of Common Market Studies* 31, no. 2 (June).

Marsden, David, and Jean-Jacques Silvestre. 1992. "Pay and European Integration." *Pay and Employment in the New Europe*, ed. by David Marsden. Brookfield, VT: Edward Elgar.

Marshall, T. H. 1975. *Social Policy*. London: Hutchison.

Misner, Paul. 1991. *Social Catholicism in Europe*. London: Darton, Longman and Todd.

Peters, B. Guy. 1992. "Bureaucratic Politics and the Institutions of the European Community." In *Euro-Politics*, ed. by Alberta Sbriaga. Washington, DC: Brookings Institution.

Pipkorn, John. 1980. "The Legal Framework of Employee Participation Methods at National and International Levels and Particularly Within the European Community." *Economic and Industrial Democracy* 1: 99–123.

Shanks, Michael. 1977. *European Social Policy: Today and Tomorrow*. Oxford: Pergamon Press.

Springer, Beverly. 1992. *The Social Dimension of 1992*. Westport, CT: Greenwood Press.

Springer, Beverly, and Dorothy Riddle. 1988. "Women in Service Industries: European Communities–United States Comparisons." In *Comparable Worth, Pay Equity, and Public Policy*, ed. by R. Kelly and J. Bayes. Westport, CT: Greenwood Press.

Thompson, E. P. 1963. *The Making of the English Working Class*. New York: Vintage Books.

Wessels, Wolfgang. 1991. "The EC Council: The Community's Decisionmaking Center." In *The New European Community*, ed. by Robert Keohane and Stanley Hoffmann. Boulder, CO: Westview Press.

Chapter 6

Environmental Concerns
and European Union

T he involvement of the European Community (EC) in environmental policy
is a recent development. During its first decades of operation, the EC had
little reason to address environmental concerns. Other issues were more urgent
and public pressure was low; moreover, the Treaty of Rome did not mandate
an EC environmental policy. Everything changed in the 1980s, and now the EC
has a "green" mandate. The Treaty on European Union adds urgency to the
requirement for action on the environment. The EC has the legal authority to
make environmental policy and public support to do so. The success or failure
of the EC to act on the environment will directly affect its social legitimacy
with citizens in the EC.

In order to analyze the development of environmental policy in the EC and the
probable role which it will play in the formation of the European Union, three
categories of information are examined following a brief background discussion
of the subject. The three categories are adapted from the Sabatier model discussed
in Chapter 2. The first category concerns the stable system parameters which
comprise the framework within which environmental policy is formulated. Three
different aspects of stable system parameters will be examined: the basic attributes
of the problem, the relevant cultural values, and the legal structure within which
the policy is formulated. The second category is the external environment, which
encompasses the changing socioeconomic system. The third category is the policy
subsystem, which includes the decision makers, the policy brokers, and the
competing advocacy groups. The chapter includes a consideration of the concepts
which are discussed in all the policy chapters. They are regime, social legitimacy,
policy-related learning, and subsidiarity.

BACKGROUND

The EC environmental program evolved from random actions to a comprehensive policy. The bases for the program, its legal standing, its principles, and its reach have all grown in complexity and importance. Today the program constitutes a major policy, and the EC is accepted as a significant actor in regard to environmental policy both in Europe and around the world.

The EC environmental policy dates from 1973, when the first action program on the environment was adopted. (An action program is a broad statement of policy accepted by the Council which is implemented through the adoption of specific directives and regulations.) Although the EC had adopted directives dealing with the environment before 1973, it had not regarded the environment as a topic to consider comprehensively. The French government, which held the presidency of the Council in 1972, called for EC action in order to ensure that national environmental policies did not hinder trade among the member states (Lodge, 1989a, p. 320). The Netherlands and West Germany, both exporting nations, supported the initiative. Politics also played a role. The 1970s was a decade of rising social consciousness in the member states, and social concerns spread to Brussels. Politicians, such as German chancellor Willy Brandt, encouraged the EC to broaden its agenda and the Commission did so.

The first action program on the environment took a comprehensive approach to the environment. The Commission was given the ongoing task of studying the state of the environment in the EC, which was broken down by sectors. On the basis of its findings, the Commission would propose policies to solve problems. According to the program, the EC derives its authority to act on environmental issues from the preamble to the Treaty of Rome, and: "the aim of a Community environmental policy is to improve the setting and quality of life, and the surroundings and living conditions of the peoples of the Community" (CEC, 1973). The program provided principles to guide policy formulation, two of which became hallmarks of EC environmental policy. The "polluter-pays" principle is well known. A major environmental disaster in Seveso, Italy, in 1976 dramatized the costs of environmental problems and the need to make the responsible parties pay. The second major principle embodied in the first action program holds that prevention is more effective than punishment. The principle did not become a major basis for action, however, until the third action program.

The second action program lasted from 1977 to 1983. It continued along the lines set out in the first program and proposed directives for remedial action on existing pollution problems. It also made the EC the overseer and protector of natural environments (Hildebrand, 1992, p. 20). The EC was in the grips of the energy crisis and an economic recession during those years, but it was able to implement many provisions of the two action programs. It adopted over seventy legislative texts between 1973 and 1983 (Rehbinder and Stewart, 1988, p. 18).

Conditions were more favorable when the third action program was drafted in 1983. Economic and political revitalization had started, and Parliament drafted a treaty to renew the vision of European integration. As environmental movements gathered strength in a number of member states, the EC established a directorate general (DG XI) especially to deal with environmental policy, which became a focal point for European action on the environment. A commissioner acquired the portfolio for oversight of DG XI and the environment. The third action program reflected the new vitality appearing in Europe. It was more ambitious in scope and more detailed, providing a precise list of priorities. It gave environmental policy greater legitimacy by freeing it from the rubric of trade policy. Hereafter, the EC could adopt measures because they served environmental objectives rather than internal market concerns. The EC was no longer limited to acting on the environment only when different national policies interfered with trade among the member states. The ambition of the program was matched by legislative output. Between February 1983 and December 1985, the EC adopted over forty directives to fulfill objectives in the program (Hildebrand, 1992, p. 22).

Conditions had changed yet again when the fourth framework program was adopted in 1987. The Single European Act removed doubts about the competence of the EC to act on environmental matters. A new and dynamic Commission had set to work to revitalize the EC by creating a single market. Free-market philosophies were in ascendancy, and the new program reflected the prevailing theories, by stating:

The Commission intends to make full use of the provisions of the new Treaty, and in particular Article 100A. It acknowledges the need to combine, by way of actions which effectively protect the environment, two of the main objectives of the Treaty, i.e. the achievement of the internal market and the development of a high level of environmental standards within the Community. The Commission is moreover convinced that the development of high environmental standards is consistent with, and sometimes necessary for, the protection and improvement of the future competitive position of Community industry. (CEC, 1987)

The EC espoused both the internal market and more ambitious environmental objectives and refused to consider that the two objectives may have been incompatible. Ambiguity characterized many areas of EC activity in that period. The Commission was eager to advance integration on a number of fronts. The internal market was the first priority, but the Commission tried to balance its requirements against those of other programs. The EC, then, differed from the United States, which also adopted a free-market orientation but slowed the growth of environmental policies.

In contrast, the fourth action program of the EC marks, in many ways, the apogee of EC environmental policy. It makes protection of the environment a basic principle which has to be respected in all EC policies. (The principle has now been incorporated into the Maastricht Treaty.) It takes a holistic approach to the environment, in marked contrast to the modest and limited ambitions of the first program. The fourth program establishes a voluntary procedure whereby member states inform the Commission of proposed environmental laws so that the EC may consider whether those laws would be more appropriate for action by the EC. (The procedure should later become legally binding.) Two principles popular among environmentalists in the 1980s were inserted into the program. "Integrated pollution control" refers to "organizational and legislative changes that enable institutions to deal with the connected nature of environmental problems" (Haigh and Stewart, 1990, p. 5). "Cross-media pollutant" refers to a pollutant which moves from one part of the environment to another to cause damage (pp. 9–10).

The history of EC environmental policy is distinguished by growth and by a constant search for legitimacy. The rate of growth was not constant, but some progress continued even in the difficult 1970s. The rate has accelerated in recent years. Today the EC adopts about one hundred pieces of legislation for the environment per year. It adopted more legislation between 1989 and 1991 than it had during the previous twenty years (Peterson and Bomberg, 1992). The policy has expanded in scope and complexity until it has now taken on the attributes of national environmental policies, extending from the protection of habitats for birds to concern for the quality of life in cities, and from participating in international conventions on global environmental problems to revisiting the original topics related to trade in the EC.

Throughout much of its history, EC environmental policy was colored by questions about its legitimacy. Gradually its legitimacy has been accepted, and the change has been reflected in the terminology of the action programs. The first one was called "a declaration of the Council and the member states participating in the Council"; the next two were "resolutions of the Council and the national representatives"; and the fourth was a "resolution of the Council" (Liberatore, 1991, p. 290). In the legal hierarchy of the EC, a declaration is weaker than a resolution. In the nuances of EC language, "the Council," as the sole provider of the fourth program, signals the emergence of the EC as an actor in its own right on environmental matters.

Most authorities on EC environmental policy comment that it is not a coherent whole, but it is characterized by fragmentation as a result of its history. That fragmentation, however, does not prevent the policy from being regarded as important. Rehbinder and Stewart, two experts on the topic, wrote that EC environmental policy, "although still fragmentary, is a rather remarkable step that has contributed substantially to the continued growth of the Community as a political system" (1988, p. 15). We return to their assessment again at the conclusion to this chapter in a consideration of the contribution of EC environmental policy to the European Union.

STABLE SYSTEM PARAMETERS

The EC environmental policy develops within a framework which helps to shape it. The framework, or parameters, consist of three relatively permanent factors:

1. The conditions or basic attributes which give rise to the need for an EC environmental policy
2. The sociocultural values which shape the demand for the policy and influence the way the policy is made
3. The constitutional rules which govern the making of environmental policy

Basic Attributes of the Policy Area

The situation in Western Europe is one which almost compels the EC to have an environmental policy. Population density, affluent life styles, advanced economic development, and small national units join together to create the necessity for international action. The facts are known, they are relatively immutable, and, therefore, action by the EC is accepted and expected.

The EC is one of the most densely populated areas in the world. It has 146 persons per square kilometer in comparison to the world average of 32 persons per square kilometer (CEC, 1992b, p. 64). Over 80 percent of the population of Belgium, the Netherlands, Germany, and the United Kingdom live in urban areas with all the associated environmental problems. Over 30 percent of the population of Germany, France, and the United Kingdom live in conurbations of 250,000 or more inhabitants.

The average household in the EC spent ECU 15,300 on consumption in 1985 (CEC, 1992b, p. 134). EC households throw away 80 percent of the products which they buy after a single use (CEC, 1991, p. 32), have a total of 124,781,000 cars (CEC 1992b, p. 205), and consume 27 percent of the energy used in the EC (p. 175). As educated, affluent people, EC residents demand a good quality of life, but their life styles produce high levels of pollution.

The economy in the EC depends heavily on the production of goods for the domestic market and for export. Industry is more important to the EC economy than it is to the economy of the United States; it produces more than one-third of the gross value added in the economy, and consumes 31 percent of the energy used in the EC. The chemical industry, with all its attendant environmental problems, plays a larger role in the EC economy than it does in the economy of the United States or of Japan. The economy of the EC also requires an extensive transportation network to facilitate trade. The member states of the EC are trading nations that export about 23 percent of their GDP (CEC, 1990a, p. 259), although they do a large volume of intra-EC trade as well. Because the existing transportation networks were developed for the needs of small countries, the EC has inherited a system which is not well adapted for current needs (Ilbery, 1986, p. 80). Goods frequently move farther than they would if channels of distribution were designed for today's economy.

No country in the EC has a large enough landmass to resolve its own environmental problems or to remain unaffected by the pollution of others. The saying that pollution knows no boundaries takes on great importance in the EC where, for example, France has an area of only 549,100 square kilometers, which is smaller than that of Texas, and shares rivers and air currents with heavily industrialized neighbors. The French government, as do all national governments in the EC, faces public demand for a clean environment but cannot satisfy that demand solely by national policies.

Relevant Cultural Values

Citizens in the EC expect public policies to protect and to clean the environment. Environmentalism is an important sociocultural value which public officials must respect. Public opinion polls consistently find that the majority of Europeans place the environment close to the top of their list of concerns (see, for example, CEC, 1992a, p. 67). Students of the subject do not agree, however, about when and why environmentalism achieved its present importance. Some believe that European environmentalism began with the industrial revolution as a reaction to its deleterious effects on the environment. Others argue that environmentalism was stimulated by publication of the Club of Rome report in the 1960s. Still others classify environmental awareness as a postindustrial value as defined by Ronald Inglehart (1977). All agree, however, that environmentalism has been an important value in the EC at least since the late 1960s.

Environmentalism is not a simple value, and people who espouse it do not constitute a cohesive group. Environmentalism is pervasive in the EC and not limited to people who call themselves environmentalists. Even environmentalists differ greatly among themselves. People who vote for green parties, for example, do so for a variety of reasons (Franklin and Rudig, 1992, pp. 129–159). In some cases, environmentalism is linked to the European peace movement (see Young, 1992, pp. 9–45, or Muller-Rommel, 1989). In others, it is espoused by groups advocating alternative forms of economic development. Some environmentalists regard themselves as left-wing politically. Others argue that they are neither left nor right in the traditional sense but are part of the "new politics." The environmental movements in the member states have different histories as well. The green movement in Germany grew from grass-roots antinuclear campaigns, developing outside mainstream politics (Spretnak and Capra, 1985, pp. 172–174). The environmental movement in the Nether-lands is associated with pacifism and the Dutch values of pragmatism and consensus building (Jamison, Eyerman, and Cramer, 1991). Environmentalism in Italy was promoted by the Radical Party and the Environment League, which was associated with the Communist Party. Both linked environmentalism with the need for a general reform of the political system. National differences also exist in the extent to which citizens demand green policies, but the differences are not great. The two countries which occupy the opposite ends of the environmental political spectrum, Ireland and Germany, both have large ma-jorities who believe that the environment is an immediate and urgent problem; for example, 70 percent of the Irish and 89 percent of the Germans responded affirmatively in a poll asking them if they regarded the environment as an immediate and urgent problem (CEC, 1992a, p. A65). The people in the EC want environmental policies but they do not necessarily all want the same ones or want them with the same intensity.

The actors who make EC environmental policy, their behavior, and the ways in which they relate to one another are determined, in part, by sociocultural values. The process by which the EC makes policy is shaped by neo-corporatist values which are prevalent in many member states (Mazey and Richardson, 1993, pp. 109–128). Groups who will be affected by a policy are involved in making it. The EC encourages the formation of European interest groups, which are generally federations of national groups. The EC even provides money to support such groups when they are deemed essential in order to ensure repre-sentation of an interest. The European Trade Union Confederation is an exam-ple. European interest groups regularly interact with the Commission and the Parliament. The small staff of the Commission relies on experts in the interest groups for information and advice.

Neo-corporatism, the value which governs the relationships between the EC and external actors, derives from a distinctive conceptualization of state and society. It is a "socio-political process in which organizations representing monopolistic functional interests engage in political exchange with state agen-cies over public policy outputs which involves those organizations in a role that combines interest representation and policy implementation through delegated self-enforcement" (Cawson, 1985, p. 8). Many scholars assert that neo-corpo-ratism characterizes policy making in much of Western Europe (Scholten, 1987). According to Mazey and Richardson, "The corporatist ambitions of the Commission are widely acknowledged" (1992, p. 116). The practice of neo-corporatist policy making values informed and responsible participation, as well as moderation and consensus building. Mazey and Richardson, in a study of groups formed to represent the interests of European industries, found that the groups behaved according to the values and rejected suggestions to use their power in aggressive and obstructionist ways. They directly discussed issues with environmental groups and appeared to be progressive on the environment (p. 125). The authors also found evidence that environmental groups have learned to moderate their stances in order to be effective in the EC (p. 126). The findings indicate that sociocultural values favor moderate behavior and help to ensure that the resulting policy is acceptable to the major actors. They also make it unlikely that the EC will create bold, innovative environmental policies.

Relevant Constitutional Rules

The Treaty of Rome and the Single European Act (SEA) provide the rules which govern environmental policy making in the EC and therefore constitute part of the stable system parameters. The ratification of the SEA in 1987 provided the EC with rules which facilitated the formation of environmental policy as noted in the previous section on background. The Treaty of Rome does not mention the environment but implies that authority to regulate it resides in the member states. Article 36 of the treaty states that member states may limit exports or imports in order to protect the health and life of persons, animals, and plants. The treaty has two provisions, however, which provided the basis for the first EC environmental policies. The famous Article 100 empowers the EC to enact directives in order to harmonize national laws or regulations when different national policies directly affect the operation of the common market. Article 235 is an implied powers clause which allows the EC to act in areas where it does not have a specific grant of authority if the action is intended to attain one of the objectives of the EC as stated in the treaty. The Council had to agree unanimously in order to pass measures under either of those articles. The Commission also believed that three other articles of the treaty provided bases for action on the environment: Article 43, which provides for a common agricultural policy; and Articles 75 and 84, which provide for a common transportation policy. Germany did not agree with the Commission, so most early legislation dealing with the environment was based on Article 100 and, to a lesser extent, on Article 235 (Rehbinder and Stewart, 1988, p. 20). The result is that environmental policy, in its formative stages, was linked to economic considerations and subsumed to them.

With the adoption of environmental action programs starting in 1973, the EC began to separate environmental concerns from economic confines. Action programs are only policy statements, but they do provide for comprehensive consideration of the environment in place of ad hoc measures. The environment in its own right became a concern of the EC and not only as an adjunct of the common market. The Commission and the Council, as well as the member states, agreed to a broad interpretation of the objectives of the treaty as provided in its preamble and Article 2 so that the EC could act to improve the quality of life. The Treaty of Rome had enough flexibility that the EC could become, by the 1980s, a significant actor in protecting the environment, but the legal basis was tenuous. The treaty also provides two principles which have remained constant. One is that the EC competence in regard to the environment is a shared competence. The member states have significant power to regulate the environment. The other is that EC environmental directives fall primarily under Article 100, meaning that they must have an economic purpose.

The Single European Act (SEA) constitutes a major step in the development of EC environmental law because it removes doubts about the competence of the EC to act in order to protect the environment. The environment is dealt with in a separate section, Title VII. Article 130 sets the objectives of EC environmental policy: to preserve, protect, and improve the quality of the environment; to contribute toward protecting human health; and to ensure a prudent and rational use of natural resources. Article 130 states that the Council shall agree unanimously when adopting a policy under this article. The SEA has two other provisions which have proved to be important for environmental policy. The SEA, along with the "White Paper on Completing the Internal Market," is the linchpin of the 1992 initiative. It revised Article 100 to add 100a so that measures necessary for the 1992 initiative may be adopted by the Council by a majority vote rather than by a unanimous one. The revision also applies to environmental proposals, if they are related to creating the internal market. The change poses a dilemma for environmentalists. If they want environmental measures to be adopted by a majority vote, they have to subsume them under the economic rubric of the common market. If, on the other hand, they opt for Article 130, in order to emphasize the right of the EC to act on purely environmental concerns, they risk a veto in the Council. The outcomes of measures accepted under Article 130 have the added attraction for environmentalists that member states may maintain national standards which provide a higher level of protection than that required by the EC. They may not do so for directives adopted under Article 100a, if the national law constitutes a barrier to the internal market.

Subsidiarity is invoked for the first time in an EC treaty in the SEA and is intended solely as a principle to guide the division of authority for the environment between the EC and the member states. The provision was little noticed at the time in contrast to its present prominence as a principle in the Treaty on European Union. According to Article 130r(4) of the SEA, "The Community shall take action relating to the environment to the extent to which the objectives referred to in paragraph 1 can be attained better at Community level than at the level of the individual Member States." In effect, the SEA gives the EC the authority to make environmental laws, but the principle of subsidiarity limits the authority and imposes the need to share the authority with the member states.

A problem which had long troubled the EC concerned national standards and trade. Different national standards create barriers to trade among the member states. The problem was partially solved by the ruling of the European Court in the famous Cassis de Dijon case, which stated that products lawfully produced and traded in one member state may also be traded in other member states. The Court ruling allowed for some exceptions, but the status of environmental standards was not clear. The Commission issued a communiqué to assure member states that they could still have national environmental standards for traded products, but the standards needed to be necessary, appropriate, and not excessive (CEC, 1980). The provision on subsidiarity in the SEA may be seen in the context of developments following the Cassis ruling. The EC was committed to removing barriers to trade among the member states. The member governments had a mandate to raise environmental standards. The SEA gave the EC the right to create EC environmental standards when the EC could better serve the objectives of improving the environment than could national governments. The distinction was not clear-cut. The important fact is that the SEA made the environment a matter of shared competence for the EC and the member states. Shared competence does not mean that the EC and the member states shall have separate and distinct spheres of operation, but rather that they will define their spheres case by case. Their authorities overlap. The test is to determine which actor can better fulfill the objectives set in Article 130 of the SEA. Subsidiarity is different from federalism because a constitution defines separate spheres for action in a federal system.

Conclusions in Regard to the Stable System Parameters

Demographic, economic, and cultural facts compel political leaders in the EC to act to protect the environment. National policies cannot resolve environmental problems. The scope of those policies is too limited, and separate national policies interfere with the creation of a single market. The EC has responded to the need for common policies, but it is restrained by its own rules and by values which guide its policy making.

The stable system parameters ensure that the EC will continue to affect, if not dominate, environmental policy. The EC's style of operation requires that it extensively communicate with European interest groups and with member states, which continue to be important actors. The parameters lead to a system which is complex, reciprocal, and participatory. They constrain the EC actors from centralizing action on the environment in Brussels, but they also ensure that the EC environmental policy process is slow and fraught with opportunities for confusion and even conflict.

THE DYNAMIC EXTERNAL ENVIRONMENT

In addition to the constants considered above, EC environmental policy is influenced by external changes which expand or contract the possibilities for such policy. A number of changes occurred in the late 1980s and early 1990s which favored the development of environmental policy. The need for global action on the environment was one of them. The Commission became an important actor in international environmental politics. The "greening" of politics was another change, as politicians and political parties jumped on the bandwagon in Brussels and Strasbourg, as well as in national capitals. On the other hand, one important change poses a threat to the development of EC environmental policy. The economic recession of the 1990s with the resulting increase in unemployment raises fears that the cost of environmental policies will harm the competitive position of European firms. Business leaders have transmitted such a message to Brussels. Two other changes which directly affect EC environmental policy are also important and need further discussion: the creation of the internal market and the adoption of the Treaty on European Union.

The policy to create the internal market (the 1992 program) is the most important policy in EC history. The program changed the legal parameters for businesses operating in the EC, and it changed the entire image of the EC. It gave the EC a mission and a credibility which all member states recognized. The program consisted of nearly three hundred directives to reform or eliminate national policies which obstructed the formation of a single market. The goal was to create an economic area in which businesses and trade could operate without regard to national borders. The ramifications of this gigantic program are enormous. Multinational corporations have restructured. Cross-border mergers and acquisitions have increased dramatically. The EC was revitalized and took on an aura of success. Although the EC has since stumbled badly over the issue of creating a single currency, the core of the 1992 initiative remains and it directly affects environmental policy.

Many governments in the EC have highly developed national policies for environmental protection. The creation of the internal market threatens the effectiveness of those policies in a number of ways. Governments who impose costly environmental regulations on firms operating in their countries put the firms at a competitive disadvantage in an integrating single market. Multinational corporations can escape the reach of national laws because the rules of the internal market allow them to locate anywhere in the twelve member states and service the entire market. If Germany, for example, places onerous restrictions on firms operating in Germany, firms can move to another country and still sell in the German market without the constraints that national borders formerly entailed. In a competitive economy, those restrictions punish countries with a high level of protection, so national governments will hesitate to raise standards. As noted above, member states have also found that their freedom to impose high environmental standards on products sold in their country has been limited by the priority given to the removing of trade barriers. The countries which impose strict environmental standards are generally countries which also have advanced industries which benefit from the single market. The governments of those countries support continued progress on the single market and therefore advocate strong action by the EC on the environment in order to ensure that they can keep both competitive firms and high environmental standards.

The Maastricht Treaty significantly changes the framework within which the EC formulates environmental policy. It ensures the legitimacy of the EC as a party to environmental policy, and it gives the EC new means with which to create a strong environmental policy. Title XVI allows the EC to adopt most environmental directives by means of a qualified majority vote in the Council. Unanimity is required only for energy issues, fiscal provisions, and certain aspects of urban policy. The treaty also gives Parliament, generally a proponent of environmental measures, a larger role in shaping action programs and other general policies. The treaty enhances the role which the EC can play in international environmental politics. It now has the same authority to conclude international environmental treaties as it already had under Article 228 for international commercial treaties. The enhancement of the EC's authority constitutes a progression from previous practices. The treaty contains an innovation which may be important: It creates the Cohesion Fund (Title XIV), which will fund environmental projects in poorer regions. Apart from its obvious environmental and business implications, the fund should increase political support for environmental measures in the Council, especially among the poorer members.

The provisions of the Maastricht Treaty for the environment have caused less controversy than have those for most other topics. If the EC has the political will to use them, the provisions could make environmental policy a much more important part of the work of the EC than it has been. Given the public support for green policies, the prospect that environmental policy will play a role in establishing the social legitimacy of the EC is promising, especially if the EC enters another period of economic growth.

THE POLICY SUBSYSTEM

The subsystem through which EC environmental policy is formulated consists of three groups: the formally appointed decision makers (the Commission, the Parliament, and the Council), advocacy groups, and power brokers. Care must be exercised in analyzing the roles which each group plays in the decision-making process.

First, the process is not "mechanical" or fixed, nor is it adversarial in the Anglo-Saxon tradition of creating "winners" and "losers." Greed, of course, does sometimes motivate national governments, or a government may act aggressively to seize a special prize, but such negative motives inform decisions less frequently than the press may imply.

Second, the term *role playing* implies that each group performs discrete functions in the decision-making process. The implication is a misleading one because consensus building, reciprocity, and "packaged deals" more characteristically influence the process.

The simple explanation that the Commission proposes, the Parliament offers an opinion, and the Council decides is also misleading. The actors do play the formal roles implied in the explanation, but the decision-making process is much less tidy. An official of the Commission once described the EC as a "vast convention," a giant network of officials, who represent both the EC and national governments, politicians, and interest groups. They interact at all stages of the decision-making process. The images of the vast convention, the interaction norm, and the giant network all need to be kept in mind as background for the following discussion of actors, advocacy groups, and power brokers.

Decision Makers

The Commission has the formal authority to initiate proposals for environmental policies. It has a specific directorate general (DG XI) to perform the work. The civil servants working in DG XI form the nucleus for EC environmental policy making. DG XI has subdivisions for the different types of environmental policies. Although the organization looks impressive, many parts of the DG XI are seriously understaffed for the increased workload of recent years and the highly technical nature of much of the work, so DG XI depends on outside experts. Indeed, many observers agree that DG XI uses more outside experts than any other directorate general. It relies on interest group representatives who have proved knowledgeable and reliable, as well as on national civil servants. *Comitology* is the name of the process which brings together national civil servants to serve on expert committees who advise the Commission on proposals (Williams, 1991, p. 158). The civil servants on the Commission have also been working more and more closely with the civil servants on the Council; in fact, they work so closely together that the Council is seldom surprised when it receives a formal proposal from the Commission. Indeed, Peter Ludlow, one of the most knowledgeable observers of the EC, argues that the conflictual model of the relationship between the Council and the Commission is misleading, because it ignores the highly institutionalized network of cooperation which exists long before the formal proposal arrives in the Council (Ludlow, 1991, p. 103).

The Commission has been able to harness that network of cooperation in order to produce a prodigious amount of work. The Commission is obviously eager to develop a wide span of EC initiatives for the environment. It has produced around two hundred successful pieces of legislation, has participated in international negotiations, and has commissioned a significant number of studies of environmental issues.

The working method of the Council is also more complex and porous than is customarily assumed. The Council has its own bureaucracy, which is smaller than that of the Commission, but whose importance has been increasingly recognized. In 1990 it had 2,008 persons working for it in seven directorates general. DG D deals with the environment, research, energy transport, and consumer protection (CEC, 1990b, pp. 26–28). Its members work with representatives from the member states, the Commission, and interest groups. The Council also has the Committee of Permanent Representatives (COREPER), which is the influential body of national representatives who regulate the agenda of the Council. Although the official members of the Council are the member governments, the Council should not be seen as simply the conduit for national interests. Peter Ludlow argues that the Council has become increasingly autonomous in relation to the member states (1991, p. 114). The vote of any participant should not always be regarded as an expression of that participant's national self-interest. Politics and political leadership lead to tradeoffs and package deals. The increased use of majority voting encourages coalitions and the exchange of votes. Strong presidents of the Council can shape outcomes as well (de Bassompierre, 1988, pp. 34–35). The norms of behavior in the Council also encourage consensus building and discourage obstruction by individual members (Wessels, 1991, p. 146).

The expansion of EC environmental policy could not have been possible without the support of the Council, which had the unanimity required to pass most of the environmental measures. Since the 1980s, the Council has made the environment a priority. In addition to being good politics, the move was also realistic in light of the inability of individual countries to solve many of their own environmental problems. Some member states, when assuming the role of the presidency of the Council, have made ambitious promises about environmental legislation which they would produce during their tenure in office. The British government made such a promise, but without great success. The Belgian government is the most recent one to promise a green presidency.

Most authorities agree that Parliament has become an effective actor in the EC (see, for example, Lodge, 1989b, pp. 58–79). Members of Parliament have developed the new powers accorded them by the SEA to compel the Council and the Commission to respect opinions and amendments proposed by Parliament. The Commission must reply to all questions submitted to it by Parliament, and it frequently revises proposals to incorporate amendments of Parliament. The Council also has been receptive to changes proposed by Parliament, but less so than has the Commission (Wessels, 1991, p. 144).

Parliament has used its new power to promote environmental issues. It is generally regarded as the nucleus of European green politics. The green party group in Parliament, while not large, is visible and active. The socialists and the people's party groups, which dominate politics in Parliament, have a green orientation as well. The environmental committee is hard-working and has a reputation for producing good reports on environmental issues, and for being the stronghold of environmentalists. Although its members represent the major party groups in Parliament, all are united as advocates of green policies (Judge, 1993, p. 209). The head of the environmental committee in Parliament, Ken Collins, is well known as a spokesperson for environmental issues. The new importance of Parliament in regard to environmental policy is matched by the attention which it now receives from interest groups and the press in contrast to earlier days when both ignored its existence.

Advocacy Groups

The advocacy groups or interest groups which try to influence EC environmental policy have increased in number and prominence in response to the growing importance of EC environmental policy. The number and type fluctuate depending on the agenda in Brussels. Some groups are formed temporarily only to influence a specific proposal under consideration. Such groups are frequently formed by interested corporations. Others are confederations of national interest groups which have a broad mandate and a permanent presence in Brussels. Still others are groups which were formed to influence another type of policy but which have added an interest in environmental measures. The European Trade Union Confederation is an example. It was created several decades ago when the EC began to draft measures affecting employees' concerns. Today it closely follows EC actions on the environment. International environmental groups, such as Greenpeace and the World Wildlife Foundation, monitor activities in Brussels and try to influence them as well.

The number of persons involved in interest groups is not as large as most assume from the number of groups. Most of the groups operate with a small staff and modest offices. The national operations of a group are usually better funded than operations of that same group in Brussels. Even the employers' association in Brussels (UNICE) fits the norm. It has a small operation in Brussels in contrast to employers' associations in most member states, which operate with large budgets. The reason for the situation may be simply that the development of interest is relatively new, and organizations have not adapted to the increased importance of Brussels; on the other hand, the reason may be that actors still find that policies which concern them are made by national governments rather than by the EC. Still another explanation, which many authorities offer, is the divisions which exist inside many groups. The groups are composites of national groups, each of which has its own agenda and norms (Mazey and Richardson, 1993, p. 118).

Interest groups need to adapt to the norms of policy making in the EC. The officials of those groups must cultivate relationships with persons in the Council, the Commission, and the Parliament because all three institutions shape policy. Interest group representatives are more than lobbyists. They cultivate positions as respected authorities and reliable advisers. Some develop reputations as experts on relevant, technical subjects and others are known as persons of vision and ideas. They generally avoid the appearance of being "too partisan." They conform to the norms mentioned previously which prevail in policy making in the EC. Those norms do not encourage adversarial tactics or the rejection of consensus building.

One of the most important environmental groups in Brussels is the European Environmental Bureau (EEB). Its members consist of 153 groups in the member states as well as in non-EC countries. They range from the French Association of Environmental Engineers to the Greek Sea Turtle Protection Society. The EEB operates under the direction of an executive committee and a small staff in Brussels which coordinates all of its work. It routinely meets with the Council and president of the Commission and members of Parliament. It also has international contacts with the United Nations and the Organization for Economic Cooperation and Development and has programs for sustainable development in Third World countries. Each year, it is responsible for the preparation of position papers by expert groups.

The EEB tried to ensure that the new Treaty on European Union would provide for a more effective and democratic environmental policy. It prepared a document for consideration by the Intergovernmental Conference which prepared the treaty (EEB, 1990). Following the signing of the treaty, the EEB published an assessment of it which reflected general disappointment (EEB, 1992). The report cites, in particular, the cumbersome and ambiguous procedure for formulating environmental policy and calls the treaty "scandalously deficient" in addressing the problem of the democratic deficit (p. 2).

The EC Committee of the American Chamber of Commerce in Brussels is a different type of interest group. It represents 130 U.S. companies operating in Europe. It is interested in the EC environmental policies which directly affect the operation of U.S. corporations and has a special subcommittee for such issues. It serves both to influence policy (frequently through contact with the U.S. delegation to the EC) and to inform its members of EC activities. It stresses its service function; for example, it regularly publishes a guide for its members, which includes information on legislation and on other interest groups as well as names, addresses, and telephone numbers for EC offices (EC Committee of the American Chamber of Commerce, 1994).

The U.S. group is, of course, not representative of other business groups in the EC, but it does share with them many of the same concerns. In general, business groups are regarded as stronger than environmental groups. They associate their concerns with the general interest in promoting a sound economy, but they do not disparage environmental values. The strategy is effective in the current situation. A study of the activity of the chemical industry revealed how, under the right conditions, an industry group can balance national and international concerns to devise a cohesive position (Boons, 1993, pp. 84–105).

Policy Brokers

Policy brokers do not exist as separate actors in EC environmental policy making. Both the Commission and the Council act as policy brokers in addition to their formal roles in the process. The long process of consultation provides ample opportunity for the Commission to resolve differences among national and interest group participants. Indeed, the Commission must be an effective policy broker in order to succeed in launching a program. It must find the differences and adjust its proposals to make them acceptable to both Parliament and the Council, each of which has its own constituencies. Proposals are frequently redrafted in this preliminary stage. Later the Commission plays policy broker between Parliament and the Council when it considers proposed amendments and seeks to reconcile differences between the two institutions. According to Peter Ludlow, the secretariat of the Council, which has grown in importance, is now a major policy broker (Ludlow, 1991, p. 115). It has a close working relationship with the Commission as well as with the member governments. It functions effectively in that relationship because the Council has gained autonomy from the national governments (p. 114). Participants in the Council from the member states have to work with the secretariat if they are to protect their interests when the Council votes on the final draft of a proposal. The policy process and the norms in the EC create conditions which are ripe for policy brokers, and both the Council and the Commission play the role at relevant moments in the process.

ENVIRONMENTAL POLICY IN THE MAASTRICHT ERA

The EC has an ambitious agenda for environmental action, but the portents are not good for the successful implementation of many of the measures, while others will be adopted only after they have been moderated. Both the Danish and Belgium governments had promised action on the environment during their tenures as president of the Council in 1993, but neither was able to achieve the adoption of a carbon and energy tax nor of the Rio Convention—two of the most visible items on the environmental agenda. On the other hand, the Commission was able to avoid dismantling the environmental controls that had been threatened earlier in the year when the British and French governments presented a list of measures which they believed violated the principle of subsidiarity. The Commission agreed to adjust (not repeal) sixteen laws from a list that had originally contained seventy-one measures, and European leaders accepted the compromise at a summit in Brussels in December 1993.

In order to provide a deeper examination of environmental policy in the Maastricht era, two quite different aspects of the subject are examined. One is the proposed packaging directive and the other is the "White Paper on Growth, Competitiveness, Employment" (CEC, 1993). The former provides a case which may be examined by means of the concepts used in the chapter. The latter, the defining document of the era now commencing, determines the place of environmental issues within the hierarchy of EC priorities.

The development of the packaging directive has been watched with care by businesses operating in the EC because of its potential impact on many business operations (CEC, 1992c). It has also been watched anxiously by environmental groups concerned about the waste crisis inside the densely populated EC. The political activity surrounding the making of the directive has been intense.

The fifth action program provides the context for the packaging directive as it does for all environmental legislation during the life of the program. The EC borrowed a concept currently in vogue in environmental circles, sustainable development, and gave the title "Towards Sustainability" to the fifth action program (CEC, 1992d). As the title indicates, the EC now wants to balance environmental concerns with the need for economic development, particularly among the poorer member states. The document opens by grimly noting that a recent report "indicates a slow but relentless deterioration of the general state of the environment of the Community notwithstanding the measures taken over the past two decades" (p. 3) and adds that international competition will worsen the problem. The EC must, therefore, adopt a more far-reaching and effective strategy characterized by three features. The first is the placing of blame for much of the problem on human behavior: "The real problems which cause environmental loss and damage are the current patterns of human consumption and behavior" (p. 6). Pollution control begins with changing values and behavior and, therefore, more emphasis will be given to education and information and less to legislation. The second feature is related to the first. Market-based instruments (measures to encourage the pricing of products to include pollution costs) will replace legislation as the primary instrument for protecting the environment. The third feature is the increased use by the EC of financial mechanisms to encourage environmental protection, the most important of which is the new Cohesion Fund. Environmental and developmental needs will be tied together for funding in poor areas under the provisions of the Cohesion Fund. LIFE is another financial instrument established by the Council to fund priority programs for the environment. Similar projects in Eastern Europe are funded under the PHARE program, the EC aid program for the region (CEC, 1992d, pp. 71 and 90).

"Shared responsibility" is an important principle in the fifth action program. "The Programme combines the principles of subsidiarity with the wider concept of shared responsibility; this concept involves not so much a choice of action at one level to the exclusion of others but, rather, a mixing of actors and instruments at the appropriate levels, without any calling into question of the division of competences between the Community, the Member States, regional and local authorities" (p. 9). All the actors are to work together in partnership. The concept of shared responsibility fits easily into the neo-corporatist style of policy making practiced in the EC. Neo-corporatist principles are also embodied in two new bodies created by the program. A consultative committee, composed of representatives of enterprises, consumers, nongovernmental organizations, and public authorities, will participate in policy formulation. An environmental policy committee, with representatives from the Commission and the member states, will oversee and advise on policy. A network of environmental inspectors and enforcement bodies of the Commission and the member states will work with the newly established European Environment Agency.

The program has five target sectors: industry, energy, transport, agriculture, and tourism. The twin themes of sustainable development and shared responsibility run through the discussion for each of the sectors. Implicit in all the discussions is a note of caution and moderation. The euphoria of the 1992 era is gone. The need for a clean environment must be balanced with other needs. The new emphasis also requires wider participation. The environment calls for an integrated effort by private and public actors and by local, regional, national, and EC governments. The environment also requires integrated pollution control and, in the interest of subsidiarity, member states must take the lead in establishing limits on polluting substances for each industrial sector. In 1993, the Commission introduced a directive on integrated pollution control to provide a framework for national action in accord with the fifth action program.

The proposed EC directive on packaging is part of the EC waste management policy which started in 1975. The EC has three responsibilities toward waste. It provides oversight to ensure that waste is dealt with properly in the member states. The EC ensures that the movement of waste among the member states is conducted in ways which do not degrade the environment. The EC also has some responsibilities to prevent waste. In 1989, the EC adopted a "A Strategy Paper on Waste Management," which identified prevention as the best solution to the difficult problem (CEC, 1989).

The proposed packaging directive, adopted by the Commission on July 15, 1992, incorporates many features of the fifth action program (Ifland and Springer, 1992). Prevention of waste is the principle of the directive. Designed to induce humans to change their patterns of consumption, it relies on control measures, rather than legislation, to achieve its objectives. In particular, it forces the inclusion of the costs of pollution control in the prices of products. It promotes shared responsibility among the relevant players.

The proposed directive is based on free-trade concepts. Different national policies to prevent packaging waste are a barrier to trade among the member states. The objectives of the proposal are to harmonize national policies, to prevent and reduce the quantity of packaging waste, and to promote sound environmental practices for the recovery of packaging waste. The provisions of the proposal include the following:

1. Targets must be set for the recovery of packaging material in the waste stream

2. Member states must establish effective systems for collecting and returning used packaging

3. Packages must be marked with standardized symbols and must provide information on the contents of the packaging material

4. Member states must establish an information system with data on all aspects of packaging-waste management

5. Member states must adopt economic instruments, such as deposits, fees, and taxes, to promote the objectives of the directive

6. The Commission must promote the standardization of packages to facilitate reuse

7. A technical committee must be created to advise and assist the EC on technical matters related to the directive

When the proposal is examined within the Sabatier framework used in this chapter, a number of important insights are gained (see Figure 6.1).

Stable System Parameters

The factors considered in the general discussion of stable system parameters played a role in shaping the packaging directive. Environmental conditions made the policy a necessity. The waste problem had reached a crisis by the 1990s. The amount of waste was increasing as the number of disposal sites was decreasing. Germany, for example, had only 385 dumps for household waste in 1984. Of those, 114 were expected to reach capacity within three years, and no one wanted a new site located in his backyard (Institute for Environmental Studies, 1991, p. 468).

Social values and norms ensured that public officials would act on the waste issue and reassured them that the public was ready to accept measures which would entail significant changes in their buying habits. Social values and norms also affected the way in which business responded to the proposal. Business groups avoided overt obstructionist responses. They worked with environmental groups and EC officials to find mutually acceptable positions.

The constitutional rules, which make the environment a shared competence between the EC and the member states significantly affected the packaging directive. Member states had enacted a number of regulations to control waste. The different national policies caused problems for businesses operating across national borders. When the Germans adopted their draconian law on packaging waste, businesses became more concerned and recognized the need for an EC directive to harmonize and restrain national regulations. Officials also recog-

Figure 6.1
A Diagram of Policy Changes in the EC Waste Management Policy Based on the Sabatier Approach

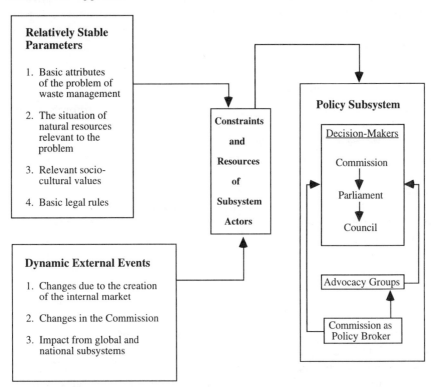

nized that the different national laws constituted a problem for internal trade. Under the principle of subsidiarity, the EC became the appropriate actor for the regulation of waste. Officials drafted the proposal under Article 100a, the relevant article for the internal market measure, which has a restraining effect on national measures if they constitute a barrier to the internal market. The article also means that Parliament has a larger role and that the vote in the Council may be by a qualified majority. The ratification of the Maastricht Treaty probably will not affect the rules relevant to that proposal. The argument to keep the proposal under Article 100a, which is unchanged by the treaty, seems to have prevailed.

THE DYNAMIC EXTERNAL ENVIRONMENT

Recent developments have impeded the passage of the packaging directive in contrast to the factors noted in the stable system parameters, which encouraged and enabled EC action on waste prevention. The economic recession is an obvious constraint on any environmental measure. It contributed to the cautious mood apparent in the latest action program. A number of provisions noted in the discussion of the proposed directive were also affected by changing circumstances. Some examples are the provisions for member states to use financial measures, the delegation of responsibilities to committees, and the importance placed on information and education factors to encourage compliance.

The Policy Subsystem

Activity surrounding drafting and passing the proposal conforms to the general picture of the process which has been described in this chapter. During the first two years of its existence, the proposal was revised four times, and redrafting continues. Parliament offered several hundred amendments which the Commission and the Council must consider if they are to build the necessary support for such a high-profile measure. Interest groups have been involved throughout the process as have officials from national governments. The types of interest groups fit into the categories noted in the general discussion.

The Packaging Chain Forum is an association of businesses directly concerned with the directive. It has been consulted by the Commission and has been successful in effecting changes. The group does not oppose the directive but wants industry to be free to use a variety of methods to deal with waste. The EC food and drink industry has also been consulted and also supports the proposal as long as it does not impose excessive costs on industry. Both groups have worked with the Commission to design a directive which they can accept and which will foreclose the possibility of more restrictive actions by national governments in some member states.

Two groups representing a different perspective are Greenpeace and the European Confederation of Food Workers. The latter supports the directive but would like it to be adopted under Article 130 of the Treaty of Rome so that national governments are free to adopt higher standards if they chose. Greenpeace has a similar position. A spokesman stated that the "dogma of free trade should not be allowed to override national environmental concerns" (Hines, 1992). The issue is whether EC policy should constitute the minimum that states may have or the maximum.

Political rules and sociological norms have created a regime composed of business groups, environmentalists, labor unions, EC officials, national officials, and members of Parliament. Together they comprise the policy subsystem which is shaping the EC directive on waste. The policy which emerges will be forged by the efforts of the Commission acting as a broker among the competing interests but also by the efforts of the secretariat of the Council, which acted as a broker to reconcile different national concerns.

In December 1993 the Council, over the opposition of Denmark, Germany, and the Netherlands, adopted the packaging directive. The fate of the directive is still not decided, however. Parliament has to consider it and will probably offer a number of amendments which will then require the consideration of the Council. During the eighteen months that transpired from conception to adoption in the Council, the directive was changed to be more acceptable to the packaging industry. The three poorest members of the EC (Greece, Ireland, and Portugal) won some exemptions. The main provisions of the directive require that within five years member states must recover between 50 and 65 percent of their waste and must recycle between 25 and 40 percent of total waste and not less than 15 percent of any category of waste. The percentages are lower than those in the original draft, but environmentalists did receive two concessions. Member states may exceed the rates set for recovery and recycling if their policies do not harm the internal market by exporting the waste. The Council also agreed that the percentages would be subject to an unspecified, but substantial, increase within ten years.

The short history of the packaging directive illustrates the numerous factors that come into play in shaping an EC policy. It also provides evidence of why it is difficult to state definitively who makes the policy. The Council has the legal power, but it is not a cohesive force on the issue. Some members formed alliances with the Commission and interest groups that had relevant political influence. The Commission controlled the outcome to the extent that it was responsible for devising the acceptable compromise. Finally, Parliament and environmental groups may still force a greening of the directive through effective political action. At the end of 1993, however, the directive existed in a form that is acceptable to the packaging lobby and the majority in the Council as well as the Commission. It is significant as a precedent, but does not represent a major step in the control of waste in the EC. The percentages set in the directive are below those already found in the most advanced states, and the EC already meets the minimum percentage of 25 percent for recycling as stipulated in the directive.

The 1993 White Paper and the Environment

The "White Paper on Growth, Competitiveness, Employment" is the major document presented to the European Council meeting in Brussels in December 1993 to provide the guidelines for EC action on the economy. The purpose of the paper is to define the scope of the crisis confronting the EC and to provide the outlines of a policy to resolve it. The crisis is defined by two related facts—high rates of unemployment and economic recession. The challenge is to restart growth through making the economy more competitive globally while simultaneously creating new employment opportunities. The document was accepted by the Council and constitutes the official statement of the priorities of the EC at this time.

The priorities accepted by the EC in the White Paper have major implications for the future of EC environmental policy. The economic cure proposed in the document appears to consist of two prescriptions. One is to increase the global competitiveness of European firms by lightening the burden on them from public charges and from regulations. The other is to restart growth by a large investment program for trans-European networks (TENs) for communication, transportation, and energy. Environmentalists find little encouragement in the priorities or the prescriptions, but there are some green passages in the White Paper that could be important depending on the way they are interpreted.

The new development model which the White Paper sets as the goal for Europe is one in which environmental industries would flourish and one in which older, polluting industries would be replaced by clean ones. The White Paper foresees a greening of the labor market. Environmental business is expected to be an important source for the three million jobs which could be added to the labor market (CEC, 1993, p. 20). The problems rest not in the model, but in the transition from the current situation and specifically in the two prescriptions. Although the discussion to lighten the costs and regulatory burden on business is cast in terms of labor market burdens, the argument could serve as well to attack the burden placed on business by environmental policies. If the primary objective is to make EC business competitive in the global economy, then environmental charges are an obstacle. In the long run, green laws lead to new businesses, but in the short run they may hurt existing firms. The argument is familiar even if it is absent from the White Paper. The other prescription concerns the TENs and the large investments needed for them. The paper reiterates the theme that environmental consequences will be considered in all programs. The difficulty arises from the competition for investments and, in particular, the impact on the Cohesion Fund. Environmental projects will have to contest with more traditional public works projects for investment funds. The Cohesion Fund is limited to TENs and environmental projects. If job creation is the primary objective as stated in the White Paper, then TENs will obtain the bulk of the funds. The scenario foreseen for the transition is not necessarily an either/or situation. Much depends on the actors who will implement the program and the environment in which they will operate. The decisions that are made in regard to growth, competitiveness, and employment will shape the parameters for EC environmental policy for the foreseeable future.

CONCLUSION

The question that remains to be addressed is what role environmental policy will play in the creation of the European Union. In one sense, the policy will have little influence even if it continues to grow in importance. The policy is developed through directives which require national legislation. Citizens are aware of the national laws which affect them, but they seldom realize that behind the national law is an EC requirement for the law. The policy, therefore, will not increase the social legitimacy of the EC, because citizens will not credit the EC for the policies. In another sense, however, environmental policy, as it will develop under the new treaty, will give more depth to the Union. The process of making the policy requires multiple actors and provides numerous points of access for participants outside the list of formal actors. The number of participants is likely to grow as the scope of environmental policy grows under the more permissive framework of the new treaty. As noted in this chapter, the range of participants is broad and their influence is strong. Labor union members, businesspersons, and environmentalists all exercise their influence, as do representatives of national governments. The treaty also enhances the role of Parliament, which has been an important meeting point for persons concerned with environmental issues. The main doubts shadowing this mildly optimistic assessment of the effect of environmental policy on the European Union arise from concerns connected with the economic recession and the development of the internal market. If the internal market continues to be the number-one priority of the EC and the recession also continues, then the development of the environmental policy will be thwarted and its contribution to the growth of the European Union lessened.

REFERENCES

Boons, Frank. 1993. "Product-oriented Environmental Policy: Challenges, Possibilities and Barriers." In *A Green Dimension for the European Community*, ed. by David Judge. London: Frank Cass.

Cawson, Alan. 1985. "Conclusion: Some Implications for State Theory." In *Organized Interests and the State*, ed. by Alan Cawson. Beverly Hills, CA: Sage Publications.

CEC. 1973. "Declaration of the Council of the European Communities and of the Representatives of the Governments of the Member States Meeting in the Council." *Official Journal*, no. C 112.

———. 1980. "Communication from the Commission Concerning the Consequences of the Judgement Given by the Court of Justice on 20 February 1979 in Case 120/78." *Official Journal*, 256/2.

———. 1987. "Resolution of the Council of the European Communities and of the Representatives of the Governments of the Member States Meeting with the Council." *Official Journal*, no. C 328/1.

———. 1989. "A Strategy Paper on Waste Management." SEC(89)934 final.

———. 1990a. *Basic Statistics of the Community*. 27th ed. Brussels: Statistical Office of the European Communities.

———. 1990b. *The Council of the European Community*. Brussels: CEC.

———. 1991. *Cities and the Global Environment*. Proceedings of a European Workshop of the European Foundation for the Improvement of Living and Working Conditions.

———. 1992a. *Eurobarometer*, no. 37

———. 1992b. *Europe in Figures*. 3rd ed. Brussels: CEC.

———. 1992c. "Proposal for a Council Directive on Packaging and Packaging Waste." COM(92)278/7.

——— . 1992d. "Towards Sustainability." COM(92)23 final.

——— . 1993. "White Paper on Growth, Competitiveness, Employment." *Bulletin of the European Communities*, Supplement 6/93.

de Bassompierre, Guy. 1988. *Changing the Guard in Brussels*. New York: Praeger.

EC Committee of the American Chamber of Commerce. 1994. *The EC Environment Guide*. Brussels: EC Committee of the American Chamber of Commerce.

EEB (European Environmental Bureau). 1990. "Greening the Treaty." Produced in cooperation with Friends of the Earth and the World Wide Fund for Nature. Brussels: EEB.

——— . 1992. "How Green Is the Treaty?" Produced by Ralph Hallo. Brussels: EEB.

Franklin, Mark, and Wolfgang Rudig. 1992. "The Green Voter in the 1989 Election." *Environmental Politics* 1, no. 4 (Winter): 129–159.

Haigh, Nigel, and Frances Stewart. 1990. "Introduction." In *Integrated Pollution Control in Europe and North America,* ed. by Nigel Haigh and Frances Stewart. Baltimore, MD: Conservation Foundation.

Hildebrand, Philipp. 1992. "The European Community's Environmental Policy, 1957 to '1992.' " *Environmental Politic* 1, no. 4 (Winter): 13–44.

Hines, Colin. 1992. "The Green View on Subsidiarity." *Financial Times*, September 16.

Ifland, Peter, and Beverly Springer. 1992. "Environmental Policy in the European Community." Unpublished manuscript.

Ilbery, Brian. 1986. *Western Europe: A Systematic Human Geography*. 2nd ed. Oxford: Oxford University Press.

Inglehart, Ronald. 1977. *The Silent Revolution: Changing Values and Political Styles among Western Publics*. Princeton, NJ: Princeton University Press.

Institute for Environmental Studies. 1991. *European Environmental Yearbook*. London: DocTer International.

Jamison, Andrew, Ron Eyerman, Jacqueline Cramer, with Jeppe Laessoe. 1991. *The Making of the New Environmental Consciousness*. Edinburgh: Edinburgh University Press.

Judge, David. 1993. "Predestined to Save the Earth: The Environment Committee of the European Parliament." In *A Green Dimension for the European Community*, ed. by David Judge. London: Frank Cass.

Liberatore, Angela. 1991. "Problems of Transnational Policymaking: Environment Policy in the European Community." *European Journal of Political Research* 19: 281–305

Lodge, Juliet. 1989. "EC Policymaking: Institutional Considerations." In *The European Community and the Challenge of the Future*, ed. by Juliet Lodge. New York: St. Martin's Press.

——— . 1989b. "The European Parliament—from 'Assembly' to Co-legislature." In *The European Community and the Challenge of the Future,* ed. by Juliet Lodge. New York: St. Martin's Press.

Ludlow, Peter. 1991. "The European Commission." In *The New European Community*, ed. by Robert Keohane and Stanley Hoffmann. Boulder, CO: Westview Press.

Mazey, Sonia, and Jeremy Richardson. 1993. "Environmental Groups and the EC." In *A Green Dimension for the European Community*, ed. by David Judge. London: Frank Cass.

Muller-Rommel, F. 1989. *New Politics in Western Europe: The Rise and Success of Green Parties and Alternative Lists*. Boulder, CO: Westview Press.

Peterson, John, and Elizabeth Bomberg. 1992. *The Politics of Prevention and Health Care*. Aldershot, England: Avesbury Press.

Rehbinder, Eckard, and Richard Stewart. 1988. *Environmental Protection Policy*. New York: Walter de Gruyter.

Scholten, Ilja. 1987. "Introduction: Corporatist and Consociational Arrangements." In *Political Stability and Neo-Corporatism*. Beverly Hills, CA: Sage Publications.

Spretnak, Charlene, and Fritjof Capra. 1985. *Green Politics*. London: Paladin Grafton Books.

Williams, Shirley. 1991. "Sovereignity and Accountability in the European Community." In *The New European Community*, ed. by Robert Keohane and Stanley Hoffmann. Boulder, CO: Westview Press.

Wessels, Wolfgang. 1991. "The European Council: The Community's Decisionmaking Center." In *The New European Community*, ed. by Robert Keohane and Stanley Hoffmann, Boulder, CO: Westview Press.

Young, Stephen. 1992. "The Different Dimensions of Green Politics." *Environmental Politics* 1, no. 1 (Spring): 9–44.

Chapter 7

Regional Policy and European Union

R egional policy differs in several respects from other policy areas on the
social agenda of the European Community (EC). For example, it is the
only one which contains funds to be disbursed to its clients and it is the only
one for which the EC has created a new institution, the Committee of the
Regions. In most respects, however, regional policy fits the profile of other
policy areas on the social agenda. It is designed to meet social needs and it links
the EC with its citizens. A successful regional policy would enhance the social
legitimacy of the EC.

EC regional policy serves a number of different objectives—political, economic, and social. Its genesis derives from economic norms of the 1950s and
1960s, as well as from political bargains struck during the negotiations for the
European Economic Community (EEC). National economic planning was
widely accepted in postwar Europe with French indicative planning providing
a much admired model of the government and the private sector cooperating to
modernize the economy. Many European economists assumed that public
policy and public money could be combined to shape a more rational and a
more just economic system. Regional development aid programs were based
on the same assumption. The famous Italian Cassa per il Mezzogiorno program
directed public money into southern Italy in an effort to end its chronic poverty
and underdevelopment. The economic assumptions of the day were carried by
Italian negotiators into the discussions that preceded the formation of the
European Economic Community. Italian negotiators bargained for provisions
in the Treaty of Rome by which the EEC would assume some responsibility for
Italian regional problems. Their success ensured Italian support for the treaty

(Willis, 1971, p. 167). Although the treaty did not specifically provide for a regional policy, it established the European Investment Bank (EIB) and the European Social Fund (ESF), which became important components of regional policy. Indeed, Willis states that "no effort was made to disguise the fact that the Bank had been created by the negotiators of the Treaty of Rome as the EEC's principal instrument for bringing the economy of the Italian South up toward the level of the rest of western Europe" (1971, p. 175). The signatories of the treaty accepted the assumption that the new Community could and should play a role in promoting regional development.

In December 1974, the Council adopted the European Regional Development Fund (ERDF), which became the core of a more fully developed EC regional policy. (The Italian and Irish participants on the Council had threatened to boycott the Council meeting if the other members did not promise to support the fund.) The ERDF provides grants to public and private organizations for development projects in designated regions. It operates within the EC institutional framework. The Commission is responsible for proposing the funding levels and for oversight, and the Council formally adopts the proposed program. (The EIB, which also dispenses money, operates as do other international banks and, therefore, is outside the direct control of the Commission or the Council.) During the first decade of its operation, the ERDF disappointed many of its early supporters. Real power stayed with the member governments and politics, more than regional need, determined the allocation of money (Keating, 1993, pp. 299–300). Both the Commission and regional governments demanded reform of the system and a stronger voice in decision making. Their demands were partially met in 1986 by the Single European Act (SEA).

The SEA was primarily intended to provide for the creation of the single market; however, the drafters of the treaty had to consider the possible impact of the single market on areas in the periphery of the market. The new high-technology industries that were expected to be the hallmark of the market are located near centers of finance, communications, and transport. A single market could exacerbate the differences between the core and the periphery in the EC, as the most advanced firms in the member countries move to the core. In order to forestall this possibility, the SEA includes a special section on economic and social cohesion which gives the Community the responsibility to act to strengthen economic and social cohesion (Article 130a). The ERDF is also designated in the treaty to "help redress the principal regional imbalances in the Community" (Article 130c).

By the end of the 1980s, the regional policy of the EC had become an important part of Community political and economic life. A policy that started as an aid to member states in pursuit of their own regional policies became a tool to bring about more balanced development for the entire area. Along the way it also became a bargaining chip in the complex political accommodations that had to be made within an EC composed of an increasingly diverse membership.

During the evolution of regional policy, its politics have changed from being primarily intergovernmental to being multilayered with many actors, although member governments continue to play and to demand a key role. Recent developments, including the ratification of the Treaty on European Union (Maastricht Treaty), will facilitate broader participation. Indeed, regional policy promises to be one of the most interesting arenas to watch for a contest between the traditional politics of intergovernmental bargaining and the new multilayered politics provided by the Maastricht Treaty. The amount of money available for regional development in the future makes the stakes of the contest attractive.

The discussion of regional policy and its role in the building of the European Union is the task of this chapter. The discussion is organized according to the format followed in the other policy chapters. The three main subheadings are stable system parameters, dynamic external environment, and the policy subsystem. Concepts, such as social legitimacy and regime, which are included in other chapters are discussed as well.

STABLE SYSTEM PARAMETERS

Three different aspects comprise the stable system parameters for EC regional policy: the basic attributes of the problem area, the relevant cultural values that shape policy responses, and the legal structure within which regional policy is made.

Basic Attributes of the Problem Area

The basic attribute for EC regional policy is, of course, the existence of regional disparities. (For a useful explanation, see Cole and Cole, 1993.) Disparities among regions are readily discernable although it is difficult to measure the extent of disparities and to assign borders. Such tasks are essential, however, if policy is to be grounded on defendable criteria. Specialists do not agree on the indicators to use for measurement, and politicians do not agree on whether the boundaries of regions should be coterminous with existing political boundaries of subnational units or determined by some measurable criteria. The task of designating regions has been contentious in the EC throughout the history of regional policy and continues to be. Member states do not have uniform policies regarding subnational units. The size and degree of legal autonomy of such units vary considerably. The EC, however, requires uniformity among the units used for regional policy in order to ensure proper distribution of funds. The issue is further complicated by the existence of the EC competition policy. Properly designated regions are exempt from EC rules that limit public assistance where such assistance interferes with free competition.

Measuring Regional Disparities. Although the EC is relatively similar to the United States in wealth and level of economic development, it has a much wider range of regional diversity. For example, the per capita gross domestic product (GDP) ratio in the United States between the richest and poorest regions is 1.5 to 1 compared to a ratio of 2.1 to 1 in the EC. The landmass of the EC is much less coherent as well. According to one method of determination, 62 of the 174 regions of the EC are at least partly islands or groups of islands, and 40 are peninsulas belonging to seven member states. "In fact, only three Member States are totally integrated into the European continent in terms of physical geography" (CEC, 1991, p. 28). In contrast, only three of the fifty states in the United States are either islands or peninsulas.

The Statistical Office of the EC established a system whereby the entire area of the EC is divided into units known formally as the Nomenclature of Territorial Units and informally by the acronym NUTS. There are three levels of NUTS: NUTS 1 consists of the largest units; NUTS 2, of medium-sized units; and NUTS 3, of smaller units. (Units within the same level are relatively, but not exactly, comparable in size.) NUTS 1 comprises 66 regions, NUTS 2 comprises 174 regions, and NUTS 3 includes 829 regions. (For the purposes of both NUTS 1 and 2, Denmark, Ireland, and Luxembourg each constitute a single region.) The area of the EC is subdivided into these categories in order that data can be compiled from relatively comparable units to aid policy makers. The most commonly used measure for relative need is per capita GDP, which is valued in purchasing power standards (PPS). While the average per capita GDP for units in NUTS 2 was 100 in 1989, the average for the ten weakest units and that for the ten strongest were 47 and 151, respectively (CEC, 1992, Annex 1, p. 3).

Some member states are critical of the NUTS system. They argue that the Commission relies too heavily on economic criteria in making decisions, ignores sociological factors, and does not consider differences among administrative units in the member states ("European Regional Incentives," 1992, p. 592). The conflict is heightened when the division of the Commission responsible for enforcement of competition policy (DG IV) interferes with national regional policies on the grounds that they harm competition in the common market. According to the authoritative study cited above, "European Commission intervention in Regional Policy in Germany has been a consistent feature for much of the past decade. . . .The significant cases of intervention by the Commission have often been concerned with area designation" (pp. 583–584).

Causes of Regional Disparity. Persons dealing with regional policy in the EC generally assume that regional disparities are caused by geographical and economic variables. Geographical variables have received the most attention, but recently economic variables have been blamed for certain types of regional disparities. Obviously, the assumptions which policy makers make regarding causation directly affect the remedies that they propose (Tomkins and Twomey, 1992, pp. 100–101).

The concepts of core and periphery have been the most influential geographical explanation of EC regional disparities. Decades ago geographers pointed out that regions distant from the core of activity in a country fail to develop equally with areas closer to the core. Geographers also noted that the same phenomenon exists in the EC. The EC has a core containing a high concentration of economic development, modern infrastructure, and advanced social indications and a periphery lacking these attributes. Many geographers refer to the core as the "golden triangle." For example, Geoffrey Parker wrote that the core comprises the "golden triangle" of Birmingham, Paris, and Frankfurt (Parker, 1975, p. 164). More recently geographers also include the new growth area that extends in an arc from Barcelona across southern France to northern Italy in their determination of the core (CEC, 1991, p. 51). All the attributes of postindustrial life are concentrated in the core. The periphery contains the regions traditionally designated as underdeveloped, which have been outside the main strands of European development throughout this century. Southern Italy, large parts of Greece, and some regions of Spain, Portugal, and Ireland remain locked in the rural life styles of another age. Regions in the periphery have received the major share of EC regional assistance funds.

In recent years, EC regional specialists have recognized that some regions are chronically poor not because of their location, but because of economic factors. Such regions had depended on one major economic activity, such as steel making or textile production. When the economic viability of the activity declined, the region lacked the resources necessary to diversify and fell into chronic recession. Such regions are scattered across the economic map of Western Europe and include sites in northern England, the Ruhr valley, Lorraine, and so on. Such regions are not geographically defined and their economic and social characteristics differ from the ones in the periphery as well. They have an industrial tradition and skilled workers and are more urban.

The EC has devised a classification system to use to distinguish different types of development programs. The system is used to determine allocations from the ERDF, the European Social Fund (ESF), the Guidance Section of the European Agricultural Guidance and Guarantee Fund (EAGGF), and the Financial Instrument for Fisheries Guidance (FIFG). These funds comprise the Structural Fund, which is the primary source of money for regional development. As revised in 1993, the classification system consists of five categories known as objectives, each of which designates a different type of problem. Objectives 1 and 2 relate specifically to the ERDF. Objective 1 encompasses regions, most of which are in the periphery and structurally backward, which have a per capita GDP that is less than 75 percent of the EC average. Objective 2 regions are those affected by industrial decline. Such regions have unemployment rates 15 percent above the EC average and a higher rate of industrial employment as a proportion of total employment than the EC average. Objective 3 regions have a high rate of long-term unemployment and a large number of persons socially excluded from labor markets. Objective 4 comprises regions which need ESF funds in order to assist workers to adapt to industrial changes and to changes in production systems. Objective 5 regions receive assistance to modernize agriculture and fisheries and to promote rural development through the creation of nonagricultural jobs, such as those in tourism (CEC, 1993e).

Relevant Cultural Values

Regional policy is a norm in Western Europe. Most national governments practice some form of regional policy and many have done so for decades. Few dispute the claim that governments have a responsibility to assist poor regions. Few believe that regional disparities will be overcome solely through the operation of free markets. A search of the literature on regional policy as well as a consideration of the language used in policy documents indicates four values that have been important to the development of regional policy and that ensure its continued prominence in the panorama of EC policies. They are social justice, democracy, cohesion and participation.

Social justice was probably the value which played the largest role in shaping social policy in postwar Europe. Seymour Martin Lipset, one of the foremost political sociologists of the era, wrote about "the end of ideology" and the consensus in support of social democratic values (see, for example, Lipset, 1968, pp. 267–304). Governments of both the left and right endorsed social democratic values and adopted policies to eradicate social injustices. Social justice also became a basic principle for the new EC. The preamble of the Treaty of Rome contains the following clauses:

- "Resolved to ensure the economic and social progress of their countries by common action to eliminate the barriers which divide Europe"
- "Affirming as the essential objective of their efforts the constant improvement of the living and working conditions of their peoples"
- "Anxious to strengthen the unity of their economies and to ensure their harmonious development by reducing the differences existing between the various regions and the backwardness of the less favored regions"

The values embodied in the above passages are expressed even more strongly in the Single European Act (SEA) and the Maastricht Treaty, both of which affirm that the EC has an obligation to provide policies to improve the quality of life of citizens. The preamble of the SEA contains the clause "Determined to work together to promote democracy on the basis of fundamental rights . . . notably freedom, equality and social justice."

Democracy is, of course, a fundamental value in the EC as in Western society in general. Proponents of regional policy argue that the policy is a necessary attribute of a democratic society. Democracy has three meanings when used in this context:

1. Democracy means equality. Chronic inequality is destructive in a democratic society.
2. Democracy means respect for the cultural identity of peoples in subnational units. Renewed interest in cultural and historical identity is directly associated with renewed interest in regionalism (Keating, 1993, p. 297).
3. Democracy means that the people who are subject to a policy should also participate in the formation of that policy.

The European Parliament is the leading proponent of democracy in the EC. The Draft Treaty Establishing European Union, which Parliament issued in 1985, is a landmark in the history of the democratic idea in the EC. The draft treaty includes the words "Convinced of the need to enable local and regional authorities to participate by appropriate methods in the unification of Europe" (CEC, 1985, Annex 1). According to the Parliament, democracy means participation, and a legitimate regional policy is one in which regional authorities and regional interests are fully involved. More recently, David Martin, vice president of the European Parliament, wrote, "I believe that power should be passed down as well as up and am very much in favor of the concept of a Europe of the Regions" (Martin, 1991, p. 16). The expression "Europe of the Regions" is used by many today to indicate that a regional policy formulated with the participation of regional authorities is a democratic imperative for the new European Union.

The principle of cohesion was enshrined in the SEA in Title V on economic and social cohesion, which states that the Community "shall aim at reducing disparities between the various regions and the backwardness of the least-favored regions." Both the SEA and the Maastricht Treaty imply that cohesion is an essential basis for European union. Cohesion, as used in Community documents, means that regional disparities must be lessened so that people in all regions will feel an identity with the Union.

Participation is the fourth principle underpinning the EC regional policy. The commitment to participation has grown through the years and finds its most recent expression in the new Committee of the Regions established under the Maastricht Treaty. The principle has broad acceptance in this era, which is characterized by popular distrust of central authorities. Traditional political parties and national elites have lost support and regional politics offers a promising alternative for many.

The meanings of the four basic values which form the basis for EC regional policy are overlapping and similar, but with separate nuances. Each expresses a deep vein in European society. Together they have shaped EC regional policy and provided it with a basis which ensures the continuity of the policy. (A recent study of persons involved in regional policy found broad support for these values [Leonardi, 1993].)

Relevant Constitutional Rules

Article 92 of the Treaty of Rome states that aid given to promote the economic development of poor areas or ones with underemployment is not incompatible with the common market. This somewhat negative endorsement, coupled with the principles of the preamble of the treaty, provided the basis on which the EC began to develop regional policy. The primary purpose of Article 92 is to ensure that member states will not engage in policies that could interfere with EC competition policy in the common market; however, paragraph 3 exempts regional policies and assumes a role for the EC as well. Section d of paragraph 3 mentions, "such other categories of aid as may be provided by decisions of the Council acting by a qualified majority on a proposal from the Commission." In addition, the Treaty of Rome established the European Investment Bank (EIB) and the European Social Fund (ESF), both of which have been important for regional development.

Although the treaty permitted the EC to have regional policies, it did not require them. In the early years, only the EIB acted to assist regional development and it operates outside the customary policy-making procedures of the EC. In 1975 the EC established the European Regional Development Fund (ERDF), which constituted the first step in the evolution of an EC regional policy. The ERDF was inside the EC policy-making process, but member states, acting through the Council, remained in control. The fund operated essentially as an adjunct of national regional policies. Almost all of its funds (95 percent) were allocated according to a quota system by which each member state was entitled to an assigned percentage of the total. Member states proposed projects to the EC, and the EC paid part of the cost of the project. The subsequent history of the fund is marked by steady pressure from the Commission to gain control and make the fund the centerpiece of a comprehensive regional policy. Through the years the quota system was gradually transformed and the emphasis in funding shifted from projects to programs (Armstrong, 1989, pp. 171–181).

The Single European Act provided a new legal structure for regional policy and prepared the way for a major reform. The SEA moved regional policy toward the top of the hierarchy of EC policies and made the EC the major actor in controlling it. The following provisions from Article 130(a,b) are particularly relevant:

- "In order to promote its overall harmonious development, the Community shall develop and pursue its actions leading to the strengthening of its economic and social cohesion"

- "Member states shall conduct their economic policies and shall coordinate them, in such a way as, in addition, to attain the objectives set out in Article 130a"

In addition, the SEA stipulates that the Commission shall draft and the Council adopt a comprehensive policy to provide the EC with the means to operate regional policy with more coordination and efficiency. The act also states that decisions regarding the operation of the ERDF shall be adopted by a qualified vote in the Council, thus reducing the power of individual national governments. As a consequence of the SEA, regional policy is no longer a supplement to national policies but a major tool to serve integration through economic and social cohesion. Moreover, the regional policies of national governments must also be directed toward the same objective.

The leaders of the EC moved quickly to implement the provisions of the SEA. In 1987, the Council agreed to double the amount of money available in the Structural Funds. In 1988, it adopted a number of regulations (Regulations 2052/88, 4253/88, 4254/88, 4255/88, and 4256/88) to provide the legal framework for the operation of the policy (CEC, 1988). The regulations constituted a major reform of the operation of the Structural Funds and established the criteria for the division of funding into the various "objectives" discussed above. The core for the operation of the new regional policy is the Community Support Framework (CSF), which is an agreement between the Commission and a member state for regional policy (Landaburu, 1992, pp. 80–83). A CSF starts with a plan developed by a member government for its regions. (The regions have been designated by the EC under one of the five "objective" categories.) A CSF is established on the basis of negotiations among a member state, the region concerned, and the Commission, which agree to a financial commitment for a multiyear period. The creation of CSFs represents several important advances for EC regional policy: It places emphasis on programs rather than projects; it gives the Commission a more significant role; it establishes the principle of partnership by which regional authorities can work directly with the Commission; and it provides a core around which other Community instruments can be coordinated. For example, the report on the CSFs for Italy for converting regions affected by industrial decline (objective 2) lists financial involvement from a number of sources, such as the EIB, the ESF, and the European Coal and Steel Community (CEC, 1990a).

The SEA and the regulations adopted in 1988 provided regional policy with a solid legal foundation and a number of basic principles which provide the parameters for EC regional policy. The most important principle is that funding should be concentrated on regions whose development is lagging. Objective 1 regions, defined as NUTS 2 regions with a per capita GDP of less than 75 percent of the EC average, are the major recipients of aid. Another basic principle is programming. The EC succeeded in changing the emphasis from projects to programs for a broader and more long-range approach to development. The programs are outlined in multiannual plans that are produced jointly by the Commission, national governments, and regional authorities (CEC, 1992, p. 9). A third principle is partnership. The Commission is an active participant rather than a passive provider of funds, and regional authorities are beginning to take an active role as well. The fourth principle is additionality. EC funds should not be used to replace national funds but rather to enhance the program or project. CSFs contain agreements on financing arrangements and help to assure the additionality of EC funds (Tomkins and Twomey, p. 106).

THE DYNAMIC EXTERNAL ENVIRONMENT

Regional policy in the EC was affected by several major changes in the EC in the late 1980s and early 1990s. One obvious change was the admission of Greece in 1981 and Spain and Portugal in 1986 as members of the EC. Their participation greatly strengthened the forces in support of regional policy. Other important developments were the adoption of the SEA, which has already been discussed, and the end of the Cold War and the unification of Germany. The EC could not ignore the economic needs of fragile, new regimes on its border, but the regional lobby opposed the redirection of regional funds. The cost of German unification posed a particularly sensitive problem. Germany, the paymaster of the EC, suddenly faced a large financial burden of its own which made it reluctant to increase its contribution to regional policy. Moreover, the new *Länder* (German states) qualified for regional funds. In 1990, the Council agreed to contribute ECU 3 billion in aid and another ECU 2.6 billion in loans from the EIB and the European Coal and Steel Community (CEC, 1992, p. 14). Two changes require a more detailed discussion because they have overwhelming importance for regional policy. They are the policy to establish the single market (SEM) and the Maastricht Treaty.

The Effect of the SEM on Regional Policy

Leaders from poor member states feared that the operation of the SEM would exacerbate the disparities between the core and the periphery. The removal of internal barriers to a single market would enable the factors of production to move freely across national borders. National firms and capital could move toward the core in order to benefit from the concentration of economic life there. Moreover, national governments would lose the right to subsidize firms, and domestic firms would be forced to compete with more productive firms from other member states. In part, the improvement in the regional fund was a compensation which these leaders demanded in exchange for support of the policy to create the internal market.

According to a study made for the EC, the impact of the SEM depends on a number of factors. If the general economic climate is poor, mobile investments are less likely to be made in new locations. Regions which have a generally competitive economy and can exploit their natural advantages will be less harmed than others. Regions which have depended on national barriers to protect their industries will be hurt. If the EC enlarges to include Scandinavian countries, industry will take advantage of SEM to locate near the new prosperous regions to the disadvantage of poor, southern countries (reported in CEC, 1991, p. 55). The same study considered the impact of the SEM on several industries that are important for poor regions in order to determine if different business aspects of an industry would be affected differently. The headquarters, research and development functions and distribution operations of an industry would tend to locate in core areas or ones containing centers of education and a good quality of life. Small and medium-sized firms as well as production units are the operations most likely to consider locating in a poor region, but both would require good infrastructure in order to operate there. None of the different industries noted in the study is likely to restructure in favor of the poor regions even though they will be more mobile. They will probably relocate to growth regions around the southern arc which form part of the new core of the EC. The prognosis for the textile and clothing industry is particularly ominous. This sector, which is highly important for poor regions, went through a severe restructuring in the 1980s, but has been hit again because of the bad global economy. Production is moving offshore and headquarters are locating in the EC near the computer and telecommunication facilities necessary to run a globally competitive industry. Portugal, with 15 percent of its GDP dependent on this sector, is particularly at risk (CEC, 1992, pp. 56–61).

Border regions account for 15 percent of the land area of the EC and 10 percent of its population (CEC, 1993b). These regions have been the focus of special attention as a consequence of the policy to create a single market. Border regions suffer from a number of handicaps. They are usually distant from political and economic centers and cut off from ties with adjacent areas across the border due to different systems of communications, laws, transportation, and so on. Borders internal to the EC will lose their raison d'etre as a result of the internal market and countries will need to compensate for the change by cultivating relationships across their borders. External border regions will be remote from the core of EC developments and many will confront the turbulence occurring in Eastern Europe. In 1990, the EC recognized that the changes resulting from the SEM and the new situation in Eastern Europe required a new initiative in order to assist border regions to adjust. The new program is known as INTERREG and it is now the largest program among those initiated by the Commission with contributions from the Structural Fund. The program operates along the lines of CSF programs except that more parties are involved. The EC determines which NUTS 3 regions are eligible. The relevant national governments and local authorities propose a plan and negotiate it with the Commission. The plan is generally implemented by national and local authorities. The Commission is represented on the Monitoring Committee which oversees the plan (CEC, 1993b). It is still too early to assess INTERREG, but it is a promising innovation that responds to the new situation in Europe.

It is probably not an exaggeration to state that regional policy achieved prominence as a direct result of the SEM policy. The negative effects of SEM, both real and anticipated, gave power to the advocates of regional policy. The response of policy makers has been prompt and ambitious. Regional policy and the internal market policy are linked as the propulsive elements fueling the development of European integration.

The Maastricht Treaty and Its Meaning for Regional Policy

If the SEM is the key to regional policy in the SEA, then monetary union is its key in the Maastricht Treaty. As noted in Chapter 3, monetary union attracted the most attention during the drafting of the treaty. Leaders of the Commission were determined to have monetary union; however, they worried about the economic consequences of the union. The relationship between economic factors and monetary ones in determining the appropriate area for a single currency is complicated and uncertain (Kindleberger, 1993, Chapters 24 and 25). The drafters of the Maastricht Treaty linked economic and monetary union (EMU) and used economic indicators as the measure to indicate readiness for monetary union. Some degree of economic union is, therefore, a prerequisite for monetary union. According to a Commission document, the principal objectives of economic policy in the treaty should be "a harmonious development of economic activities, a continuous and balanced expansion, an increase in stability, an accelerated raising of the standards of living, and economic and social cohesion" (CEC, 1990b, p. 21). The Commission also stated that regional disparities would pose an economic and political threat to the union "so particular attention has to be paid to an effective Community policy aimed at narrowing regional and structural disparities" (p. 25). The Commission further noted that regional disparities can exist over long periods unless sufficient measures are taken to overcome them (p. 26). Consequently, regional policy becomes an economic imperative for a Community in the process of creating a monetary union.

The twelve heads of state who signed the Treaty on European Union agreed to achieve the convergence of their economies and the economic and social progress of their peoples by "reinforced cohesion." Economic and social cohesion is one of the basic objectives listed in Article 2, which contains the common provisions of the treaty. Member states agree to pursue economic policies in accord with the objectives listed in Article 2 (Article 102a). Title XIV (which replaces Title V of the SEA) includes the provisions for regional policy. Most are unchanged from the SEA, but Article 130d orders the Council to create "a Cohesion Fund to provide a financial contribution to projects in the fields of environment and trans-European networks in the area of transport infrastructure." (This potentially important new instrument is discussed more fully below.) The treaty leaves unchanged the policy-making procedure set forth in Articles 130d and 130e of the SEA except to give the new Committee of the Regions the right to be consulted on proposals for regional policy. In regard to the crucial issue of voting rights, the treaty requires unanimity by the Council for the adoption of general policies, but a qualified majority vote suffices for specific policies regarding the ERDF.

The treaty contains two additional sections relating to regional policy. Article 198a provides for a Committee of the Regions, which has the right to give opinions as noted above and which may be consulted by the Council or the Commission on regional issues. France, Germany, Italy, and the United Kingdom each have twenty-four members on the committee; Spain has twenty-one; Belgium, Greece, Netherlands, and Portugal each have twelve; Denmark and Ireland each have nine; and Luxembourg has six. (One of the first controversies to arise regarding the new body is the selection of its members. The treaty gives the authority to the Council and the member states, but regional authorities want a role in the selection of participants in order to ensure the representation of regional interests which may not be the same as those of the national government.)

The other relevant provision in the treaty is the protocol on economic and social cohesion. The protocol reiterates the position of the EC on the subject as stated in the treaty and EC policy, but also declares that the EC will be more flexible in the future in regard to the administration of its policies and will take greater account of the different capacities of the member states. The protocol appears to be a gesture to reassure poor states that the EC is prepared to respond to the problems which these states may have in the future as a result of the demands for economic convergence.

In conclusion, the Maastricht Treaty continues on the track first set in the SEA in many respects, but it also marks a major advance in others. Most of the changes in regard to policies and policy making were not a surprise to persons familiar with the subject. Even the provisions for the new Cohesion Fund and the Committee of the Regions do not take the EC into new territory. The most significant development regarding regional policy in the treaty is that the treaty makes regional policy the linchpin for the next stage of integration. Economic and social cohesion is tied to currency unification and together they constitute the objective which the treaty sets for integration.

THE POLICY SUBSYSTEM

The policy subsystem for regional policy appears to be poised for major changes and a new politics. The subsystem has changed from one dominated by national governments to one in which both the Council and the Commission have powerful roles. The principle of partnership requires a further broadening in the subsystem. The regional actors will become more assertive and conditions appear to be ripe for them to gain more influence. The three aspects of the policy subsystem—decision makers, advocacy groups, and power brokers—are discussed. The discussion should provide evidence to support the assertion that the subsystem for regional policy is changing and regional authorities are becoming important actors in policy making.

Decision Makers

Despite the important roles of other participants, the Council is and has been the preeminent actor in regional policy for two basic reasons. One is the fact that regional policy was an adjunct to national policies and that the primary decisions were national. The other is that the stakes in regional policy are monetary. Council members and interested national groups bargain fiercely for a share of the funds which then are applied directly to national programs or projects. Council members are not only the recipients of regional funds, they are also the providers.

In 1988, the Council was the main arena for complex negotiations that led to important reforms in the funding sources for the EC, in the budget process, and in regional policy. The reforms were interlinked. Council members agreed to provide a new "own resource" in order to increase EC revenues. Then the Council, the Commission, and the Parliament agreed that budget expenditures should not exceed revenues, but that they would increase funds available for regional policy (see Shackleton, 1991, or Nugent, 1989). The result of the 1988 reforms is to limit somewhat the powers of the Council because the reforms provide parameters for the annual budget negotiations. The reform has not ended; however, regional policy still depends on budget politics, an area in which member states continue to be dominant.

The Commission's role in regional policy is carried out primarily by the commissioner responsible for regional policy and by DG XVI (the directorate general for regional policies formed in 1968). The role of the Commission as an institution has grown in scope and authority since the 1960s. It has gradually extended its control over funds by increasing the percentage of the funds not directly allocated to member states. The Commission has the right to initiate special programs such as INTERREG which it oversees and funds out of the money not allocated to the member states. The 1988 reforms doubled the amount of money available for the Structural Funds and it increased from 5 to

9 percent the amount directly controlled by the Commission. The Commission has extended its authority by forging an alliance with regional authorities who want a counterbalance to the power of national governments. In addition, according to Gary Marks, the poorest member states welcome a more active role by the Commission because they need the expertise which the Commission can supply (1993). Today, the Commission's responsibilities include the drafting of proposals for regional policy, the implementation of special programs, the oversight and assessment of the entire policy, and the coordination of contacts among all the participants. In pursuit of its responsibilities, the Commission gathers information, commissions studies, and hires its own experts. One authority calls the Commission a policy entrepreneur because it brings about policies and laws by building support for them; it sets broad goals and ensures their acceptance; and it devises strategies to take advantage of opportunities. It accomplishes all of this by bringing regional policy into the public arena and creating political support beyond the narrow confines of its legal authority (Deeken, 1993).

The European Parliament is the third institution to have a formal role in the making of regional policy. Its powers in regard to regional policy are not changed by the Maastricht Treaty. The Treaty of Rome gave Parliament important power over the budget, which is, of course, relevant for regional policy. Most regional policies are adopted by the cooperation procedure established by the SEA. The procedure provides Parliament with two opportunities to consider a proposal and the right to reject a proposal, in which case it may be adopted only by unanimous agreement in the Council. In 1990 Parliament enacted new rules so that it could utilize more effectively the powers provided by the SEA. As a result, cooperation with the Commission is easier and Parliament operates more efficiently (CEC, 1993d, p. 372). Parliament has used its authority to champion regional development and in so doing allies itself with the Commission. For example, when the Commission tried to compel the government of the United Kingdom to respect the principle of additionality, Parliament adopted a resolution in support of the principle (CEC, 1993d, p. 149). Parliament has also acted on its own to promote EC regional policy. It recently adopted an "own initiative resolution" calling for the creation of an EC center which could provide information and monitor regional planning (p. 148). As noted previously, Parliament equates regional policy with democracy and, therefore, it advocates greater decentralization in the operation of regional policy. At the present time, the composition of Parliament is weighted heavily toward representatives of parties sympathetic to regional concerns, including sixteen members who are elected from regional parties. (The number will probably increase in 1994 following the election of a new Parliament.)

The regional committee in Parliament is responsible for studying and drafting preliminary opinions on proposed regional policies. It also serves as a contact point between Parliament and regional interest groups and as a watchdog for regional interests when budget proposals are before Parliament. Lobbyists from regional authorities routinely contact members of the committee when they want Parliament to amend a regional proposal, and they believe that they have a good working relationship with many of its members.

Proponents of regional policy are found in all three of the major EC institutions. Consequently, regional policy is in a strong position compared to other policies discussed in this book. The three institutions differ, however, in their reasons for supporting regional policy. The regional faction in the Council supports regional policy in part because it has important monetary consequences for them. Other members of the Council do not oppose it because regional policy is based on widely held values and because it is now linked to the success of the internal market and progress toward monetary union, which they do support. The Commission advocates regional policy as an essential building block for European integration, and Parliament advocates a decentralized and participatory regional policy as an essential building block for a democratic European Union. The differences among the three are not ones that prevent compromise; the prognosis for continued development of EC regional policy, therefore, is optimistic.

Advocacy Groups

The most distinctive feature of the advocacy groups concerned with regional policy is the extent to which they are nurtured and supported by the Commission, in contrast to the typical relationship between interest groups and governments. They are also distinguished by being almost totally composed of public authorities whose primary responsibility is to operate local or regional governments. Private interest groups are a smaller and newer part of the panorama of advocacy groups for regional policy. Another distinguishing feature is the fact that the advocacy groups are almost entirely groups that support regional policy. Few groups oppose such policy. (Those that do exist direct their attention to the budget process rather than the debate over regional policy.) The groups differ only in regard to the types of regional policy that they want or in the allocation of existing funds.

The most visible advocacy groups are the regional governments, many of which have offices in Brussels to maintain contacts with relevant persons in the EC. These groups are not interest groups as customarily defined but they act as interest groups in Brussels. Regional governments hire specialists to operate the offices and to lobby. They want preferential treatment from the EC and frequently want to bypass their own national governments in regard to EC programs. The relationship between the regional government and the EC may be bilateral (for example, the representative of the Kent Local Council contacts DG XVI regarding funding for a program) or multilateral, in which case two or more regional authorities jointly approach the EC. For example, the local authorities at either end of the tunnel under the English Channel have jointly sought EC assistance for programs to train their safety teams working inside the tunnel to speak each other's language. Another example is the Coalfield Communities Campaign, which links local authorities in coal-mining areas in the United Kingdom, Belgium, France, Germany, and Spain to promote an EC initiative for these areas.

Interest groups representing the private sector have not been active in Brussels because national governments rather than the EC allocate funds to private firms participating in regional projects. Now that the Commission has a larger scope for its own initiatives, labor unions, employer's associations, and even environmental groups are beginning to lobby in Brussels on regional policies. The latter groups want to ensure that regional policies promote sustainable development by combining regional development with environmental awareness. They also want local citizens to have the right to appeal when regional policies are not properly implemented (EEB, 1992, p. 7). Environmental groups lobbied unsuccessfully for a provision in Article 130a of the Maastricht Treaty requiring respect for environmental objectives in economic and social cohesion policies (EEB, 1990, p. 11).

Experts in the Commission believe that participation by interest groups is necessary for the successful implementation of regional policies. A study contracted by the Commission confirmed that belief (Leonardi, 1993). One of the reports in the study noted that local social networks involving public and private interests played an important role in the successful outcome the Integrated Mediterranean Programs (Bianchi, 1993, pp. 64–65). Others note that the lack of credible regional or local bodies is a problem in several member states. The Commission has several initiatives to overcome this weakness, one of which is noted below. The Commission has also been a proponent of partnership as required in the CSFs. According to Regulation 2052/88, competent authorities from the national, regional, and local areas shall work together with the Commission in partnership to prepare, finance, monitor, and assess operations in a CSF (Article 4). Although the national governments have the authority to designate the other participants, the Commission has encouraged wider and more independent participation.

Two new developments should be discussed even though neither fits the usual image of interest groups and their behavior. One is the European Cooperation Networks project, which was established under Article 10 of the revised regulations of the ERDF. Article 10 enables the Commission to cofinance pilot projects to promote exchanges of experiences and to facilitate cooperation among European cities and regions. Some thirty-seven networks are now operating in the EC with funding from the Commission. A network is created either at the initiative of an international organization such as the European association of cities and regions or at the initiative of a group of local authorities who have a common concern. The goal of a network is to assist poor regions by cooperation to transfer know-how and by cost savings through joint programs. One of the networks was initiated by several chambers of commerce in France and Italy, which decided to share their knowledge in processing scientific information with five poor regions in Greece, Ireland, and Spain through the operation of pilot programs. In another case, nine seaside regions joined to form COAST, a European cooperation network. The participants work together on solutions for their environmental and employment problems (CEC, undated). Each network is different in its membership and its special focus but all receive EC funding and are composed of local groups which also lobby the EC on other aspects of regional policy. They do not involve national governments. Because they make and operate their own regional policies, they are not advocacy groups per se, but they also lobby the Commission for funds and assistance to promote their interests. Perhaps they constitute a new type of EC advocacy activity.

The new Committee of the Regions is another entity that does not easily fit under the rubric of this section, but neither does it fit elsewhere. Representing another effort by the EC to encourage broader participation in policy making, it replaces a committee of regional representatives that advised DG XVI. The Committee of the Regions is mandated by the Maastricht Treaty, which gives each country an assigned number of participants to make a total of 189 members. The participants are nominated by the national governments and appointed for four-year terms by the Council (Article 198a). Both the Commission and local authorities want the participants to be elected in their areas, but the British government, in particular, has resisted any diminution of national authority. One legal specialist in the Commission believes that despite this dispute the Committee of the Regions has the potential to become a significant actor in shaping EC regional policy if its members have the political will. The Council or the Commission has the authority to set a time limit for the committee to provide its opinion on a proposal. Although the time limit prevents the committee from obstructing action, it gives it bargaining leverage with the Council or the Commission if either wants a prompt and positive opinion from the committee to bolster the political impact of a proposal. Much will depend on the status of the participants and the success of the new body in creating a favorable public image. Parliament provides a useful model for the endeavor.

Policy Brokers

The Commission is obviously the policy broker for regional policy. Indeed, the history of the Commission and regional policy is, in large part, a history of different approaches which the Commission has used to bring all interested parties together in a working relationship. Most conflict takes place among the member governments inside the Council when the budget allocations are made.

The Commission has worked to lessen the scope for conflict by having the Council agree to broad principles to guide the allocations and thereby decreasing the possible choices. This approach has been used successfully for the allocation of Objective 1 funds.

Conclusion

The policy subsystem is undergoing transformation. The Council retains the main legal power, but it is not a cohesive group. It would be wrong, though, to envisage the Council as divided into two blocs on regional policy, because all member states benefit from some portion of the policy. The governments from poor states, however, form the strongest group in support of regional policy. They can veto general policy proposals which require unanimity and they form a bargaining unit for measures that require a qualified majority (which includes budget proposals). The poor states also find allies in the Commission and in the Parliament (although sometimes individual member states may have bitter disputes with the Commission over the allocation of funds). If the Council is the legal power, the Commission is the political power. With multiple tasks and multiple contacts, it operates at the core of regional policy. Parliament and the new Committee of the Regions constitute the focal points for regional interests. Parliament has been the leading exponent of a decentralized, participatory regional policy. The newer actors in the policy subsystem are the regional governments and interest groups, which constitute the advocacy coalition for regional policy. They have an ally in the Commission and together they pose a challenge to the authority of national governments.

REGIONAL POLICY IN THE MAASTRICHT ERA

The rationale for a European Union as envisioned in the Maastricht Treaty depends on economic and social cohesion. Even before the treaty was ratified, work began on restructuring regional policy for its vital role. The two most important changes are the reform of the Structural Funds, the principal instrument for regional policy, and the proposal of a program for economic and social cohesion.

The reform of the Structural Funds continues the work started by the 1988 reforms. The reform is both monetary and legal. The European Council, meeting in Edinburgh in December 1992, agreed to provide ECU 140 billion for the fund for the years 1994 to 1999. The amount is double the amount available for the most recent period, 1989 to 1993, and will constitute more than a third of the entire budget of the EC. The bulk of the money (70 percent or ECU 93 billion) is directed to Objective 1 regions. (Belgium, France, Germany, Greece, Ireland, Italy, Portugal, Spain, and the United Kingdom have Objective 1 regions according to the latest list.) Objective 2 regions will receive slightly over 20 percent and Objective 5b regions will receive slightly less than 10 percent of the total. The size of the Structural Funds will make them an important factor in economic development. Structural Funds already play an important role in the economies of some member states. EC funds equaled 3.5 percent of GNP in Portugal (CEC, 1992, p. 14), and the city of Birmingham received almost three times more aid as an assisted area from the EC than it did from the British government in the years 1984 to 1992 ("Twisting Cartography of Distress," July 24–25, 1993).

The legal reform takes the form of amendments to the framework regulations of 1988 (CEC, 1993c). The reform leaves unchanged the basic principles that guide the Structural Funds, concentration, partnership, additionality, and programming. The most important result of the legal changes will be that Structural Funds will be available to new regions and to new kinds of activities. The amendments also simplify and speed up the procedures to obtain assistance. The definitions of Objectives 1 and 2 regions was not changed. Objective 3, which had funded measures to combat long-term unemployment, was changed to include measures to assist the employment of young people (formerly Objective 4) and the integration of persons who have been socially excluded from the labor market. The new Objective 4 modifies the operation of the European Social Fund to include measures to aid workers to adapt to industrial change and to changes in the production system. Objective 5a funds measures to modernize agriculture but now also those to modernize and restructure fisheries. Objective 5b is to promote rural development by aiding the structural adjustment of rural areas (CEC, 1993e). All of the programs will now run for six years with the exception of those funded under Objectives 2 and 4, which will be for two three-year programs (with the possibility of adjustment after the first three years).

The EC may now provide for 85 (rather than 75) percent of total public expenditure on an Objective 1 project when the project is in Greece, Ireland, Portugal, or Spain (countries entitled to money from the Cohesion Fund). Furthermore, the EC may expedite the planning stage for programs. Negotiations for CSFs and for operational programs may occur simultaneously rather than in sequence, thus, shortening the time required and simplifying the negotiations. The amendments make three other changes which will be important:

1. Member governments are required to designate representatives from economic and social groups to participate as partners in the entire process
2. Member states shall include an environmental assessment in their plans
3. Funding by the ERDF may now include investment in health, education, research and technological development, and trans-European networks (TENs)

The changes in the regulations governing the Structural Funds broaden the scope for Commission action with a counterbalancing narrowing of the scope for action by individual national governments.

Cohesion is a basic principle of the EC and is embodied in both the SEA and the Maastricht Treaty. It is designated as essential for integration, but its meaning is not explicitly defined in the documents. Cohesion is generally referred to as economic and social cohesion but economic and social criteria for cohesion are not provided. Iain Begg, who has studied the subject extensively, concludes that cohesion must be perceived as a political rather than an economic concept (Begg, 1993, p. 3). The lack of cohesion refers to regional disparities that are based on visible but unquantified differences of wealth, of levels of economic development, of labor markets, and of societal characteristics. Cohesion also implies linkage in reference to trans-European networks. Lack of cohesion, therefore, is economic and social isolation; regions lacking cohesion have poor transportation and communication links with the core and do not partake of the quality of life found in the core. The sense of EC documents on the subject is that cohesion must be created or the legitimacy of the European enterprise will be threatened. In this sense, the concept is political, as Begg has asserted.

Cohesion is not the same as convergence as defined in the Maastricht Treaty. Indeed, cohesion and convergence can be contradictory. The criteria for convergence which countries must meet for monetary unification are price stability, sustainable government financial position, a stable exchange rate, and stable interest rates (Article 109j of the Maastricht Treaty). National governments in poor countries that adopt convergence policies (such as an austerity program) could actually worsen cohesion between their country and the rest of the EC. Critics of the convergence criteria argued this point and demanded measures to counteract the risk.

The Cohesion Fund, established by the Maastricht Treaty, is intended to supply extra funds to countries where development policies are at risk due to the need to meet convergence requirements. The fund is a new source of assistance in addition to the Structural Funds and the European Investment Bank. The fund assists countries with a per capita GDP less than 90 percent of the EC average and with a program to meet the convergence criteria. Greece, Ireland, Portugal, and Spain were designated as cohesion countries. The fund will supply ECU 15 billion to the four in the period from 1993 to 1999. (Over 50 percent of the fund will go to Spain, between 16 and 20 percent will go to Greece and Portugal, and less than 10 percent to Ireland.) The fund will provide between 80 and 85 percent of the costs of designated projects (CEC, 1993a). According to the protocol on economic and social cohesion in the Maastricht Treaty, the projects aided by the Cohesion Fund shall be in the fields of environment and trans-European networks. The results of the first period will be assessed in 1996.

Although ECU 15 billion is not a large amount of money, the impact of the fund should be significant. The money is targeted to only two types of projects. Moreover, the cohesion countries will receive about ECU 70 billion in the same period from Structural Funds and the EIB has been urged to increase its loans to them as well. A project receiving money from the Cohesion Fund cannot receive money from the Structural Fund as well, but other projects in the country can and will obtain such money. As a result, cohesion countries will benefit from a significant amount of new funding.

The Cohesion Fund must be used for projects in the fields of environment and trans-European networks. Environmental projects are easily recognized, but trans-European networks are a more obscure concept. It is, however, a prominent one in Brussels today. Title XII of the Maastricht Treaty gives the EC the responsibility to create TENs in the areas of transport, telecommunications, and energy infrastructure. The EC is supposed to promote the interconnection and interoperability of national networks and to give particular attention to the need to link peripheral, landlocked, and island regions with the core of the Community (Article 129b). Article 129c gives the EC three means by which to fulfill its responsibility. First, it shall establish comprehensive plans, which shall be adopted by the Council according to the new procedure established in Article 189b. (This procedure, called the co-decision procedure, provides more power to Parliament than other existing procedures do.) Second, the EC shall take such measures as are necessary to ensure the operability of the networks such as setting common standards. Finally, the EC may help to finance national projects that fit within the comprehensive plan.

Title XII gives the EC important new responsibilities in areas formerly controlled by member governments. TENs are directly relevant to regional policy not only because poor regions are most likely to lack modern networks but also because the Cohesion Fund was created for the purpose of funding the development of networks in these regions. The prompt allocation of a budget for the Cohesion Fund demonstrated the willingness of the Council to advance the program.

The importance of trans-European networks increased dramatically with the adoption of the important new "White Paper on Growth, Competitiveness, Employment." The paper is a major policy statement of the EC, comparable to the "White Paper on Completing the Internal Market" of the previous decade. The purpose of the paper is to "lay the foundation for sustainable development of the European economies, thereby enabling them to withstand international competition while creating the millions of jobs that are needed" (preamble). Trans-European networks are at the center of the development program. They will increase the competitiveness of the economies and building them will create jobs. To fund the program the EC will provide approximately ECU 5.3 billion per year from its budget, including money from the Structural Funds, the Cohesion Fund, the research and development budget, and a special TENs budget. The EC will also provide funds from non-budget sources and issue Union Bonds, while the EIB will provide loans. The total from all EC sources will be ECU 20 billion per year (CEC, 1993f, p. 33). Member governments as well as the private sector will supply additional funds.

The TENs program is a gamble. It is not the innovative program that was heralded in preliminary announcements. Indeed, it has a strong resemblance to old-fashioned public works programs. The importance of the program is not its contribution to global competitiveness, but its impact on the development of regional policy. In this regard, the program has important implications. It contributes to the formation of an EC regional policy in place of national regional policies partly financed by the EC. Regions are to be linked to Europe rather than to their national capitals. The program will also increase the ties between the EC and regional authorities. A large number of regional specialists will need to work closely with Brussels in order to implement the program. Finally, the program provides the Commission with a major role as the central coordinator. In all of these respects, the TENs program constitutes a force to compel EC regional policy along the track which it has followed since the 1988 reforms.

CONCLUSION

Regional policy is the most important of the EC policies for citizens, because of its place in the hierarchy of EC policies and its relationship to economic and monetary objectives. The SEA linked regional policy to the internal market; the Maastricht Treaty links it to monetary union. Economic and social cohesion is accepted as a prerequisite for economic and monetary union. The large increase in the budget for regional policy gives evidence of the commitment of EC leaders to the policy.

The objectives of regional policy have changed along with its status. EC regional policy used to be merely a supplement to national regional policies. Politically useful and socially just, it helped member governments integrate backward regions into the national economy. Now it is an economic imperative for an EC committed to economic and monetary union. It helps backward regions to integrate into the EC. The comprehensive TENs plan is the latest example of the transition in regional policy objectives, but the transition is by no means complete and national actors do not necessarily accept the direction of change.

The process of policy making is also undergoing change. National governments control most of the money, but the Commission fills multiple roles in the process from initiator to monitor. As regional policy has grown more complex and more "European," the formation of the policy has also become more complex. Regional authorities and private interests have roles and increasing amounts of authority. Gary Marks, in an insightful study, calls the new process "multi-level governance" (Marks, 1993). Other authorities on the subject use different names, but generally agree with his analysis. Devolution is one characteristic of the process of making EC regional policy.

The principle of subsidiarity is easily expressed in the new process. The Commission referred to the principle in its proposals to amend the 1988 regulations by stating, "Subsidiarity is the guiding principle during the present period and will continue to apply in the next" (CEC, 1993c, p. 17). Subsidiarity in the context of regional policy means a pooling of resources and participatory policy making. It does not mean the devolution of responsibility to national actors. The regional policy that is necessary for economic and monetary union as conceptualized in Brussels necessitates the economic and social cohesion of regions to the EC core.

One question that remains to be considered is the contribution which regional policy makes to the European Union. Regional policy has been consciously used by EC leaders to enhance the social legitimacy of the EC. They reminded the Irish before their referendum on the Maastricht Treaty of how much Ireland gains from the policy. They notify localities of the role of EC funds in development projects in their area. These efforts probably have some impact, but the championship of regional authorities by the Commission and Parliament probably are more effective. The Commission and Parliament are aided in this regard by the rising popularity of regional government and the comparable decline of popularity of national elites. The fact that Brussels also has a respectable amount of money to allocate strengthens the effort.

The Maastricht Treaty and the 1993 White Paper constitute important documents in the development of regional policy and place it in the foundation for the new European Union. They also ensure that the construction of economic and social cohesion involves a range of participants operating in regional, national, and EC localities.

REFERENCES

Armstrong, Harvey. 1989. "Community Regional Policy." In *The European Community and the Challenge of the Future*, ed. by Juliet Lodge. New York: St. Martin's Press.

Begg, Iain. 1993. "The Emergent European Market and Economic and Social Cohesion." Paper presented at the European Studies Association Conference, Washington, DC, May 27–29.

Bianchi, Giuliano. 1993. "The IMPs: A Missed Opportunity? An Appraisal of the Design and Implementation of the Integrated Mediterranean Programmes." In *The Regions and the European Community*, ed. by Robert Leonardi. London: Frank Cass.

Cole, John, and Francis Cole. 1993. *The Geography of the European Community*. London: Routledge.

CEC (Commission of the European Community). 1985. "Draft Treaty Establishing the European Union." In *An Ever Closer Union* (Annex 1), Brussels: European Perspectives Series.

————. 1988. "Council Regulation of 24 June 1988 on the Tasks of the Structural Funds and Their Effectiveness and on Coordination of Their Activities Between Themselves and with the Operation of the European Investment Bank and Other Existing Financial Instruments." Number 2052/88.

————. 1990a. "Community Support Frameworks, 1989–91, Italy."

————. 1990b. "Economic and Monetary Union." Communication of the Commission, August 21, 1990.

————. 1991. *Europe 2000*. Communication from the Commission to the Council and the European Parliament.

————. 1992. "Community Structural Policies: Assessment and Outlook." COM(92)84 final.

————. 1993a. "The Cohesion Fund: A Sign of Solidarity in the Future of European Union," prepared by Peter Schmidhuber. *Frontier Free Europe*, April.

————. 1993b. "INTERREG." *Info Background*. Undated copy supplied by DGX VI.

————. 1993c. "The Operation of the Community Structural Funds, 1994–99." (Revision of the Council Regulations Governing the Operation of the Community Structural Funds.) Working paper containing the drafts of the proposed revisions, not numbered.

————. 1993d. *XXVIth General Report on the Activities of the European Communities 1992.* Brussels: CEC.

————. 1993e. "What Changes to the Regulation Governing the Structural Funds." *Info Background*, February/March.

————. 1993f. "White Paper on Growth, Competitiveness, Employment." *Bulletin of the European Communities,* Supplement 6/93.

————. Undated. *European Cooperation Networks*. Packet prepared by the directorate general for regional policies.

Deeken, John. 1993. "Regional Policy and the European Commission: Policy Entrepreneur or Brussels Bureaucracy?" Paper presented to the European Community Studies Association Conference, Washington, DC, May 27–29.

EEB (European Environmental Bureau). 1990. "Greening the Treaty." Produced in Cooperation with Friends of the Earth and the World Wide Fund for Nature. Brussels: EEB.

"Environmental NGOs' Declarations Addressed to the European Council." 1992. Edinburgh, December. Brussels: EEB.

"European Regional Incentives." 1992. Report of the European Policies Research Centre of the University of Strathclyde. *Journal of Regional Policy* (English edition of *Mezzogiorno D'Europa*) 12 (July–December).

Keating, Michael. 1993. "The Continental MESO: Regions in the European Community." In *The Rise of Meso Government in Europe,* ed. by L. J. Sharpe. London: Sage.

Kindleberger, Charles. 1993. *A Financial History of Western Europe. 2nd ed.* New York: Oxford University Press.

Landaburu, Eneko. 1992. "The Reform of the Structural Funds: The First Year of Implementation." In *Economic and Social Cohesion in Europe,* ed. by Achille Hannequart. London: Routledge.

Leonardi, Robert, ed. 1993. *The Regions and the European Community*. London: Frank Cass.

Lipset, Seymour. 1968. *Revolution and Counter-Revolution*. Garden City, NY: Anchor Books.

Marks, Gary. 1993. "Structural Policy and Multi-level Governance in the European Community." In *The State of the European Community*, ed. by Alan Cafruny and Glenda Rosenthal. Boulder, CO: Lynne Rienner.

Martin, David. 1991. *Europe: An Ever Closer Union*. Nottingham, England: Russell Press.

Nugent, Neill. 1989. *The Government and Politics of the European Community*. Durham, NC: Duke University Press.

Parker, Geoffrey. 1975. *The Logic of Unity*. 2nd ed. London: Longman.

Sabatier, P. 1988. "An Advocacy Coalition Framework of Policy Change and the Role of Policy-Oriented Learning Therein." *Policy Sciences* 21: 129–169.

Shackleton, Michael. 1991. "Budgetary Policy in Transition." In *The State of the European Community*, ed. by Alan Cafruny and Glenda Rosenthal. Boulder, CO: Lynne Rienner.

Tomkins, Judith, and Jim Twomey. 1992. "Regional Policy." In *European Economic Integration*, ed. by Frank McDonald and Stephen Dearden. London: Longman.

"Twisting Cartography of Distress." 1993. *Financial Times*, July 24–25.

Willis, F. 1971. *Italy Chooses Europe*. London: Oxford University Press.

Chapter 8

Citizenship and European Union

The Treaty on European Union introduces the concept of "citizenship of the Union." One of the objectives of the new treaty is "to strengthen the protection of the rights and interest of the nationals of the Member States through the introduction of a citizenship of the Union." The implications of European citizenship cannot be fully understood at this time, but the potential importance of it for European integration is significant. The objectives of this chapter are to provide a brief summary of the concept of citizenship, to survey its development in the history of the European Community (EC), and to study it as a policy area. The study of the policy area will employ the format used to study other policy areas in the book. The study, however, is not strictly comparable to the others because citizenship is a relatively undeveloped topic for the EC. The policy area for citizenship is defined broadly to encompass related topics such as individual rights, immigration issues, and the growing concern over social exclusion. The findings will provide insights into the meaning of European union in the Maastricht era.

THE CONCEPT OF CITIZENSHIP

The essence of citizenship is the right to participate in the life of a state (Closa, 1992, p. 1139). The concept is primarily a political one, but it also has social and economic connotations. In Western society, citizenship, as a political concept, implies the right to vote and the right to related freedoms such as the freedom of association and free speech. Citizenship is related to the belief that the people are the source of legitimate political power and "the people" is equivalent to the nation (MacIver, 1947, pp. 184–185). Citizenship is conferred at birth by *jus sanguinis* (family lineage) or *jus soli* (place of birth), depending on the fundamental law of the political system.

Citizenship in Western Europe is generally assumed to confer on individuals social and economic rights as well as political rights. The constitutions of a number of European countries state, for example, that citizens have the right to work. (See, for example, the Italian constitution, Article 4.) The welfare state is expected to protect its citizens from the extremes of inequality or poverty. The attributes of economic and social citizenship are less clearly defined than those of political citizenship, but they play an increasingly important role in the concept of citizenship as it is understood in Western Europe.

Citizenship and legitimacy are two sides of the same coin. The definition of citizenship given in the paragraph above is based on the assumption of a legitimate state, one with the sovereign power to confer citizenship. Citizens confer legitimacy on their political system and the political system confers citizenship on them. The modern meanings of citizenship and legitimacy have evolved in tandem in European history. Citizens, in contrast to subjects, participate in the political life of the state. One of the attributes of a legitimate state is the provision for effective participation by its citizens.

Citizenship is customarily singular. Persons are citizens of only one sovereign entity. Persons acquiring a new citizenship usually relinquish their former citizenship. Federal systems present a challenge, however, to the generalization. Sovereignty is shared between the federal government and the subunits. Citizenship is conferred by the federal government but exercised in both the larger unit and one of the subunits. Citizenship in the European Union is only partly comparable to federal citizenship because the member states and not the Union are the conferring authorities.

The concepts of citizenship and human rights are linked in European history as are the concepts of citizenship and legitimacy. The definitions of citizenship and human rights have broadened throughout history, and the responsibility of governments to protect and promote citizenship and human rights has grown as well. The abuse by the Nazi government of its citizens and of human rights led to international agreements following World War II to bind governments before the international community to uphold their obligations. The European Convention for the Protection of Human Rights and Fundamental Freedoms, adopted in 1950, has been an important reference point in Western Europe.

CITIZENSHIP IN THE HISTORY OF THE EC

The Treaty of Rome does not include the concept of citizenship or related human rights. The omission may seem surprising given the concern about human rights in postwar Europe, but the Council of Europe and the European Convention for the Protection of Human Rights and Fundamental Freedoms were already in existence to ensure basic rights (CEC, 1992c). The purpose of the Treaty of Rome was to establish an economic community which would be one of a growing number of communities to bind peoples and provide them with a shared destiny. The treaty does have a number of provisions, however, that provide grounds for later development.

The preamble of the treaty refers to the Charter of the United Nations and also states that the members will pool their resources in pursuit of peace and liberty thus placing the document within the existing framework of values. Moreover, the treaty provides for institutions compatible with the needs of a democratic society. The Parliament, with its representative and supervisory functions, and the Court, with effective judicial powers, provide a foundation on which the concept of citizenship has grown. In addition, the treaty states that any European state may apply for membership but the criteria that have guided the selection have been those established by the Council of Europe and include democracy, rule of law, and respect for human rights.

The most important contribution of the Treaty of Rome to the concept of citizenship is in the field of economic citizenship. The treaty gives individuals rights to free movement and to freedom from discrimination on the basis of nationality or sex (Articles 7, 48, 119, and 220). The rights apply to employees and self-employed persons who are nationals of member states. A number of directives and rulings by the European Court have subsequently elaborated the meaning of the rights (CEC, 1988b, pp. 249–252).

Early in the 1960s, Parliament began work on a procedure to provide for the direct election of members of Parliament. The effort led to a long controversy over who would be allowed to vote and what authority should control the procedures. The controversy obstructed direct elections until the late 1970s, when the search for a uniform procedure was abandoned and each member state allowed to determine its own procedure. The result was not very satisfactory to supporters of integration, but it established the principle, however weakly, that the nationals of the member states have the right to participate in the political life of the EC.

The idea of European citizenship continued to be discussed in many documents throughout the 1970s and into the 1980s, when it was elaborated in a major document called "A People's Europe" (CEC, 1985b). The document provided a number of facets to the idea of EC citizenship including the right of residence throughout the EC for nationals of a member state, the right to petition Parliament, the right to select the Parliament by a uniform electoral procedure, and the right to participate in local elections. The European Court was active during the same period in defining rights and broadening the meaning of the Treaty of Rome to include respect for fundamental rights (ECJ, 1974, 1975).

Two documents are landmarks in the history of citizenship in the EC in the 1980s: the Single European Act (SEA) and the Community Charter of the Fundamental Social Rights of Workers (CEC, 1989). The first treaty of the EC to mention human rights, the SEA also increased the authority of the directly elected Parliament.

The Charter of Social Rights was a victory for the supporters of economic citizenship in the EC. The document does not have the force of law, but it gives the EC a moral responsibility (shared with member states) to protect a number of economic rights, such as consultation rights for employees in their work-places and equal treatment of male and female employees (Springer, 1992, pp. 88–96). The public debate which took place over the document raised aware-ness of the EC. Most labor unions held discussions or issued brochures on the subject. The EC subsequently adopted an action program to implement the charter, but failed to win acceptance for specific provisions.

At the end of the 1980s, the concept of citizenship in the EC was still underdeveloped despite past progress. Nationals of member states had limited rights of residence in other member states and no right to vote when living in a member state of which they were not a national. They also had few economic and social rights guaranteed by the EC.

The remaining portion of this chapter is organized as previous chapters have been organized. It includes three sections, the first of which, entitled stable system parameters, explains the context within which the policy is made. The context is composed of the following long-term factors which give rise to the policy and shape it: the basic attributes of the policy area, the relevant cultural values, and the legal structure within which the policy is made. The second section contains an explanation of recent changes in the external environment that affect the development of the policy. The third section presents the actors involved in making the policy. Citizenship policy in the Maastricht era is discussed in the final part of the chapter.

STABLE SYSTEM PARAMETERS

Basic Attributes of the Problem Area

Throughout the history of the EC, interested persons have discussed the need to provide for citizenship in the EC. Participants in the discussion have been divided in their assessment primarily because they differed in their belief about the objective of European integration. The consideration of citizenship cannot be separated from a consideration of the purpose of integration. So long as agreement cannot be reached on integration, agreement on citizenship will be missing as well. The introduction of the European Union complicates the matter. Citizenship in the EC and citizenship in the Union have different connotations. Because the EC has attributes of sovereignty, citizenship in the EC can be expressed through legal rights and protections such as the right to participate in elections to Parliament. In contrast, the European Union is not an entity recognized in international law; therefore, the concept of citizenship in the

Union is amorphous and dependent on intergovernmental agreement for its definition.

The European Union is superimposed over existing member states with deep traditions of participatory democracy and broadly defined concepts of citizenship. The construction of the Union raises the question of whether or to what extent the Union should replicate the policies and processes that distinguish Western European democracies. The construction also raises questions about how to distinguish citizenship in the Union from citizenship in the member states. The principle of subsidiarity applies, but it is not a clear guide for decisions about the allocation of responsibilities.

The attitudes and expectations of the people in the member states form part of the parameters in which citizenship policy is made. Europeans have been passive observers of the construction of the EC even though they have steadily indicated support for European integration on opinion polls. They have not demanded citizenship or expressed interest in participation in the EC, judging by participation rates in elections to the Parliament. Public interest was only aroused by the media campaign in support of the 1992 program and some were concerned by the subsequent rush of legislation in Brussels. Plans to eliminate national borders frightened many when they considered the threat to public security. New power and new activity in Brussels worried citizens because they felt remote from the levers of control. Concern about the democratic deficit spread. The negative vote on the Maastricht Treaty in Denmark, the weak endorsement which the treaty won in France, and falling indicators of public support for integration warned that the legitimacy of the Union was in question.

The basic attributes of the problem area are ones which will make the development of the policy difficult. The policy will unfold without a model to guide it and without a generally accepted objective. The citizenship policy being developed in the Union is without a counterpart. Europeans have deeply held traditions regarding citizenship, but they are all directed toward national citizenship. They have had little experience with European integration. Citizenship policy may increase their involvement in European integration, but the context within which the policy will be made is not supportive of rapid progress on the policy.

Relevant Cultural Values

The cultural values related to citizenship policy require little explanation. The basic democratic values of Western society, they are widely accepted by the people and respected by legitimate governments. They include the right of citizens to participate in the political system, to have a responsible government, and to receive from that government a secure and just society. These values have taken shape through history largely in relation to national governments. More recently, some individuals have tried to change the EC in order to ensure the expression of the values within its operation. They write about the democratic deficit (see, for example, Williams, 1991). The main concern is to ensure democratic accountability through a strong Parliament because it is the only institution directly accountable to the people. Some people, however, argue that reform of Parliament is not adequate. They say that the EC must also adopt policies which protect and promote the interests of individuals. They advocate a "social Europe."

Given the broad acceptance of democratic values, it is unlikely that the EC can acquire legitimacy among the people unless it addresses some of the detrimental aspects of its own policies and provides rights that complement the ones which people already have as citizens in the member states. The prevailing value system supports the development of a citizenship policy which provides for participation and also gives expression to the social and economic aspects of citizenship that are valued in Europe. The latter aspects include equality and social justice as noted earlier in this chapter. Europe may now be at the stage where the protection of social and economic citizenship will need to pass from member governments to the EC. Stephan Leibfried wrote that if the existence of a single market forces a "downward spiraling of national citizenship benefits," people will demand "social citizenship" in the EC (Leibfried, 1992, p. 113).

Relevant Constitutional Rules

The Treaty of Rome and the Single European Act (SEA) are silent on the subject of citizenship. The Treaty of Rome does provide the basis for the development of citizenship policy as noted in the historical section. It is somewhat surprising that the SEA does not mention citizenship in light of interest in the topic during the time when the treaty was drafted. Individuals are dealt with in the treaties primarily in their capacity as workers. The EC, therefore, had only weak and indirect authority to act in regard to citizenship issues. The SEA provided Parliament with new legislative power, but the exercise of that power was limited to measures dealing with the internal market. Despite this weakness, Parliament held numerous debates on issues related to citizenship and gained publicity for the issue. Pressure began to build for treaty revisions to provide the EC with the power to act on the subject.

The creation of the internal market, however, which was mandated by the SEA, provided grounds for new concerns regarding citizenship. The new market had implications for the right of residence, border security, freedom to supply services across borders, and the protection of workers in an open market. Member states began to negotiate agreements on topics such as asylum and frontier-free areas (the Schengen Agreement in 1990). These intergovernmental agreements were useful, but many believed that action by the EC was called for.

THE DYNAMIC EXTERNAL ENVIRONMENT

The external environment affecting citizenship policy changed dramatically in the years between 1989 and 1993 because of the end of the Cold War and the ratification of the Maastricht Treaty. The two events concern very different subjects, but they are interrelated. The collapse of the communist regimes in Eastern Europe led to a need to redefine Europe and the place of Western Europeans within it. The drafting of the Maastricht Treaty took place against that background and gave a new relevance to the question of citizenship.

The Chaos in Eastern Europe

The end of the Cold War presented Western Europe with one of its most serious crises since the end of World War II. The situation tested the limits of national governments to respond and forced them to seek cooperative responses through the EC. The chaos that ensued in Eastern Europe after 1989 threatened to inundate the member states of the EC with large numbers of persons fleeing the economic collapse of their countries. National governments either had to admit the Eastern Europeans into their countries, where unemployment was already a serious problem, or had to reject them and bear the onus for inhuman actions against individuals who had suffered under communist regimes. In order to avoid the dilemma, the member states turned to the EC to draft a common policy. The EC was already at work on a common visa policy as a part of its internal market program, but support for the policy was weak. The crisis in Eastern Europe gave a new incentive to the work.

The Eastern Europeans who were admitted to member states of the EC added to the large numbers of immigrants already there and created another problem for the EC. Anti-immigrant feeling threatens social stability in the member states, makes it more urgent to define citizenship and its rights.

The Maastricht Treaty

Four passages in the preamble of the Treaty on European Union (the Maastricht Treaty) indicate that European integration now encompasses citizenship and its related rights:

- "Confirming their attachment to the principles of liberty, democracy and respect for human rights and fundamental freedoms and of the rule of law"
- "Resolved to establish a citizenship common to nationals of their countries"

- "Reaffirming their objective to facilitate the free movement of persons, while ensuring the safety and security of their people, by including provisions on justice and home affairs in this Treaty"
- "Have decided to establish a European Union"

It is important to recall that the treaty has three parts or pillars in addition to the general provisions with which it opens. The legal structures for implementing policies differ greatly if the policy falls under the part dealing with the European Community or the part dealing with justice and home affairs. Different aspects of citizenship are dealt with in different parts of the treaty and consequently will be implemented by different procedures. Inevitably, controversies will arise over the boundaries separating the responsibilities of the EC from those of the member states acting under the European Union. The common provisions of the treaty charge all institutions to respect citizenship in the Union in order to strengthen the protection of the rights and interests of the nationals of its member states.

The section of the treaty which deals with the European Community contains the most important passage on citizenship. Part 2 of Title II, called "Citizenship of the Union," states that every person holding the nationality of a member state shall be a citizen of the Union (Article 8). The treaty extends a number of rights to citizens of the Union, but such rights are not absolute. The Commission must report to the Parliament, the Council, and the Economic and Social Committee every three years regarding the applications of the provisions in Article 8. The Commission may propose measures to strengthen or to add to rights. The Council may adopt the proposals by a unanimous vote after consulting Parliament. Such measures shall be recommended to member states for adoption in accordance with their constitutional requirements.

The EC has the authority to legislate in regard to citizenship according to Title II of the treaty. Some of the rights associated with citizenship in Title II are ones already provided by the Treaty of Rome, such as the right of free movement. Other rights are new and include the right to diplomatic protection and voting rights. The procedure by which the voting rights are to be adopted is unclear, but Carlos Closa believes that they may be implemented by multilateral agreement rather than by EC procedures (Closa, 1992, p. 1159).

Issues related to citizenship are also covered in Title VI, which is titled "Provisions on Cooperation in the Fields of Justice and Home Affairs." Title VI is part of the European Union but not part of the EC. Member states agree to cooperate in regard to policies for asylum, external border controls, immigration, illegal residents, drug addiction, and crime. Action on the foregoing subjects must be in accord with the European Convention for the Protection of Human Rights and Fundamental Freedoms and the Convention on the Status of Refugees of July 1951.

The topics covered in Title VI are interrelated with those of Title II and progress will need to be made simultaneously. For example, member states will be reluctant to eliminate internal borders (a Title II subject) unless all members are confident that each will be equally rigorous in pursuit of illegal residents (a Title VI subject). The elimination of internal borders is also related to common rules for entrance into the EC and mutual trust among the member states regarding effective enforcement of the rules. Article 100c of Title II gives the EC the authority to legislate common visa requirements for entrance into the EC.

The treaty extends the competence of the EC to subjects that will make the EC more relevant to its citizens. The EC has competence in the areas of education, culture, and public health. The EC is prohibited by the treaty, however, from adopting measures on these subjects if they require harmonization of national policies. The role of the EC is to encourage action by members, not to replace it.

Directives concerning some subjects related to citizenship—the free movement of workers, education, culture, and health—must be adopted by a new co-decision procedure which provides Parliament with increased power (Article 189b). Parliament has the power to veto a proposal if an absolute majority of its members vote to do so. Proposals arising under Article 189b are initiated by the Commission and adopted by the Council. (A qualified majority vote is needed for adoption by the Council.)

The procedure for adopting proposals under Article 8, which deals with citizenship, is more complicated. Policies regarding citizens' rights to free movement and the right to residence are proposed by the Commission, receive the assent of Parliament, and are then adopted by the Council unanimously (Article 8a and b). The assent procedure makes Parliament a key player in the process because it can, by a simple majority, block the adoption of a proposal (Weiler, 1992, pp. 14–15). Both the Commission and the Council need to respect the position of Parliament. Parliament and the ombudsman also have important roles in regard to the right to petition. Citizens directly petition Parliament, which develops its own procedures for handling petitions. Parliament appoints the ombudsman and receives an annual report from the officer, but the Court of Justice has the power to dismiss the ombudsman following a request from Parliament. Parliament also has the responsibility to draft the rules by which the ombudsman operates, but the Commission must be consulted and the Council must give its approval by a qualified majority vote (Article 138e). One procedure differs significantly from the others. Member states are instructed by Article 8c to negotiate procedures to implement the right to diplomatic representation. Finally, the rights in Article 8 may be supplemented or extended as noted above.

In conclusion, the Maastricht Treaty creates the concept of citizenship in the European Union and gives the EC responsibility to enact the policies necessary to give meaning to the various facets of the concept. The EC gains important new competences related to citizenship which will make the EC more relevant to the people. Parliament gains both new scope for action and new authority in the formulation of policy. The contributions of the treaty are undermined, however, by the many and complex procedures which it establishes. The treaty lacks the transparency which is essential for democratic accountability.

THE POLICY SUBSYSTEM

The policy subsystem comprises decision makers, advocacy groups, and policy brokers. The policy subsystem has not had a long history and it is less fully developed than other policy subsystems considered in this book. Now that citizenship is fully subsumed under the legal framework of the EC, its policy subsystem may enter a dynamic phase.

Decision Makers

The three primary decision makers are the Commission, the Council, and Parliament. (The European Court plays an important role in regard to citizenship, but it is not a decision maker.)

The Commission is organized around functional areas with a commissioner and a directorate general (DG) responsible for an area. As noted in previous chapters, the Commission has a commissioner and a DG for the environment, for social policy, and for regional policy. The organizational structure ensures that individuals have the responsibility and the expertise to study and to draft the necessary policy. The commissioner and the civil servants working in the DG frequently act as advocates for the policy area. Citizenship, only recently gaining its status as a policy area, lacks the power base which a commissioner and a DG can provide. No commissioner and no DG have, as a primary responsibility, the development of citizenship policy. Different aspects of the policy are scattered among the responsibilities of several commissioners and their DGs. The fragmented structure requires the president of the Commission to exercise leadership in order to ensure coordination. The Commission also coordinates the operation of many external groups that are attached to a policy area. For example, asylum policy already has a number of groups that have worked on the policy for several decades. The members of the groups are drawn from the governments of the member states and from the Commission. In 1992 the commissioner responsible for oversight of the groups was Martin Bangemann, whose primary responsibility was industrial affairs (EP, 1992). The example illustrates two points. One is that the Commission does not have a central locus for handling citizenship policy. Instead, it utilizes a number of already existing procedures. The other is that the Commission is not an island. Although it has the power to initiate policy, it does so in cooperation with a number of other actors.

The Council is a dominant player in regard to citizenship policy. Council members are intimately concerned with citizenship issues and some have been very influential. The Spanish government, under the direction of Prime Minister Felipe Gónzales Marquez, was primarily responsible for the section on citizenship in the Maastricht Treaty. Belgium, Greece, Portugal, and Denmark contributed as well. The European Council, at its meeting in Rome in 1990, endorsed the concept of citizenship and the related rights which were later included in the treaty (CEC, 1991b, pp. 86–87).

The Council has a more comprehensive role in regard to justice and home affairs than it does for policies arising under the EC. Member states share with the Commission the right of initiative on issues concerning justice and home affairs. If the members agree by a two-thirds majority vote, they may adopt conventions concerning the subject and may designate the Court to have jurisdiction over disputes arising from such conventions. The Council must associate with the Commission in its work and the two must keep Parliament informed on developments (Article K). The Council started work on issues related to justice and home affairs even before the treaty was ratified. Two topics that attracted early consideration were the need for a policy on asylum and an action plan on Europol (the network among European police) (CEC, 1993b). Given the present environment, the Council can be expected to continue providing leadership in this area.

The Parliament has long been the advocate of citizenship and human rights in the EC. It established a working group on human rights in the 1960s and in January 1992 it created a Committee on Civil Liberties and Internal Affairs (CEC, 1993c, p. 366). Parliament keeps the subject of citizenship before the media through debates on issues of the day such as immigration and through the submission of written questions to the Council and the Commission. In 1989, Parliament, on its own initiative, adopted the "Declaration of Fundamental Rights and Freedoms" (CEC, 1992c, pp. 38–42).The document lists rights commonly contained in such documents in Europe, but also includes newer rights such as the right to just working conditions, workers' right to information in the workplace, and the right to environmental and consumer protection. Parliament asked that the document be incorporated into the treaties and that citizens be given access to the European Court of Justice to protect their rights (CEC, 1990, pp. 354–355).

The Maastricht Treaty makes Parliament an even more important participant in the policy area. Parliament's role is, perhaps, larger and more diverse than that of the Commission in this one policy area, but the Council is the primary actor, given its control of issues concerning justice and home affairs. Parliament has two important tools in the assent procedure: (1) its oversight of the ombudsman, and (2) its responsibility as the receiver of petitions. If Parliament uses the tools with the will with which it used the tools given it by the SEA, citizenship will gain a prominent place on the EC agenda.

Advocacy Groups

Advocacy groups have not had a major policy area around which to form, but some groups are active. One is the Economic and Social Committee (ESC). It is not strictly an interest group in the American sense, because it is an EC institution. Composed of persons representing special interest groups, it acts as a conduit for the views of these groups regarding EC policies. It has 189 members who are divided into three groups: representatives of employers, workers, and various groups such as those representing agriculture, the professions, and consumers. The ESC has consultative rights under the Treaty of Rome and prepares formal opinions on proposals submitted to it for consideration. It does not have the stature of the Parliament, but some of its reports have been influential and it was the creator of the important Community Charter of the Fundamental Social Rights of Workers (Springer, 1992, pp. 88–92).On its own initiative, the ESC issued a report titled "The Citizens' Europe," which made a significant contribution to the work on citizenship (CES, 1992a, 1992b). According to the ESC, "European citizenship must represent more than just the sum of twelve national citizenships" (CES, 1992a, p. 1). The task is to construct a durable, transnational model of citizenship based on European values and culture including humanistic principles. The EC must address the democratic deficit and ensure social justice to give meaning to European citizenship (CES, 1992a, p. 2). The ESC worked on "The Citizens' Europe" report for almost eighteen months and adopted it unanimously except for five abstentions in a plenary session. The report constitutes one of the most fully developed discussions of European citizenship available from an EC institution.

Europe has a number of groups concerned with different aspects of citizenship policy, but one group has emerged as the most visible and active. The Euro Citizen Action Service (ECAS), based in Brussels, acts as a central clearinghouse for citizen complaints about interferences with the right to free movement (ECAS, 1993). The group criticized the Commission for failing to act against member states when they obstruct the elimination of passport controls. The group has also filed a case in the Court (Hill, 1994).

Policy Brokers

The Commission is the primary policy broker for citizenship, as it has been for other policy areas. Although the Commission has not been the leader, it has facilitated the making of the policy by coordinating and supporting the work of other actors. Its support for citizenship and human rights in the EC is unquestioned. Since 1979, the Commission has advocated the incorporation into EC law of the European Convention for the Protection of Human Rights and Fundamental Freedoms. It cooperated with other EC institutions on the 1986 "Declaration Against Racism and Xenophobia" and the 1977 "Joint Declaration on Fundamental Rights" (both are reprinted in CEC, 1992c, pp. 31 and 35). Laura Cram studied the means by which the Commission operates in regard to social issues. She found that the Commission conducted research, provided forums for groups to interact, and built a constituency of support. Its style was consensus building and the avoidance of "head-on clashes with powerful interests" (Cram, 1993, p. 16).

CITIZENSHIP AND RELATED POLICIES IN THE MAASTRICHT ERA

The initial EC involvement in citizenship leads to concerns for a number of related issues. Social exclusion, immigration, poverty, and so forth, are all under consideration by the EC. Three different aspects of the policy area are considered below in order to illustrate the development of the concept. They are political rights, social exclusion, and immigration. Each deals with a different facet of citizenship.

Political rights have been the hallmark of citizenship and some leaders of the EC have worked for decades to provide uniform and meaningful political rights to citizens in the EC. In 1960 Parliament proposed a draft convention on the direct election of members of Parliament and included in the draft the right of citizens to vote or run for Parliament in the member state where they reside. Through the years certain principles have been generally accepted: Member states control their own principles for determining citizenship (the EC does not interfere), and nationals of the member states have the right to elect representatives to the European Parliament. Agreement could not be reached on other issues. One concerned the right of citizens to vote or run for office where they reside rather than in the country of nationality. The same issue has been raised concerning municipal elections. Another issue has been whether members of Parliament should be elected by a uniform electoral system operating in all member states. The Maastricht Treaty ends the debate: it gives nationals the right to vote and run for Parliament and local office in their place of residence, but the right must be implemented by subsequent legislation. The EC has proceeded cautiously to adopt new legislation. The Commission proposed legislation to allow citizens to vote where they reside, but did not propose uniform residence requirements. Member states determine residence requirements so long as they do not discriminate between their citizens and residents from other member states. Luxembourg, which is the only member to have a high percentage of nationals from other member states, has a long residence requirement. The goal of a uniform electoral system remains elusive as well. The early results may be disappointing to many, but the policy is unfolding in the gradual, incremental style that characterizes EC policy making.

Social exclusion is a concept that has moved into the limelight in recent years. It refers to poverty in modern societies which is multifaceted and excludes individuals, groups, and regions "from those exchanges, activities and social rights which are an inherent part of social integration" (CEC, 1992a, p. 3). The poverty is caused by changes in the labor market and in family structure and by long-term unemployment. About 15 percent of the population in the EC exists in social exclusion.

An EC poverty program is not new. The EC adopted a multiyear poverty program in 1975. Subsequent programs have primarily included three types of activity—research and data collection, funding of pilot projects, and the coordination of national programs (see, for example, CEC, 1991a). The most recent program is "Poverty 3" (1989–1994) with a budget of ECU 55 million. The program includes the same three-pronged approach of the earlier ones, but on a larger scale. Two organizations have been created to assist the Commission in its work. One is the Observatory on National Policies to Combat Social Exclusion, which is staffed by independent experts who compile national reports on social exclusion and publish an annual volume (see, for example, CEC, 1992b). The other group consists of consultants who assist the Commission in overseeing the poverty program and in coordinating research on the subject. Organized as a European Economic Interest Grouping (a form of economic collaboration recognized by EC law), they are known by the name of "Animation and Research." The group publishes *Poverty 3-News* ten times a year ("Animation and Research," 1993).

In 1993 the commissioner for social affairs proposed a new program for the years 1994 to 1999 with a budget twice that of the previous program. He justified his proposal on the grounds that research shows that social exclusion must be tackled in a comprehensive fashion. He believes that it is unacceptable to leave large numbers of people in poverty (CREW, 1993, p. 8). In keeping with the now familiar pattern, the Commission wants to involve a wide cast in the program. Partnership is the operational word. The Council and local authorities have been asked to participate as well as employers and labor unions. Each has been assigned a role under the direction of the Commission. The policy is linked to regional policy and other social policies and was launched with a publicity campaign to raise public awareness of the problem.

Immigration from non-EC countries has been regulated by member governments; however, responsibility is shifting to Brussels. The EC is interested in part because of the relationship between citizenship and immigration and in part because immigration has economic and social consequences.

More than ten million persons from non-EC countries reside in the EC (*International Migration Challenges in a New Era*, 1993, p. 42). The number is expected to increase because of the economic dislocations in Eastern Europe and the large surplus labor population in North Africa. The average per capita income in Eastern Europe is only about 30 to 40 percent of the average in the EC (CEC, 1993b, p. 65). Authorities expect some ten million people to emigrate from Eastern Europe to the EC in the 1990s (Collins, 1993, p. 305). The situation in regard to North Africa and sub-Saharan Africa is less noticed, but perhaps more serious. According to a leading French demographer writing about the causes of migration from Africa to Europe, "The gap [between the two banks of the Mediterranean] is the greatest ever seen in the history of mankind, and it has serious social and political implications" (Chesnais, 1990, p. 22). Such dramatic commentary is common in scholarly and popular publications and people are increasingly focusing on immigration as a major security and economic problem for Western Europe.

The EC stands at the intersection of two of the three major zones of international migration pressure. (The third is the Rio Grande region.) About one million people are entering the EC per year. Member states of the EC no longer believe that they can cope with the immigration problem by themselves and have turned to the EC. The United Nations High Commission for Refugees has also called on the EC to be the primary actor in developing a European immigration policy (*International Migration Challenges*, 1993, p. 62). The EC has responded with a major new policy initiative.

In the past, the EC dealt only with the migration of nationals of member states within the EC. National governments regulated the migration of non-EC country nationals. The EC began to develop a migration policy in the 1980s as a necessary component of the policy to create an internal market. The EC leaders also foresaw "that a migration policy at the European level may gradually take place as an integral part of the move towards European citizenship" (CEC, 1985b, p. 6). They believed that the EC would primarily service and coordinate the efforts of member governments. In 1990, five member states signed the Schengen Agreement, in which they agreed to abolish internal controls and to adopt common external border checks and procedures including common visa requirements for non-EC country nationals. In 1988, the Council established the Immigration Group to bring together cabinet ministers in the member governments who are responsible for immigration issues. The group was to consider steps for the abolition of border controls. The issue was discussed as an aspect of the internal market (CEC, 1988b). The next year, the situation changed dramatically and the floodgates to migrants from the east were opened. Migration policy became an urgent issue.

Asylum policy was one of the related aspects of immigration policy that caused difficulties for the EC. The number of persons seeking asylum escalated and asylum policies differed greatly among the member states. Between 1988 and 1992, two million people claimed asylum in Europe, over half of them in Germany. In 1992 alone, 550,000 persons claimed asylum in Europe and 400,000 of them claimed it in Germany (CREW, 1992, p. 7). The member states of the EC adopted the Dublin Convention in 1990, which contains rules for granting asylum and for defining which member state had jurisdiction for the procedure. In November 1993, the Council met for the first time under the Maastricht Treaty to try to obtain greater agreement on the asylum issue. The effort fell apart, however, over national differences.

The EC is having a difficult time making progress on immigration policy. Many subtopics such as asylum are associated with it. A whole infrastructure of supporting policies needs to be in place and each step opens up a new area of complexity. For example, Europol needs to be functioning to the satisfaction of the member states before governments will relinquish border controls. Another obstacle is the division of responsibility between the EC and the European Union operating through the European Council. Parliament criticizes policy making by the European Council, which, it charges, operates in secret without parliamentary scrutiny. Another difficulty is that the Union is a new participant in a policy area already crowded by other actors. The Council of Europe and the United Nations High Commission for Refugees already have policies to which some EC member states adhere. The Union must harmonize its policy with the already existing international framework.

Despite the difficulties, the EC and the member states have made some progress. They agreed at the Maastricht summit to set up a work program on immigration policy. At the Edinburgh summit, they adopted a "Declaration of Principles Governing External Aspects of Migration Policy" in which they agreed to work to remove the causes of migration and to encourage people to remain at home. They also agreed to reinforce efforts to combat illegal immigration and to work with governments from which such immigrants come to ensure that they may be safely returned home (reprinted in Appendix B of *International Migration Challenges*, 1993, pp. 100–102).

The experiences which the Union has had concerning political rights, social exclusion, and immigration warn that citizenship is a complex and difficult policy area. Pressures from the external environment compel the Union to act, but a system is not yet in place to facilitate successful policy making.

CONCLUSION

The Maastricht Treaty introduces the concept of European citizenship, thereby linking people with the Union. The link is essential if the Union is to gain legitimacy. European citizenship enhances the democratic credentials of the Union. The development of a policy for citizenship, however, promises to be slow, and conflict and confusion will characterize the effort. Many factors impede progress. The responsibility is new and a regime is not yet in place to structure its development. Moreover, progress on citizenship issues has to be accompanied by progress on a number of related issues. The policy requires an infrastructure of supporting policies, many of which require intergovernmental cooperation and trust in areas, such as law enforcement, where past experience is lacking. The legal basis for the policy provided by the treaty divides authority between the EC and the European Council acting as an intergovernmental institution. The two entities have different concerns and respond to different political interests. Parliament has an important role in the EC and emphasizes human rights concerns. The European Council reflects the worries of national leaders responding to economic problems and to voter demands for security. External pressures arising from the chaos in Eastern Europe compel the Union to hasten its work on the policy despite the fact that it is better adapted to an incremental and consensus-building form of policy making. As a result of all of these factors, the development of a citizenship policy presents a serious challenge to the Union and one that must be met in the public eye. The related issues are highly emotional matters in contemporary Europe.

The EC, as a pillar of the Union, has important new areas of competence in regard to citizenship. As a consequence, the EC is engaged in activities that bring it into closer contact with the people. The EC is pursuing its responsibilities by a number of routes of which the legislative one is not necessarily the most used. Much of what the EC, and especially the Commission, are doing is preparatory. The EC is conducting research and gathering data, forming public opinion by media campaigns, and building a network into the interested community. It is employing the partnership approach, which has been noted in other policy areas as well, and delegating to the partners responsibility for policy. The authority of the EC in regard to its new competences is circumscribed, however, by the principle of subsidiarity. Member states retain a large measure of control and they appear ready to retain maximum authority. They want uniform action, but they may seek it through the auspices of the European Council as provided by the Maastricht Treaty.

The definition of citizenship which is operational in the Union reflects European values and experiences, and includes political, social, and economic aspects. A Dutch scholar provides a current definition: "Citizenship revolves around three issues: *social inclusion and participation* (who belongs to the group and has the right to participate in the community and who does not), *civic competence . . .* and *reciprocity of rights and duties*" (van der Veen, 1993, p. 78). He also explains that the social rights contained in citizenship stress the duties of the community toward the individual (p.78). The point is an important one to note because it explains the relevance of the EC policy on poverty and other social issues. The ramifications of the Union's responsibility for citizenship are sweeping. The responsibility will carry the EC into areas which will give it more political prominence, but which are also fraught with controversy. The boundaries between acts to create an internal market and acts to fulfill the social duties of citizenship are not distinct and action in the two areas may be incompatible.

Although the EC has worked on issues related to citizenship for many years, the European Union is only beginning the work to devise a comprehensive citizenship policy. It is a pioneering effort with no precedent. Citizenship in the Union is an addition to citizenship in a member state. Individuals have dual citizenship, but it differs from dual citizenship in a federal system. In the Union, primary citizenship is in the member state, in a federal system, primary citizenship is in the higher entity. The creation of citizenship in the Union is a necessary step toward European integration, but the development of the concept will take many years. How the work progresses will determine, to an important extent, the depth of the integration effort.

REFERENCES

"Animation and Research." 1993. *Poverty 3-News*. Lille, France.
Chesnais, Jean-Claude. 1990. "The Africanization of Europe?" *The American Enterprise*, May/June, 22–25.
Closa, Carlos. 1992. "The Concept of Citizenship in the Treaty on European Union." *Common Market Law Review* 29: 1137–1169.
Collins, Doreen. 1993. "Briefing." *Journal of European Social Policy* 3, no. 4: 297–308.
CEC (Commission of the European Community). 1985a. "Guidelines for a Community Policy on Migration." *Bulletin of the European Communities*, Supplement 9/85.
———.1985b. "A People's Europe." *Bulletin of the European Communities*, Supplement 7/85.
———. 1988a. "Communication of the Commission on the Abolition of Controls of Persons at Intra-Community Borders." COM(88)640 final.
———. 1988b. *A Guide to Working in a Europe Without Frontiers*. Prepared by Jean-Claude Seche.
———. 1989. "Community Charter of Fundamental Social Rights." COM(89)248 final.
———. 1990. *XXIVth General Report on the Activities of the European Communities*. Brussels: CEC.
———. 1991a. "Final Report on the Second European Poverty Programme, 1985–1989." COM(91)29 final.
———. 1991b. "Intergovernmental Conferences: Contributions by the Commission." *Bulletin of the European Communities*, Supplement 2/91.
———. 1992a. "The Commission's Programme for 1992." *Bulletin of the European Communities*, Supplement 1/92.
———. 1992b. "The Community's Battle Against Social Exclusion." *European File*, 4/1992.
———. 1992c. *The European Community and Human Rights*. Prepared by Christiane Duparc. Brussels: CEC.
———. 1992d. *Observatory on National Policies to Combat Social Exclusion*. Second Annual Report.
———. 1993a. *Employment in Europe*. Brussels: CEC.
———. 1993b. "European Council in Brussels." DOC/93/7.
———. 1993c. *XXVIth General Report on the Activities of the European Communities 1992*. Brussels: CEC.
CES (Economic and Social Committee of the European Communities). 1992a. "Information Report on the Citizens' Europe." CES 955/91 final.
———. 1992b. "Opinion on the Citizens' Europe." CES 1037/92.
Council and Commission of the European Communities. 1992. *Treaty on European Union*.

Cram, Laura. 1993. "Breaking Down the Monolith: The European Commission as a Multi-Organization." Paper presented to the European Community Studies Association, Washington, DC, May 27–29.

CREW (Centre for Research on European Women). 1992. *CREW Reports* 12, no. 12.

——— . 1993. *CREW Reports* 13, no. 10.

ECAS (Euro Citizen Action Service) . 1993. "ECAS Report." Brussels.

ECJ (European Court of Justice). 1974. "Nold v. Commission." ECR 491, case 4/73.

——— . 1975. "Rutili v. Minister for the Interior." ECR 1219, case 36/75.

EP (European Parliament). 1992. "Answer Given by Mr. Bangemann on Behalf of the Commission." 936/92, O.J.93/C 58/23.

Hill, Andrew. 1994. "Euro-Citizens Condemn Open Border Delay." *Financial Times,* January 6.

International Migration Challenges in a New Era. 1993. A Report to the Trilateral Commission, no. 44. New York: Trilateral Commission.

Leibfried, Stephan. 1992. "Europe's Could-Be Social State: Social Policy in European Integration after 1992." In *Singular Europe,* ed. by William James Adams. Ann Arbor: University of Michigan Press.

MacIver, R. M. 1947. *The Web of Government.* New York: Macmillan.

Springer, Beverly. 1992. *The Social Dimension of 1992.* Westport, CT: Greenwood Press.

van der Veen, Romke. 1993. "Citizenship and the Modern Welfare State: Social Integration, Competence and the Reciprocity of Rights and Duties in Social Policy." In *Work and Citizenship in the New Europe,* ed. by Harry Coenen and Peter Leisink. Aldershot, England: Edward Elgar.

Weiler, Joseph. 1992. "After Maastricht: Community Legitimacy in Post-1992 Europe." In *Singular Europe,* ed. by William James Adams. Ann Arbor: University of Michigan Press.

Williams, Shirley. 1991. "Sovereignty and Accountability in the European Community." In *The New European Community,* ed. by Robert Keohane and Stanley Hoffmann. Boulder, CO: Westview Press.

Chapter 9

Conclusion

A n Italian commented after the unification of Italy that Italy had been created and now it was time to create Italians. A similar comment could be made in contemporary Europe. The European Union has been created and now the task is to create a sense of citizenship among the nationals of the member states. The objective of this book has been to assess the relationship between the Union and its citizens by examining four policies of the Union which are relevant to people living in the member states. The policies concern the environment, employment, regional issues, and citizenship. The four policies are compared in this final chapter and some conclusions are offered. (In the interest of simplicity, the four policies are referred to collectively as "people policies.")

THE MAASTRICHT TREATY AND THE ROLES OF THE INSTITUTIONS

The Maastricht Treaty provides the legal foundation for a new era of European integration. According to the findings in this study, the treaty contributes to integration in some respects, but not in all. The treaty gives the Union greater legitimacy to act in areas relevant to the people. Most important, it makes the nationals of the member states citizens of the Union, thereby giving the people a new stake in European integration and rights and privileges in the Union. Citizenship as defined in Europe includes economic and social rights as well as political ones. Consequently, the Union acquires new responsibilities vis-à-vis its citizens. In addition, the treaty mobilizes citizens to participate in policy making by providing for alternative forms of policy making. Indeed, the treaty may provide for a new era in which less reliance is placed on formal policy making and more on new participatory forms. Individuals participate in the social dialogue to make employment policy, in regional governments to make regional policy, and in interest groups to make environmental policy. Consultation, participation, and social partnership are all processes provided by the treaty by which citizens are involved in Union policy making.

The treaty strengthens the democratic credentials of the Union by giving Parliament more influence over people policies and by providing for their adoption in the Council by a qualified majority vote. The new voting procedures and the opt-out protocol for the British facilitate the adoption of popular employment directives. The assent procedure and the co-decision procedure allow Parliament to block unpopular proposals.

On the negative side, the Maastricht Treaty disappointed persons concerned about the democratic deficit. It failed to make Parliament a coparticipant with the Council in all aspects of policy making. It also introduces undue complexity into policy making, as procedures for the adoption of directives vary depending on the subject of the directive. Transparency is therefore a victim of the treaty. The treaty also introduces awkward distinctions between the European Community (EC) and the Union. People are citizens of both and both have obligations for the citizens, but the line between the obligations of the EC and those the Union is unclear. The procedures by which the two fulfill the obligations are quite different. The division is a political expediency, but one with costs for the relationship between the Union/Community and the citizens.

A number of interesting observations are possible regarding the roles of the institutions. First, the relationship among the institutions changes in different policy areas. It is, perhaps, most harmonious in regard to environmental policy because participants agree on the need for action. Members of the institutions have frequent contacts, and the bureaucracies of the Commission and the Council interact on environmental policy. The Commission is a fairly effective policy broker on regional policy but less so on employment policy. The Commission and Parliament find common cause in regard to employment policy and citizenship issues. The Council takes the initiative on citizenship issues and the Commission plays a more passive role than it does in other areas. In all cases, the formal relationship among the institutions is supplemented by frequent informal contacts.

Each institution in the Union has its own characteristics in regard to people policies. The Commission is the steadfast institution. Once it adopts a proposal, it perseveres—redrafting, consulting, and building support. The proposal on worker participation is the best example: the Commission has worked on it for more than two decades to devise an acceptable policy. The Commission has a network of experts and interest groups which it mobilizes to participate in policy making. The Commission is initiator, activator, coordinator, and policy broker. The incremental style of policy making, which characterizes EC policy according to many scholars, is orchestrated by the Commission.

Parliament is the conscience of the Union. It is green on the environment, social democratic on employment issues, the advocate of poor areas on regional policy, and the champion of human rights on citizenship policy. Of course, it contains opposition voices, but the socialist and Christian democratic views largely coincide on those subjects, and the two parties dominate Parliament. The Maastricht Treaty gives Parliament new powers to make people policies, including a limited veto power. Parliament can now compel both the Commission and the Council to respect its position. The new offices of Parliament provide for frequent meetings between members of Parliament and representatives from the other institutions. The new status of Parliament is reflected in the attention which the media gives it. Parliament schedules highly publicized debates on controversial issues. Parliament is an advocate for people policies and has helped to advance them. It has gained authority and respect but continues to be the junior participant in the triad of EC policy makers.

The Council remains preeminent as an EC policy maker, but its domination should not be exaggerated. The Commission, through the power of initiative, sets the terms and orchestrates the support, and Parliament mobilizes public awareness. The Council can refuse to consider a proposal, but the Commission will then frequently wait for a more friendly Council and submit it again in revised form. Most participants in the Council do not want to appear to be "anti-Europe" (Margaret Thatcher excepted). Regional policy, however, calls forth nationalistic behavior among the Council members, who contest for regional funds. In general, however, the Council operates more often according to interactive norms than to adversarial ones.

The Maastricht Treaty may have a greater impact on the operation of the Council than on that of other institutions. Two provisions in the Maastricht Treaty are relevant. The European Council has the responsibility for justice and home affairs, but it exercises the responsibility outside the confines of the EC. The new procedure rests on intergovernmental agreement (including vague obligations to respect the views of Parliament and the Commission). It is uncertain how the Council will exercise the responsibility. If the Council follows a unilateral course on sensitive issues such as citizenship policy, relations with the other institutions could be strained. The second provision of the treaty is the protocol on social policy. The provision of an opt-out clause, by which eleven members of the Council can adopt a policy that affects only the eleven when the British opt out, introduces a wild card into Council operations. The dynamics of the procedure could affect not only the operation of the Council, but also the relations of the Council with other institutions, which would face the choice of working with a Council of eleven or a Council of twelve. The Commission, for example, can draft employment policies that meet the wishes of eleven members or temper them to encourage British participation. Employment policy and citizenship policy provide the test cases for new developments in the Council.

Interest groups are not EC institutions, but they need to be considered when discussing the institution. They are an important adjunct of policy making. Ten years ago a graduate student going to Brussels was discouraged from researching interest groups in the EC on the grounds that they did not exist. Today they exist in great numbers and in various forms. They operate as lobbies, but also as participants in the policy process by advising the drafters of policy and providing expert information. They have a quasi-institutional role. Major interest groups operate in each of the policy areas studied. Their style of operation does not necessarily accord with the model based on American experiences. The adversarial norms associated with advocacy groups are not common in Brussels. The groups interested in employment policy could be characterized as adversarial, but not the groups involved with environmental policy. Corporatist norms are more characteristic. The Commission encourages groups to work together and to build consensus. Two other observations are valid. EC interest groups serve to aggregate interests somewhat as political parties do in national politics. They also reconcile differences among their national members in order to present a united position in Brussels. As a result, they perform an aggregatory function for the Commission.

THE POLICIES—COMMONALITIES AND DIFFERENCES

The study of policy making in four areas provides useful insights into commonalities and differences. The organization of the findings into uniform categories facilitates comparisons. The categories required that consideration be given to numerous factors and brought into focus relevant factors which would otherwise have been missed.

A number of commonalities can be cited, but six have been selected because they illustrate important points:

1. All four policies were affected by changes in the dynamic external environment. The Maastricht era coincides with a major disruption in Europe. The Union has refocused policies in order to ameliorate the effects of the disruption. The "White Paper on Growth, Competitiveness, Employment" is the hallmark of the era.

2. Common values shape expectations regarding policies. Values rooted in European history shape EC policies. EC employment policy differs from that in the United States. Regional, environmental, and citizenship policies all have a distinctive orientation as well. The values are widely held and lead to expectations that public authorities should adopt people policies. If national governments are not effective, then the EC should act.

3. The policies of the Union extend into numerous areas of everyday life. A type of spillover effect, as defined by the neo-functionalists, appears to operate. Union responsibilities in the human area cannot be encapsulated into defined spheres. The spillover is most apparent in regard to citizenship, the responsibility for which is affected by immigration, police cooperation, and so on.

4. In general, Union policies evolve incrementally and through consensus building. The legal structure for policy making as well as European values shapes the process and obstructs the adoption of bold new policies. On the other hand, proposals are not rejected definitively, but remain in the system awaiting appropriate revision or the creation of a consensus of support.

5, 6. The final two points need to be discussed together and they are, perhaps, the most important observations of the study. Policy making in the Union has multiple forms and involves multiple actors. The policy process is complex, multilayered, and based on traditional as well as innovative models. The current emphasis on innovative forms gives the impression that a retreat from legislation is occurring in Brussels. In part, the development may be an attempt to counter the fear expressed in the media that too much authority is shifting to Brussels. In part, the leaders of the Union may be devising new forms in order to mobilize support for European policies. One result of the development is that many people now participate in policy making. Networks of participants extend from the institutions and groups in Brussels to civil servants and interest groups in the member countries. The offices that regional governments operate in Brussels and the new Committee of the Regions are examples of the mobilization.

The differences among the policy areas are fairly obvious. Employment policy is a topic where the Commission has failed to establish a consensus despite years of effort. The cleavages between labor and management and between Continental and Anglo-Saxon values were too wide. A new consensus has been formed as a result of the unemployment crisis, however, and may help to bring the sides together. The opt-out provision in the Maastricht Treaty stands as a monument to the lack of consensus and may actually delay further convergence. Citizenship policy is another area in which consensus is weak, but the reasons for the weakness are different. One is the relative newness of the topic. Another is that the subject, because of its broad meaning in the EC, includes many and diverse subtopics. In addition, citizenship policy involves some of the most sensitive issues in European politics today. The immigration issue is preeminent among them. The Union has much at risk in regard to the citizenship policy, because it is acting in an area of high politics that has implications for the basic security concerns of national governments. Moreover, the Maastricht Treaty does not provide the Union with explicit guidelines for making citizenship policy.

Environmental and regional policies benefit from a greater degree of acceptance and from more clearly defined procedures for policy making than do the other two policies. Of the four subjects, environmental policy has the broadest base of support. Green values are generally accepted and member governments know that national environmental policies must be supplemented by Community action. Progress on EC environmental policy is likely to continue in the incremental mode that characterizes much of EC policy making. Regional policy is the most important of the four policies. It has been in operation for many years and serves the interests of the member states as well as the cause of European integration. The unique and interesting aspect of the policy in the Maastricht era is the new role for regional authorities and groups. The growing authority of regional actors in the EC parallels a trend throughout in Europe which has been called, "one of the most important institutional changes in the modern Western state that has occurred over the past couple of decades" (Sharpe, 1993, p. 1).

The differences among the policy areas arise from four basic factors:

1. The environment in which the policy is made varies for each area, as do the problems that give rise to the policy and the social values and norms of behavior that affect the policy.
2. The procedures by which the policies are made are different. The Maastricht Treaty, which introduces additional possibilities, exacerbates the problem.
3. The stake holders are different. Regional authorities, employers' associations, national governments, and so forth, have different needs and expectations in regard to possible outcomes of the policies.
4. The outcomes of the policies differ. In some cases the outcome is monetary, in some cases it is regulatory, and in others it is moral suasion.

OBSERVATIONS REGARDING THE CONCEPTS EMPLOYED

The framework based on the Sabatier approach for policy studies, which was employed in this study, made two important contributions (Sabatier, 1988). It provided a uniformity among the chapters so that generalizations and comparisons could be made more easily. It also ensured that a wide variety of variables were incorporated into the study to provide a more valid picture of policies and the process by which they were made. Sociological, economic, and historical factors frequently affected the policies studied. The requirement to consider the legal structures for each policy was also beneficial. It brought into focus some reasons for policy differences and some concerns for problems resulting from the Maastricht Treaty. The requirement to consider advocacy groups was useful, but also risked inserting a distortion in the study. Interest groups are vital participants in policy making; however, the expression *advocacy groups* has a connotation that is more valid for studies of U.S. policy than for those of European. The political culture in Europe shapes groups into corporatist and consensus-seeking behaviors. The concept of policy-related learning, another contribution by P. Sabatier, was particularly useful in explaining the evolution of regional policy. Overall, the framework was valuable and researchers should consider comparable approaches in order to experiment with ways to build a body of information.

Insights gained from the scholars discussed in Chapter 2 were useful and valid for the study. Neo-functionalism still makes a contribution to understanding the EC and its unique features. Most policies develop incrementally and a number of actors are involved in the development. In addition, the expression *turbulent fields*, which E. Haas added when he reconsidered neo-functionalism, can help explain citizenship policy and the problems associated with its development (Haas, 1975, p. 23). The assertion by R. Keohane and S. Hoffmann that EC policies may have either supranational characteristics or intergovernmental ones depending on the subject was supported in the study. Their "preference-convergence hypothesis" is useful and warns researchers to anticipate differences when studying a number of policies (Keohane and Hoffmann, 1991, p. 25).

Several concepts contributed to understanding findings of the study, two of the most important of which are regime and social legitimacy. The concept of regime can account for differences between environmental policy making and citizenship policy, for example. The work of M. List and V. Rittberger makes an important contribution to understanding the role of regimes in regard to environmental policy (List and Rittberger, 1992). Social legitimacy is a concept that is fundamental to the study (Weiler, 1992, p. 20). Social legitimacy is acquired by a political system when its citizens perceive that their government respects and guarantees important values. The study in this book is based on the assumption that social legitimacy is a goal of the EC and that the people policies contribute to attainment of the goal.

The work of P. Schmitter best describes the Union in the Maastricht era according to the findings in this book (Schmitter, 1992). Political life is a complex mixture of actors, interests, and conditions. Policies are made in a number of ways and involve a number of actors. The Union is unique and its political life responds to many pressures and not solely to those from national governments. Integration, therefore, should not be conceptualized as a single process. According to the findings in this book, the extent and nature of integration in the Union vary in the different policy areas.

CONCLUDING REMARKS ON THE EUROPEAN UNION
AND ITS CITIZENS

European integration has reached a plateau following the rapid development in the 1992 era. The Maastricht Treaty provides the basis for a new era of integration by reforming the institutions and adding to the areas of competence. The inclusion of citizens and regions as participants in the Union is another feature of the new era. The treaty also facilitates the adoption of policies directly relevant to the people. The treaty, however, adds undue confusion to the policy-making process and obstructs public understanding. The benefits of the treaty will be lessened if the policy process is not simplified.

The contributions which the policies studied in this book make to integration are limited. Regional policy is probably the only one which has a direct impact on citizens. The relatively small output of the other policies has been in the form of directives which must be transposed into national law before citizens feel their effects. On the other hand, the Union must continue to develop policies in these areas if integration is to proceed, because such policies provide the basis for social legitimacy.

Policy making, as distinct from policy, is another contributor to integration. The process mobilizes large numbers of people and creates networks through-out the region. The growth of interest group activity is significant and needs to be more fully examined. The political life in Brussels is still remote from most citizens, but the distance is diminishing through these networks.

In conclusion, the Maastricht Treaty creates the European Union and European citizens, but the relationship between the two is at a rudimentary stage. An underlying social basis exists for progress. Common values and norms generally support common policies. Some progress has been noted in the study of policies relevant for citizens. Leaders of the Union have launched a number of initiatives. On the other hand, current conditions as well as problems arising from the treaty itself are likely to continue to hinder progress.

REFERENCES

Haas, E. 1975. *The Obsolescence of Regional Integration Theory*. Berkeley, CA: University of California Press.

Keohane, R., and S. Hoffmann. 1991. "Institutional Change in Europe in the 1980s" In *The New European Community*, ed. by R. Keohane and S. Hoffmann. Boulder, CO: Westview Press.

List, M., and V. Rittberger. 1992. "Regime Theory and International Environmental Management." In *The International Politics of the Environment*, ed. by A. Hurrell and B. Kingsbury. Oxford: Clarendon Press.

Sabatier, P. 1988. "An Advocacy Coalition Framework of Policy Changes and the Role of Policy-Oriented Learning Therein." *Policy Sciences* 21.

Schmitter, P. 1992. "Interests, Powers and Functions: Emergent Properties and Unintended Consequences in the European Polity." Unpublished paper.

Sharpe, L. 1993. "The European Meso: An Appraisal." In *The Rise of Meso Government in Europe,* ed. by L. Sharpe. London: Sage Publications.

Weiler, J. 1992. "After Maastricht: Community Legitimacy in Post-1992 Europe." In *Singular Europe,* ed. by William James Adams. Ann Arbor: University of Michigan Press.

Bibliography

Abu-Lughod, J. 1989. *Before European Hegemony*. New York: Oxford University Press.

Almond, G. 1993."The Study of Political Culture." In *Political Culture in Germany*, ed. by D. Berg-Schlosser and R. Rytlewski. New York: St. Martin's Press.

Anderson, R. 1973. *Modern Europe: An Anthropological Perspective*. Palisades, CA: Goodyear Publishing.

"Animation and Research." 1993. *Poverty 3-News*. Lille, France.

Armstrong, Harvey. 1989. "Community Regional Policy." In *The European Community and the Challenge of the Future*, ed. by Juliet Lodge. New York: St. Martin's Press.

Bailey, J., ed. 1992. *Social Europe*. London: Longman.

Barber, Lionel. 1993. "A New Lightness to His Touch." *Financial Times*, December 13.

Barnouin, Barbara. 1986. *The European Labour Movement and European Integration*. London: Frances Pinter.

Begg, Iain. 1993. "The Emergent European Market and Economic and Social Cohesion." Paper presented at the European Studies Association Conference, Washington, DC, May 27–29.

Bendix, Reinhard. 1974. *Work and Authority in Industry*. Berkeley: University of California Press.

Berg-Schlosser, D., and R. Rytlewski. 1993. "Political Culture in Germany: A Paradigmatic Case." In *Political Culture in Germany*, ed. by D. Berg-Schlosser and R. Rytlewski. New York: St. Martin's Press.

Bianchi, Giuliano. 1993. "The IMPs: A Missed Opportunity? An Appraisal of the Design and Implementation of the Integrated Mediterranean Programmes." In *The Regions and the European Community*, ed. by Robert Leonardi. London: Frank Cass.

Boons, Frank. 1993. "Product-oriented Environmental Policy: Challenges, Possibilities and Barriers." In *A Green Dimension for the European Community*, ed. by David Judge. London: Frank Cass.

Cawson, Alan. 1985. "Conclusion: Some Implications for State Theory." In *Organized Interests and the State*, ed. by Alan Cawson. Beverly Hills, CA: Sage Publications.

CEC (Commission of the European Communities). 1973. "Declaration of the Council of the European Communities and of the Representatives of the Governments of the Member States Meeting in the Council." *Official Journal*, no. C 112.

———. 1975. "Employee Participation and Company Structure in the European Community." *Bulletin of the European Communities*, Supplement 8/75.

———. 1980. "Communication from the Commission Concerning the Consequences of the Judgment Given by the Court of Justice on 20 February 1979 in Case 120/78." *Official Journal*, 256/2.

———. 1985. "Draft Treaty Establishing the European Union." In *An Ever Closer Union*, Annex1. Brussels: European Perspectives Series.

———. 1985. "Guidelines for a Community Policy on Migration." *Bulletin of the European Communities*, Supplement 9/85.

———. 1985. "A People's Europe." *Bulletin of the European Communities*, Supplement 7/85.

———. 1985. "White Paper on Completing the Internal Market." COM(85)310 final.

———. 1987. "Resolution of the Council of the European Communities and of the Representatives of the Governments of the Member States Meeting with the Council." *Official Journal*, no. C 328/1.

———. 1988. *A Guide to Working in a Europe Without Frontiers*. Prepared by Jean-Claude Seche. Brussels: CEC.

———. 1988. "Communication of the Commission on the Abolition of Controls of Persons at Intra-Community Borders." COM(88)640 final.

———. 1988. "Council Regulation of 24 June 1988 on the Tasks of the Structural Funds and Their Effectiveness and on Coordination of Their Activities Between Themselves and with the Operation of the European Investment Bank and Other Existing Financial Instruments." Number 2052/88.

———. 1988. "Social Dimension of the Internal Market." SEC(88)1148 final.

———. 1989. "A Strategy Paper on Waste Management." SEC(89)934 final.

———. 1989. "Community Charter of the Fundamental Social Rights of Workers." COM(89)248 final.

———. 1990. *Basic Statistics of the Community*. 27th ed. Brussels: Statistical Office of the European Communities.

———. 1990. "Commission Opinion of 21 October 1990 on the Proposal for Amendment of the Treaty Establishing the European Economic Community with a View to Political Union." COM(90)600 final.

———. 1990. "Community Support Frameworks, 1989–91, Italy."

———. 1990. *The Council of the European Community*. Brussels: CEC.

———. 1990. "Economic and Monetary Union." Communication of the Commission, August 21, 1990.

———. 1990. *XXIVth General Report on the Activities of the European Communities*. Brussels: CEC.

———. 1991. "Amended Proposal for a Council Directive on the Establishment of a European Works Council in Community-scale Undertakings or Groups of Undertakings for the Purposes of Informing and Consulting Employees." COM(91)345 final. September 16.

———. 1991. *Cities and the Global Environment*. Proceedings of a European Workshop of the European Foundation for the Improvement of Living and Working Conditions.

———. 1991. "Declaration of the Commission on the Two Intergovernmental Conferences on Political Union and on Economic and Monetary Union." IP(91)1063.

———. 1991. *Employment in Europe, 1991*. Brussels: CEC.

———. 1991. *Europe 2000*. Communication from the Commission to the Council and the European Parliament.

———. 1991. "Final Report on the Second European Poverty Programme, 1985–1989." COM(91)29 final.

———. 1991. "Intergovernmental Conferences: Contributions by the Commission." *Bulletin of the European Communities*, Supplement 2/91.

———. 1992. "Conclusions of the Presidency." Report issued by the Commission on the European Council, Lisbon, June 26–27.

———. 1992. "The Commission's Programme for 1992." *Bulletin of the European Communities*, Supplement 1/92.

———. 1992. "The Community's Battle Against Social Exclusion." *European File*, 4/1992.

———. 1992. "Community Structural Policies: Assessment and Outlook." COM(92)84 final.

———. 1992. *Employment in Europe, 1992*. Brussels: CEC.

———. 1992. *Eurobarometer*. no. 37.

———. 1992. *The European Community and Human Rights*. Prepared by Christiane Duparc. Brussels: CEC.

———. 1992. *Europe in Figures*. 3rd ed. Brussels: CEC.

———. 1992. "Second Annual Report." *Observatory on National Policies to Combat Social Exclusion*.

———. 1992. "Proposal for a Council Directive on Packaging and Packaging Waste." COM(92)278/7.

———. 1992. "The Principle of Subsidiarity." SEC(92)1990 final.

———. 1992. "Towards Sustainability." COM(92)23 final.

———. 1992. *Trade Union Information Bulletin* 4.

———. 1992. *Treaty on European Union*. Luxembourg: Office of Official Publications of the European Communities.

———. 1993. "The Cohesion Fund: A Sign of Solidarity in the Future of European Union," prepared by Peter Schmidhuber. *Frontier Free Europe*, April.

———. 1993. *Employment in Europe, 1993*. Brussels: CEC.

———. 1993. "EU Launches Major Employment Creation Drive: 15 Million New Jobs Is the Target." Press release of the Office of Press and Public Affairs, Delegation of the Commission of the European Communities, Washington, DC, December 9.

———. 1993. "European Council in Brussels." DOC/93/7.

———. 1993. "Green Paper: European Social Policy Options for the Union." COM(93)551 final. November 17.

———. 1993. "INTERREG." *Info Background*.Undated copy supplied by DGXVI.

———. 1993. "The Operation of the Community Structural Funds, 1994–99." (Revision of the Council Regulations Governing the Operation of the Community Structural Funds.) Working paper containing the drafts of the proposed revisions, not numbered.

———. 1993. *XXVIth General Report on the Activities of the European Communities 1992*. Brussels: CEC.

———. 1993. "What Changes to the Regulation Governing the Structural Funds." *Info Background*, February/March.

———. 1993. "White Paper on Growth, Competitiveness, Employment." *Bulletin of the European Communities*, Supplement 6/93.

Undated. *European Cooperation Networks*. Packet prepared by the directorate general for regional policies.

CES (Economic and Social Committee of the European Communities). 1992. "Information Report on the Citizens' Europe." CES 955/91 final.

———. 1992. "Opinion on the Citizens' Europe." CES 1037/92.

Chamberlain, Neil. 1980. *Forces of Change in Western Europe*. London: McGraw-Hill.

Chesnais, Jean-Claude. 1990. "The Africanization of Europe?" *The American Enterprise*, May/June, 22–25.

Cipolla, C. 1973. *The Fontana Economic History of Europe*. Vol. 3. London: Collins/Fontana Books.

Closa, Carlos. 1992. "The Concept of Citizenship in the Treaty on European Union." *Common Market Law Review* 29: 1137–1169.

Colchester, N., and David Buchan. 1990. *Europower*. New York: The Economist Book—Random House.

Cole, John, and Francis Cole. 1993. *The Geography of the European Community*. London: Routledge.

Collins, Doreen. 1993. "Briefing." *Journal of European Social Policy* 3, no. 4: 297–308.

Council and Commission of the European Communities. 1992. *Treaty on European Union*.

Coutu, D., K. Hladik, D. Meen, and D. Turcq. 1993. "Views of the Business Community on Post-1992 Integration in Europe." In *The European Challenges Post 1992,* ed. by Alexis J. Jacquemin and David Wright. Aldershot, England: Edward Elgar.

Cram, Laura. 1993. "Breaking Down the Monolith: The European Commission as a Multi-Organization." Paper presented to the European Community Studies Association, Washington, DC, May 27–29.

CREW (Centre for Research on European Women). 1992. *CREW Reports* 12, no. 12.

——— . 1993. *CREW Reports*, 13, no. 10.

Davie, G. 1992. "God and Caesar: Religion in a Rapidly Changing Europe." In *Social Europe*, ed. by J. Bailey. London: Longman.

Davis, H. 1992. "Social Stratification in Europe." In *Social Europe*, ed. by J. Bailey. London: Longman.

Deeken, John. 1993. "Regional Policy and the European Commission: Policy Entrepreneur or Brussels Bureaucracy?" Paper presented to the European Community Studies Association Conference, Washington, DC, May 27–29.

Delors, J. 1991. "The Principle of Subsidiarity: Contribution to the Debate." In *Subsidiarity: The Challenge of Change*. Maastricht: European Institute of Public Administration.

de Bassompierre, Guy. 1988. *Changing the Guard in Brussels*. New York: Praeger.

de Rougement, D. 1966. *The Idea of Europe*. New York: Macmillan.

Draft Treaty on the Union. 1991. 1722/1723 of Europe Documents Series: Agence Internationale D'Information Pour La Presse.

——— . 1991. *Economist*, November 30, 47–49.

EC Committee of the American Chamber of Commerce. 1992. *The EC Environment Guide*. Brussels: EC Committee of the American Chamber of Commerce.

ECAS (Euro Citizen Action Service). 1993. "ECAS Report." Brussels.

ECJ (European Court of Justice). 1974. *Nold v. Commission* ECR 491, case 4/73.

——— . 1975. "Rutili v. Minister for the Interior." ECR 1219, case 36/75.

EEB (European Environmental Bureau). 1990. "Greening the Treaty." Produced in cooperation with Friends of the Earth and the World Wide Fund for Nature. Brussels: EEB.

——— . 1992. "Environmental NGOs' Declarations Addressed to the European Council," Edinburgh, December. Brussels: EEB.

——— . 1992. "How Green Is the Treaty?" Produced by Ralph Hallo. Brussels: EEB.

EP (European Parliament). 1990. "Interim Report on the Intergovernmental Conference in the Context of Parliament's Strategy for European Union." Committee on Institutional Affairs. PE 137.068/final.

——— . 1990. "Interim Report on the Principle of Subsidiarity." Committee on Institutional Affairs. PE 139.293/final.

———. 1992. "Answer Given by Mr. Bangemann on Behalf of the Commission." 936/92, O.J.93/C 58/23.

Esping-Andersen, G. 1990. *The Three Worlds of Welfare Capitalism.* Cambridge, England: Polity Press.

European Council in Lisbon. 1992. "Conclusions of the Presidency." June 26–27, Brussels: CEC.

"European Regional Incentives." 1992. Report of the European Policies Research Centre of the University of Strathclyde. *Journal of Regional Policy* (English edition of *Mezzogiorno D'Europa*) 12 (July–December).

"The Federalists Fight Back." 1991. *Economist,* November 30, 1991, p. 48.

Franklin, Mark, and Wolfgang Rudig. 1992. "The Green Voter in the 1989 Election." *Environmental Politics* 1, no. 4, (Winter): 129–159.

Gardner, D. 1991. "Astonishing Compromise Threatens to Create a Brussels Benefit for the Legal Fraternity." *Financial Times*, December 12, 1992, p. 2.

Giner, S., and M. Archer, eds. 1978. *Contemporary Europe.* London: Routledge & Kegan Paul.

Gorges, Michael. 1992. "Euro-Corporatism after 1992." Paper presented to the American Political Science Association, September 3–6.

Green, Maria. 1993. "The Politics of Big Business in the Single Market Program." Paper presented at the annual conference of the European Community Studies Association, Washington, DC, May 27.

Gustafsson, B., and M. Lindblom. 1993. "Poverty Lines and Poverty in Seven European Countries, Australia, Canada and the USA." *Journal of Social Policy* 3, no. 1.

Haas, Ernst. 1968. *The Uniting of Europe.* 2nd ed. Stanford, CA: Stanford University Press.

———. 1964. *Beyond the Nation State.* Stanford, CA: Stanford University Press.

———. 1975. *The Obsolescence of Regional Integration Theory.* Berkeley, CA: University of California Press.

Haigh, Nigel, and Frances Stewart. 1990. "Introduction." In *Integrated Pollution Control in Europe and North America,* ed. by Nigel Haigh and Frances Stewart. Baltimore, MD: Conservation Foundation.

Harding, S. P., and D. Phillips, with M. Fogarty. 1986. *Contrasting Values in Western Europe.* London: Macmillan.

Heater, D. 1992. *The Idea of European Unity.* Leicester, England: Leicester University Press.

Heller, Agnes. 1992. "Europe: An Epilogue?" *The Idea of Europe*, ed. by B. Nelson, D. Roberts, and W. Veist. New York: Berg.

Hildebrand, Philipp. 1992. "The European Community's Environmental Policy, 1957 to '1992' " *Environmental Politics* 1, no. 4 (Winter): 13–44.

Hill, Andrew. 1994. "Euro-Citizens Condemn Open Border Delay." *Financial Times,* January 6.

Hines, Colin. 1992. "The Green View on Subsidiarity." *Financial Times*, September 16.

Hodges, Michael, and Stephen Woolcock. 1993. "Atlantic Capitalism Versus Rhine Capitalism in the European Community." *West European Politics* 16, no. 3.

Holland, M. 1993. *European Community Integration.* New York: St. Martin's Press.

Hurd, Douglas. 1992. "Europe after Maastricht." Speech given at Cambridge University, February 7. Published by the British Information Services. New York, February 10.

Ifland, Peter, and Beverly Springer. 1992. "Environmental Policy in the European Community." Unpublished manuscript.

Ilbery, Brian. 1986. *Western Europe: A Systematic Human Geography.* 2nd ed. Oxford: Oxford University Press.

Inglehart, Ronald. 1977. *The Silent Revolution: Changing Values and Political Styles among Western Publics.* Princeton, NJ: Princeton University Press.

———. 1990. *Culture Shift in Advanced Industrial Society.* Princeton, NJ: Princeton University Press.

Institute for Environmental Studies. 1991. European Environmental Yearbook. London: DocTer International.

The Internal Market after 1992. 1992. Report to the EEC Commission by the High Level Group on the Operation of the Internal Market (The Sutherland Report).

International Migration Challenges in a New Era. 1993. A Report to the Trilateral Commission, no. 44, New York: Trilateral Commission.

Jamison, Andrew, Ron Eyerman, and Jacqueline Cramer, with Jeppe Laessoe. 1991. *The Making of the New Environmental Consciousness.* Edinburgh: Edinburgh University Press.

Judge, David. 1993. "Predestined to Save the Earth: The Environment Committee of the European Parliament." *A Green Dimension for the European Community,* ed. by David Judge. London: Frank Cass.

Keating, Michael. 1993. "The Continental Meso: Regions in the European Community." In *The Rise of Meso Government in Europe,* ed. by L. J. Sharpe. London: Sage.

Keohane, R., and S. Hoffmann. 1991. "Institutional Change in Europe in the 1980s." In *The New European Community,* ed. by R. Keohane and S. Hoffmann. Boulder, CO: Westview Press.

Kindleberger, Charles. 1993. *A Financial History of Western Europe.* 2nd. ed. New York: Oxford University Press.

Krasner, S. 1983. "Structural Causes and Regime Consequences." In *International Regimes,* ed. by S. Krasner. Ithaca, NY: Cornell University Press.

Landaburu, Eneko. 1992. "The Reform of the Structural Funds: The First Year of Implementation." In *Economic and Social Cohesion in Europe,* ed. by Achille Hannequart. London: Routledge.

Landua, E. C. 1985. *The Rights of Working Women in the European Community.* Brussels: European Perspectives Series of the European Community.

Lange, Peter. 1993. "Maastricht and the Social Protocol: Why Did They Do It?" *Politics and Society* 21, no. 1.

Leibfried, Stephan. 1992. "Europe's Could-Be Social State: Social Policy in European Integration after 1992." In *Singular Europe,* ed. by William James Adams. Ann Arbor: University of Michigan Press.

Leo XIII (pope). 1891. *Rerum Novarum.* Reprinted in *St. Thomas Aquinas on Politics and Ethics,* ed. by Paul Sigmund. New York: W. W. Norton, 1988.

Leonardi, Robert, ed. 1993. *The Regions and the European Community.* London: Frank Cass.

Liberatore, Angela. 1991. "Problems of Transnational Policymaking: Environment Policy in the European Community." *European Journal of Political Research* 19: 281–305.

Lichtheim, George. 1970. *A Short History of Socialism.* New York: Praeger.

Lipset, Seymour. 1968. *Revolution and Counter-Revolution.* Garden City, NY: Anchor Books.

List, M., and V. Rittberger. 1992. "Regime Theory and International Environmental Management." In *The International Politics of the Environment,* ed. by A. Hurrell and B. Kingsbury. Oxford: Clarendon Press.

Lodge, Juliet. 1989. "EC Policymaking: Institutional Considerations." In *The European Community and the Challenge of the Future,* ed. by Juliet Lodge. New York: St. Martin's Press.

———. 1989. "The European Parliament—from 'Assembly' to Co-legislature." In *The European Community and the Challenge of the Future,* ed. by Juliet Lodge. New York: St. Martin's Press.

Ludlow, Peter. 1991. "The European Commission." In *The New European Community,* ed. by Robert Keohane and Stanley Hoffmann. Boulder, CO: Westview Press.

MacIver, R. M. 1947. *The Web of Government*. New York: Macmillan.

Mackenzie Stuart, Lord. 1991. "Assessment of the Views Expressed and Introduction to a Panel Discussion." In *Subsidiarity: The Challenge of Change*. Maastricht: European Institute of Public Administration.

Majone, Giandomenico. 1993. "The European Community Between Social Policy and Social Regulation." *Journal of Common Market Studies* 31, no. 2 (June).

Mally, G. 1973. *The European Community in Perspective*. Lexington, MA: Lexington Books.

Marks, Gary. 1993. "Structural Policy and Multi-level Governance in the European Community." In *The State of the European Community*, ed. by Alan Cafruny and Glenda Rosenthal. Boulder, CO: Lynne Rienner.

Marsden, David, and Jean-Jacques Silvestre. 1992. "Pay and European Integration." In *Pay and Employment in the New Europe*, ed. by David Marsden. Brookfield, VT: Edward Elgar.

Marshall, T. H. 1975. *Social Policy*. London: Hutchison.

Martin, David. 1978. *General Theory of Secularization*. Oxford: Blackwell.

———. 1991. *Europe: An Ever Closer Union*. Nottingham, England: Russell Press.

Mazey, Sonia, and Jeremy Richardson. 1993. "Environmental Groups and the EC." In *A Green Dimension for the European Community*, ed. by David Judge. London: Frank Cass.

Misner, Paul. 1991. *Social Catholicism in Europe*. London: Darton, Longman and Todd.

Monnet, J. 1978. *Memoirs*. Trans. by J. Mayne. New York: Doubleday.

Moravcsik, A. 1991. "Negotiating the Single European Act." In *The New European Community*, ed. by R. Keohane and S. Hoffmann. Boulder, CO: Westview Press.

Morris, A. 1993. "Europe 2000: Union or Fragmentation?" Occasional Papers, no. 14. Jean Monnet Council—George Washington Forum in European Studies, Washington, DC.

Mowat, R. 1973. *Creating the European Community*. New York: Harper & Row.

Muller-Rommel, F. 1989. *New Politics in Western Europe: The Rise and Success of Green Parties and Alternative Lists*. Boulder, CO: Westview Press.

Nugent, Neill. 1989. *The Government and Politics of the European Community*. Durham, NC: Duke University Press.

Papke, S. 1992. "Who Needs European Unity and What Could It Be?" In *The Idea of Europe*, ed. by B. Nelson, D. Roberts, and W. Veit. New York: Berg.

Parker, Geoffrey. 1975. *The Logic of Unity*. 2nd. ed. London: Longman.

Pentland, C. 1973. *International Theory and European Integration*. New York: Free Press.

Peters, B. Guy. 1992. "Bureaucratic Politics and the Institutions of the European Community." In *Euro-Politics*, ed. by Alberta Sbriaga. Washington, DC: Brookings Institution.

Peterson, John, and Elizabeth Bomberg. 1992. *The Politics of Prevention and Health Care*. Aldershot, England: Avesbury Press.

Pipkorn, John. 1980. "The Legal Framework of Employee Participation Methods at National and International Levels and Particularly within the European Community." *Economic and Industrial Democracy* 1: 99–123.

Pryce, R. 1987. "Past Experiences and Lessons for the Future." In *The Dynamics of European Union*, ed. by Roy Pryce. London: Croom Helm.

Pryce, R., ed. 1987. *Dynamics of European Union*. London: Croom Helm.

Pryce, R., and W. Wessels. 1987. "The Search for an Ever Closer Union: A Framework for Analysis." *The Dynamics of European Union*, ed. by R. Pryce. London: Croom Helm.

Puchala, D., and R. Hopkins. "International Regions: Lessons from Inductive Analysis." 1983. *International Regimes*, ed. by S. Krasner. Ithaca, NY: Cornell University Press.

Rehbinder, Eckard, and Richard Stewart. 1988. *Environmental Protection Policy*. New York: Walter de Gruyter.

Rose, Richard. 1993. *Drawing Lessons in Public Policy*. Chatham, NJ: Chatham House Publishers.

Sabatier, P. 1988. "An Advocacy Coalition Framework of Policy Change and the Role of Policy-Oriented Learning Therein." *Policy Sciences* 21: 129–169.

——— . 1991. "Towards Better Theories of the Policy Process." *PS: Political Science and Politics* (June): 147–156.

Salvatorelli, L. 1970. *The Risorgimento: Thought and Action.* New York: Harper & Row.

Santer, J. 1991. "Some Reflections on the Principle of Subsidiarity." In *Subsidiarity: The Challenge of Change.* Maastricht: European Institute of Public Administration.

Schmitter, Philippe. 1992. "Interests, Powers and Functions: Emergent Properties and Unintended Consequences in the European Polity." Unpublished paper.

Scholten, Ilja. 1987. "Introduction: Corporatist and Consociational Arrangements." *Political Stability and Neo-Corporatism*, ed. by Ilja Scholten. Beverly Hills, CA: Sage Publications.

Shackleton, Michael. 1991. "Budgetary Policy in Transition." In *The State of the European Community*, ed. by Alan Cafruny and Glenda Rosenthal. Boulder, CO: Lynne Rienner.

Shanks, Michael. 1977. *European Social Policy: Today and Tomorrow.* Oxford: Pergamon Press.

Sharpe, L. 1993. "The European Meso: An Appraisal" *The Rise of Meso Government in Europe*, ed. by L. Sharpe. London: Sage Publications.

Spicker, P. 1991. "The Principle of Subsidiarity and the Social Policy of the European Community." *Journal of European Social Policy* 1, no. 1.

Spretnak, Charlene, and Fritjof Capra. 1985. *Green Politics.* London: Paladin Grafton Books.

Springer, Beverly. 1992. *The Social Dimension of 1992.* Westport, CT: Greenwood Press.

Springer, Beverly, and Dorothy Riddle. 1988. "Women in Service Industries: European Communities—United States Comparisons." In *Comparable Worth, Pay Equity, and Public Policy*, ed. by R. Kelly and J. Bayes. Westport, CT: Greenwood Press.

"Subsidiarity in the Constitution of the EC." 1992. Extract from a speech by Sir Leon Brittan to the European University, Florence, Italy, June 11.

Taylor, P. 1989. "The New Dynamics of EC Integration in the 1980s." In *The European Community and the Challenge of the Future*, ed. by Juliet Lodge. New York: St. Martin's Press.

Taylor-Gooby, P. 1991. "Welfare State Regimes and Welfare Citizenship." *Journal of Social Policy* 1, no. 2.

Thompson, E. P. 1963. *The Making of the English Working Class.* New York: Vintage Books.

Tomkins, Judith, and Jim Twomey. 1992. "Regional Policy." In *European Economic Integration*, ed. by Frank McDonald and Stephen Dearden. London: Longman.

Treaty on European Union. 1992. Version produced by the combined effort of the general secretariat of the Council and of the Commission. Luxembourg: Office for Official Publications of the European Communities.

Tushnet, Mark, ed. 1990. *Comparative Constitutional Federalism.* Westport, CT: Greenwood Press.

"Twisting Cartography of Distress." 1993. *Financial Times*, July 24–25.

van der Veen, Romke. 1993. "Citizenship and the Modern Welfare State: Social Integration, Competence and the Reciprocity of Rights and Duties in Social Policy." In *Work and Citizenship in the New Europe*, ed. by Harry Coenen and Peter Leisink. Aldershot, England: Edward Elgar.

Weiler, Joseph. 1992. "After Maastricht: Community Legitimacy in Post-1992 Europe." In *Singular Europe*, ed. by William James Adams, Ann Arbor: University of Michigan Press.

Wessels, Wolfgang. 1991. "The EC Council: The Community's Decisionmaking Center." In *The New European Community,* ed. by Robert Keohane and Stanley Hoffmann. Boulder, CO: Westview Press.

Williams, Shirley. 1991. "Sovereignty and Accountability in the European Community." *The New European Community,* ed. by Robert Keohane and Stanley Hoffmann. Boulder, CO: Westview Press.

Williamson, David. 1991. "General Strategy of EPU." In *The Agenda of the Intergovernmental Conferences: What Can Be Achieved?* Proceedings by Gabriele Jauernig. Brussels: Centre for European Policy Studies.

Willis, F. 1971. *Italy Chooses Europe.* London: Oxford University Press.

Woodcock, G. 1972. *Pierre-Joseph Proudhon: His Life and Work.* New York: Schocken Books.

Young, Stephen. 1992. "The Different Dimensions of Green Politics." *Environmental Politics* 1, no. 1 (Spring): 9–44.

Index

ABOUT THE AUTHOR

BEVERLY SPRINGER is Professor of International Studies at the American Graduate School of International Management in Arizona and editor of *The International Executive.* She is the author of *The Social Dimension of 1992* (Greenwood, 1992).

ISBN 0-313-28815-1

90000>

EAN

9 780313 288159

HARDCOVER BAR CODE